COLLECTOR'S GUIDE TO

TINKER TOYS

CRAIG STRANGE

COLLECTOR BOOKS

A Division of Schroeder Publishing Co., Inc.

Searching For A Publisher?

We are always looking for knowledgable people considered to be experts within their fields. If you feel that there is a real need for a book on your collectible subject and have a large comprehensive collection, contact Collector Books.

Book design by: Karen Long
Cover design by: Beth Summers

TINKERTOY® is a trademark of Hasbro, Inc. ©1995 Hasbro, Inc. All rights reserved. Used with permission.

Printed by IMAGE GRAPHICS, INC., Paducah, Kentucky

 Dedication

This book is dedicated to my wife Susan, for without her support and encouragement this book would not have become reality.

 Acknowledgments

I would like to thank the following persons, institutions, and companies for their assistance in the preparation of this book.

Anne and Ted Lewis
David Lewis
Kristan H. McKinsey,
    Collections Curator
Mark Burnette
Lonnie and Joanne Litwiller
Gale and Wayne Bailey
Kathy and Robert Trenter
Frank Tolford
Arlan Coffman
Larry J. Basting
Hope A. Maxon
Kathy Ade
Margaret Bryant Witt
John Wright
Arlene R. Grewe
Paul Gardner
Julias Gardner
Gerry Linnemann and Pat Velasco
    of Phototronics, Inc.
John Novick of Harvard School
Mrs. A. Tyskaling
Bill Powell
Senator Paul Simon
Michael Kelly
Ken Hoos

Betty L. Strange
Nathan E. Strange
Steve Strange
Anne Williams, AGCA
Muriel Bielmolt
Anne Pashow
Gary Serby, Director of Public
    Relations, Hasbro/Playskool
Edna M. Collette
Mrs. Rollie Schmitt
Sheridan Shore Yacht Club
Chicago Historical Society
Smithsonian Institution
Library of Congress
Glencoe Public Library
Chicago Public Library
Milwaukee Public Library
The Center for Research Libraries
Playthings Magazine
Geyer McAllister Publishing
Harvard School, Chicago
Pat Kelly
Spalding Inc.
David Katz
Kelly Devlin

I would like to thank the Evanston Historical Society for their assistance in the preparation of this work, and their permission to photograph items from the Society's archives for this book.

A special thanks to Hasbro/Playskool for their help and gracious permission to use trademarked, and copyrighted company materials.

🧍 Foreword 🧍

Tinkertoy construction sets may be one of the simplest toy concepts ever marketed, and they have also been among the most popular. Their colorful components have a direct appeal to children, whose imaginations produce elaborate structures and mechanisms from the small geometric pieces.

The story of Charles H. Pajeau and the Toy Tinkers of Evanston, Illinois, is much like the playthings they produced — colorful, straightforward, imaginative. It is a story which, until this time, has not been gathered together and told in full.

This book is the result of considerable effort and love on the part of its author. A childhood affection for a favorite toy was reawakened, starting him on a journey of learning and discovery, which he now shares with children of all ages. Craig Strange diligently pursued a variety of sources for the particulars of the Toy Tinkers business — former employees and their descendants, photographs, business and legal records, and period publications, to name just a

few. Each time he thought he had exhausted the search, additional and important information surfaced. His thorough efforts are reflected in the following pages.

Most readers will be surprised to learn that the Toy Tinkers initially made their reputation from a whole line of toys that included figural and action toys in addition to the Tinkertoy construction sets. This book splendidly details the developments of the company for both the serious collector and the arm chair enthusiast. The history of Tinker Toys deserves to be told. Though the concepts upon which they were based were simple, they derived from an honest concern for children. The telling of this story lends even greater appreciation to the toys and the people who made them.

Whirly Tinker—A whirling pull toy that affords great delight to the children, two men mounted on disks dance as pulled along, hardwood, highly colored, polished, rustproof metal trimmings and frame work, each in pkg., k. d., easily put together.

Kristan H. McKinsey
Collections Curator
Evanston Historical Society
Evanston, Illinois

Contents

♟ Value Information ♟

These estimates of value are offered for illustrative purposes only. It is up to the individual to decide what they are willing to pay for a given item at a given point in time.

Value is determined by a buyer and seller when a sale is completed. The price the seller is willing to accept, and the buyer will agree to, determines that item's value at that point in time.

Values vary over time and from location to location.

No guide can hope to reflect all situations and geographic locations. You are the final arbiter of what price for which you should sell, and what you should pay.

It is assumed that all items are complete and with the original packaging where so stated. Any missing pieces would reduce the estimated values found here.

The values listed here are for items in from **good** to **excellent** condition.

♟ Preface ♟

The deeper I delved into the history of the Toy Tinkers of Evanston, Illinois, the more intrigued I became. Growing up very near to the home of the Tinkertoy, I was amazed to find that the company had produced more than construction sets. The people and products of the company fascinated me, and drove me to learn all that I could about them. I was lucky enough to locate several former employees of the Toy Tinkers, and discover from their accounts what it was like to be a Toy Tinker. Information was also derived from over four years of research that took me to historical and governmental archives all over the United States. From census data to microfilm records, any clue about the Toy Tinkers of Evanston, Illinois, was checked and followed as far as it would lead. That information also told a great deal about the times in which the company was formed, and the firms with which it competed. I have attempted to weave all of the data and findings into one clear account of the Toy Tinkers. Part of the drive to learn involved collecting examples of the products produced by the Toy Tinkers, so that I might have a clearer understanding and a tangible connection to the past. I hope that others will share my fascination with the people and products of the Toy Tinkers of Evanston, Illinois, and find as much pleasure in reading the following account as I found in producing it.

The Toy Tinkers of Evanston, Illinois, produced a dizzying array of toys and other products from 1914 to 1952 under the direction of Charles H. Pajeau. I have attempted to catalog the company output during those years, yet am certain that there are items produced that I have not been able to locate. Even as the deadline for this book approached, I was still finding new items and names that I had not come across before.

Charles H. Pajeau was a prolific inventor, and the Toy Tinkers are also known to have bought toy ideas from other inventors. There are undoubtedly many toys which were considered for production that never made the cut, and likely several more which were made and sold, but were not listed in the sources that I was able to find. Somewhere there may be company files of the early Toy Tinkers, and in time we may learn about these unknown toys.

Even among the toys identified here, there are often many variations of a single toy. The explanation for this can run from improved production methods to changing a toy to make it patentable, although often it was simply a matter of making the toy more competitive against interlopers. Companies like Fisher Price and Hustler Toy Corporation as well as foreign competition, finally pushed the Toy Tinkers out of producing the pull toys, and ultimately the rest of their line, until just the construction sets were left. But at that point the company was the undisputed ruler of the construction set category, holding the record for production of a single toy for several years.

The Toy Tinkers drew a distinction between a "Tinkertoy," one of the stick-and-spool construction sets, and a "Tinker Toy," which could be any of the toys produced by the company including the construction sets.

Toy making in 1914 and later was a labor-intensive business in the days before mold-injection toys, and other current means of mass production. The Toy Tinkers employed automation of the construction set parts early on, which served to make it a profitable toy. Many of the other toys were more labor demanding, and thus when one was not a hit, it could cost the company dearly.

The hand assembly work could also explain some of the variations noted by collectors of Tinker Toys. The monotony of putting the same item together over and over again might have caused an occasional error by the assembler, placing a red wheel where a blue was to be for example.

In the company's first year of nationwide sales, which was only their second year in business, they produced 900,000 Wonder Builder Tinkertoy sets.[22] By 1936 the company was claiming to have made 50,000,000 friends, and by 1972 production was about 100,000,000 toys.[161] Of that number, toys other than the construction sets would account for at least 20,000,000 of the items produced by the Toy Tinkers. That is a lot of bead dolls, games, and pull toys.

In the process of marketing these millions of toys the company also produced a lot of catalogs, posters, and display materials to entice children and adults to buy Tinker Toys. The single most important factor I have found in locating the early Tinker Toys is being able to recognize them. Once you know what you are looking for, it is much easier to find. I and several other collectors have recently located hundreds of Tinker Toys and related items, in addition to the construction sets which tend to be very easy to find. By using this guide you will have a better understanding of the age of the toys and the canister sets, and be able to make an educated decision about purchasing them.

It is not uncommon for dealers or flea market sellers to misidentify Tinker Toys, often believing them to be from an earlier or later period. With the availability of this history, I hope that much of the confusion and lack of knowledge about Toy Tinkers products will be cleared away. The more people that are aware of the toys and the company, the more likely it is that we will fill in some of the blanks about the history of the Toy Tinkers of Evanston, Illinois.

TOM TINKER said to Belle one day. "Come on down to the beach and play. We'll wade and swim and skip and run, And shovel sand—that's lots of fun."

"Hurrah," cried Belle, "I'll race you there And you can beat me if you dare. We'll take the other Tinker Toys, And play all day with the girls and boys."

Every reader of CHILD LIFE will want to see our jingle folder. Send us your name and address so that we can mail the one we are saving for you. There are several new members of the Toy Tinker family. You'll see them in the folder.

THE TOY TINKERS
EVANSTON, ILL.

Drag-on Tinker

Pony Tinker

Introduction to the History of Tinker Toys

The city of Chicago had grown from humble beginnings by incorporating the communities which surrounded it on all sides. On the north side of Chicago the expansion had taken it to the city of Evanston, where Howard Street marked the boundary between the two cities. Attempts were made to entice Evanston to join up, but it would have none of that.

In 1913 the suburban communities north of Chicago were a mix of truck farms, industries, businesses, and residential areas. Evanston had a variety of homes, apartment buildings, boarding houses, and hotels from which to choose. The residents were varied too, with commuting business, working class, and some very well-to-do people. The train lines made travel to Chicago easy, and played a large part in the development of surrounding towns. Evanston also had the well-known Northwestern University, plus the reputation as a dry community. If you wanted a drink you needed to cross Howard Street on Evanston's southern border, or go west to find a tavern in Glenview or Niles Center (called Skokie after 1940).

The downtown of Evanston was of good size and offered most of the services required by the residents. If more were needed one could catch the train into Chicago. Evanston offered a quiet setting with city conveniences; it was the best of both worlds. An assortment of buildings were found there, so when Charles Pajeau and his partner Robert Pettit needed a home for their young business venture they located a suitable structure. Charles had a great fondness for Evanston so it was natural that he should wish to establish a new company there.

Just as the pair was developing their product, the world was getting ready to undergo some major changes.[1] Starting in about 1890 the German toy industry became a major exporter with a large part of their production going to the United States and South America. Continuing until the start of the First World War in 1914, German toys were such a force that they kept many domestic industries from fully developing. These toys looked good and were produced very cheaply, mostly in the homes of workers with very few being factory made, then were brokered by toy cooperatives to foreign buyers. The prices were so low that few American concerns attempted to compete against the German dolls, mechanical toys, and games. If you saw a good-quality game before the First World War, you could bet it came from the Spear Toy House in Germany. No American game came close in quality or style. France and Germany produced the finest dolls and the best mechanical toys were sure to be German. Although some argued that German mechanical toys looked great, their mechanisms were not as sturdy as those produced in the United

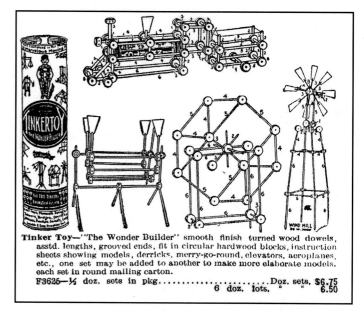

Plate 1

1920 Tinkertoy wholesale advertisement.

States. Another concern was the repair of toys from abroad. If a part was needed you might wait months for its arrival, if the part could be located at all.

In 1914 about 10% of the toys sold in the United States were of domestic origin, and of rougher appearance than the slick European imports.[2] The other 90% were imported from Europe and Japan, with the bulk coming from Germany and Austria. Russia also contributed some toys.

When the war began, things changed fast in the toy world. By August of 1914, an article in the *New York Times* newspaper announced that toy imports were hit hard and there was concern about supplying the demand for Christmas.[3] An unnamed representative of Schwartz Brothers lamented that if the war situation did not change soon, then America would have to make its own toys. He felt that American workers lacked the years of experience common to foreign workers.

Until the war, Germany was annually producing $25,000,000 worth of toys for export, with the bulk going to America. By 1916 the annual American import of German toys amounted to only about $2,500,000. The British Navy successfully restricted the flow of goods from Germany, and in the process provided a great favor to American toy manufacturers. The longer the war continued, the better established the domestic toy industry became. The Toy Manufacturers of the United States was organized in 1916 as a trade group that promised it was not intent on price fixing or controlling the toy market.[4] The group simply wished to improve and promote the quality of domestic goods in the United States and around the world (Plate 2).

Among the founding members were A.C. Gilbert, H.C. Ives, A.D. Converse, and A.F. Schoenhut; all were big names in the domestic toy business. In 1916, 65% of the $25,000,000 in the toys sold in America were of American production, and the quality had substantially improved over only a couple of years.[5]

In 1920 the numbers were even better with domestic production equaling 90% of all toys sold in the United States.[1] However, the wartime prejudice against German toys was starting to evaporate, and since the war was over, American goods again faced competition. The difference from earlier times was that now most of the U.S. firms were sufficiently established to stand up to the test and compete efficiently. A few others were only able to make a profit in the shelter of an isolated market and soon passed from the scene. The Toy Tinkers were among the former, with a popular product line featuring the Tinkertoy. The Toy Tinkers did a great business in other toys up

The benevolent plot of two kindly old gentlemen

A plot! And against the children of America! Yet judging from the merry faces of Uncle Sam and Santa Claus it bodes no ill.

In fact, they've decided between 'em that American youngsters should have American playthings —and together—for this Christmas —they've made the most splendid things in the whole wide wor!d.

Parents too are conspiring with the two jolly old gentlemen. They know that if little Bobby is to become a *real* American man—and Jane is to become a *real* American woman, the toys they play with two-thirds of the day must be *Real* American Toys.

This Christmas buy American-made Toys for your children.

THE TOY MANUFACTURERS OF THE U. S. A.

FLATIRON BUILDING NEW YORK

American-Made Toys

Plate 2

Author's collection.

Public relations advertisement for The Toy Manufacturers of the U.S.A., circa 1919.

until the Great Depression, when demand began a slow decline for their product line. The Tinkertoy was always a steady seller, but the tastes in toys began to change.

The Toy Tinkers were less sensitive to those changes after 1929.[6] Many of the toys introduced were quickly discontinued, and the product line started to shrink in number. The Toy Tinkers were late to catch the trend of products featuring cartoon characters with the introduction of Disney Snow White Tinkersand sets in 1938, and Mickey Mouse and Goofy Tinkersand sets at about the same time. An earlier trend in 1935 may have portended the decline of the Toy Tinkers, when department stores and wholesalers began to wait longer and longer before placing orders with toy manufacturers. Whereas it was typical for orders to be submitted in March or April in 1914, by 1935 orders were being placed in August and September for November delivery.[7] This required toy companies to build up large inventories and hope that what they produced would be what the stores wanted, or wait until the last minute to jump frantically into production.

The uncertainty and errors in judgment by the Toy Tinkers ultimately led to the decision to produce only one line of toys. That line was the Tinkertoy construction set in all of its variations. By 1941 the Tinkertoy sets were the only item listed for sale by the Toy Tinkers of Evanston, Illinois. Another idea that came too late for the company was the Industrial Design and Registration Bureau.[6] The bureau offered protection against copycat products by U.S. concerns, but this occurred after just about everyone in the industry had tried their hand at a knock-off of the Tinkertoy.

One trend that the Toy Tinkers did see coming was electrical propulsion, which was a natural for the Tinkertoy construction sets.[6] Whether with batteries or a wall plug, toys were moving more than ever using electricity. Toy Tinkers introduced both wind-up and electric motors for the construction sets to operate windmills, vehicles, or any other design. With the wind-up motor you could make a car that could actually move by itself.

Something else was going right for the company, as another trend became apparent. With the Depression becoming a memory the population grew again. The early signs of the baby boom were seen as the Second World War approached. Sales of the construction sets began to increase dramatically, more than offsetting the other toys which had been dropped from the line. The sales curve followed the bulge in the population, going ever higher to almost 3 million sets a year when the company was sold in 1952.[8] By 1971 sales had dropped to about 1 million sets annually, reflecting the end of the baby boom.[9] Despite this downturn in sales and several new transfers of ownership over the years, the Tinkertoy and the major impact it made on the toy world endure still today with sales again climbing.

The founders of the Toy Tinkers of Evanston, Illinois, were men of different backgrounds and temperaments drawn together by a common desire. Charles H. Pajeau and Robert Pettit met while commuting by train from Evanston to Chicago for work.[10] On those long rides they discussed a lot of different topics, but the one that seemed to spark between them was a mutual dislike for their respective occupations. Charles hated the monument business. He would tell people, "Monuments stink!"[9] Robert truly hated the job of trader down at the Board of Trade. This common feeling ultimately brought the two together into the toy business. Charles supplied the creative ability and Robert provided the cool business head.

The Pajeau family arrived in the United States from France most likely in the early 1840s. Other relations may have arrived earlier, with some living in Canada perhaps as early as 1791. Some other spellings for relations were Pageau, Pasho, Pashow, Page, and there may be others.[11] Joseph Pajeau was born in New York State in June of 1846.[12] He was very probably born in or near New York City, as that would be the likely entry point of his father into the United States. Joseph's mother was born in Quebec, Canada. In 1872 Joseph married Mary L. Cochrane of New Hampshire. Mary was born in January, 1852. Her mother was from New Hampshire and her father from Ireland. On August 18, 1875, Charles Hamilton Pajeau was born to Joseph and Mary. Most sources list Charles' place of birth as New Ipswich, New Hampshire.

Joseph was in the granite business, not uncommon for a resident of the Granite State. By 1881 the Lakeside City Directory for Chicago listed him as a travel agent, boarding at 2017 Indiana Avenue in Chicago.[13] 1883 found him listed in the Evanston City directory as a dealer and designer of granite monuments.[14] His home was now in Evanston, Illinois, at 719 Grove. The Pajeaus lived in Evanston while Joseph commuted to his Chicago business until late 1888, when the family moved back to the city, taking a house at 2229 Prairie Avenue.

It is probable that this move was made so that 14-year-old Charles would be able to take advantage of the superior schooling available at the Harvard School for Boys.[15, 16, 17] The school was located at 2101 Indiana Avenue, on the corner of 21st Street. It was the place where the sons of Chicago's successful businessmen prepared for entrance to college, or gained the skills needed to carry on the family business.

A graduate of the Harvard School was not required to take an entrance examination if he wished to enter Harvard University, the University of Michigan, Amherst College, the University of Wisconsin, or Williams College. The school's five-year higher department course (the equivalent of today's high school) covered foreign language, math, geometry, history, natural science, as well as manual training. The manual training typically involved woodworking. The intent was to teach students to design and build useful and practical items utilizing what they had learned in school. For example, students applied their math and geometry knowledge in the construction of wood projects. This experience was to prove especially important in the future of Charles H. Pajeau.

Charles' last year at the Harvard School was 1891. He completed three years of the five-year course, and went on to complete his education at Hyde Park High School.[18] After his graduation from Hyde Park High School in 1893, Charles went to work at his father's monument business at 100 Washington in Chicago. Charles began as a clerk, and by the next year had advanced to the job title of draftsman. In 1895 he was listed as a designer, and the following year he was the manager for his father's business. Charles started his own business in 1897 out of his father's offices. Named Charles H. Pajeau and Company, the new business involved bicycles. This may have been when he invented the two-wheel scooter for which the patent office refused to issue him a patent.[19] Charles ultimately realized only $100 profit for this invention. He felt that he had been short-changed for his efforts.

By 1898 Charles was again listed in the Lakeside City Directory of Chicago as a designer of monuments, the bicycle business now seemingly a memory. The proud day arrived in 1899 when Joseph changed the business name from Joseph Pajeau Monuments to Joseph Pajeau and Son. That same year on October 11, Charles married Miss Grace C. Fuller.[20] Grace was born in Chicago in 1878 to Lottie J. and Alanzo M. Fuller, a Chicago merchandiser.[21] Charles and Grace lived with Charles' parents in the Pajeau house until 1901. At that time, Charles and Grace moved to 4832 Ellis Avenue in Chicago. They remained at the Ellis Avenue address until 1907, when their daughter Grace was four years old, and Charles chose to return to his childhood town.

Charles' work required him to make a daily commute to Chicago. He found several sides of the monument business displeasing, and longed for another means of supporting his wife and child.[22] As a relief from his unhappy situation, he experimented with the invention of toys, which he began to manufacture in 1904.[23]

In 1906 he patented and started the manufacture of what became know as the "The Yankee Doodle Sulky," a two-wheeled sulky for children — a low cart with a long handle — used by parents to take their babies to the grocery store and such.[24] The unique point of this sulky was that it would not tip over, as others were prone to do.

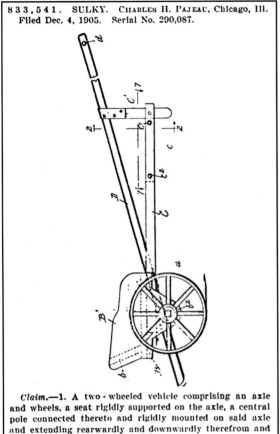

833,541. SULKY. CHARLES H. PAJEAU, Chicago, Ill. Filed Dec. 4, 1905. Serial No. 290,087.

Claim.—1. A two-wheeled vehicle comprising an axle and wheels, a seat rigidly supported on the axle, a central pole connected thereto and rigidly mounted on said axle and extending rearwardly and downwardly therefrom and adapted to support the vehicle from overturning when the front end of the pole is elevated above the normal draft-line.

Plate 3

Patent application drawing of "Yankee Doodle Sulky" designed by Charles H. Pajeau.

Unfortunately, 1912 saw the failure of the specialty house which had been exclusively contracted for all of his sulky output. After the financial smoke cleared, he was out of the sulky business, and short several thousand dollars. All the while he kept up the monument business, and now returned to it full time. Still he longed for another way to earn his living, and he continued to devise toys. He learned an important lesson from the sulky affair. The cost of packaging and freight had come to equal the cost of production for his sulky. Charles would now concentrate on smaller products, and when it came time to ship them he wanted the U.S. mail to take care of it, not the expensive freight handlers.

The Pettit family had a long history going back at least

to Revolutionary War times, when Col. Charles Pettit was, by one account, Governor of New Jersey.[10] Other sources identified Charles Pettit as Pre-Revolutionary War Deputy Secretary of the Province of New Jersey.[25] During the Revolutionary War, he was appointed as Assistant Quartermaster General by act of the Continental Congress in 1778.[26] Robert's father, Henry Pettit, was the General Superintendent of the Pennsylvania Railroad.[10] Robert was born on May 20, 1881, in Altoona, Pennsylvania. He graduated from the Harverford School in 1901, and then attended Princeton from September 1901 to 1903.[27, 28] In 1904 Robert's friend Andrew Hazelhurst graduated from Princeton and returned home to Evanston. That same year, Robert joined his friend in Evanston, where Robert presumably met Miss Rachel Kimberly Hazelhurst, Andrew's sister.[28] He knew when he met her that she was the love of his life. He refused his family's requests for his return to the East Coast, and on June 7, 1905, Rachel became his wife.

That same year Robert became a member of the Evanston Club, located at 603 Grove Street in Evanston.[29–34] It was a gentlemen's club where one could play cards, billiards, bowl, or just socialize. New members were voted on, and the membership ebbed and flowed over the years. It was especially hard hit during the Great Depression, when several members resigned for financial reasons. It does not appear that Robert ever served as an officer of the club; he simply availed himself of the club's facilities, as was a member's right. He remained a member up until his death in 1943. He also belonged to the University Club in Chicago.

Robert first appears in the Lakeside City Directory of Chicago in 1906, listed as a broker with offices at 6 Sherman.[13] From 1905 to 1907, he was a full-time grain trader at the Board of Trade. From 1908 to 1909, he operated the Gifford-Pettit Manufacturing Company, an auto truck manufacturing concern.[28]

In 1909 Robert was listed as the secretary of James Motor Express Company at 7 LaSalle Street in Chicago.[28] He operated this motor express service, which ran between Evanston and Chicago, until 1915, when he sold the business. Then, in 1912, he was listed as a trader at the Trader's Building in Chicago. It is most likely that he had already met Charles by this time, as they lived within six blocks of each other on the same street in Evanston, and both commuted to Chicago.

The two men were of different dispositions. Charles was a jokester who loved slight of hand, and did not mind poking fun at himself. He liked parties and was an extrovert when around his friends. Robert was very quiet and businesslike. He was a low-profile person who took care of the day-to-day business, and left Charles to grab the spotlight. Charles was the best publicity man a company could have. He was energetic, creative, and he truly believed in his product.

Late in 1913 Charles and Robert started work on the idea of developing the toy construction set that would become known as the Tinkertoy. Charles was a keen observer, noting how children played with and used their toys.[8,9] He saw that children from well-to-do families quickly grew bored with expensive toys. These toys often would have only one motion or function, and the repetitive nature became tiresome. Charles also noticed that poor children would invent playthings from what they could find. In one instance he saw children playing with pencils and thread spools. The youngsters spent hours devising various objects and games using these simple items. That set him to thinking about the possibilities of a modified form of sticks and spools.

Another observation which Charles made was that children liked to learn.[35] They were eager for the chance, but they did not like to be taught. They enjoyed taking things apart to see how they work, and then reassembling them. Even more, they liked to try new combinations with the disassembled object. Given the opportunity to use their imaginations, children devised a variety of new forms for the object. Executed properly, the spool and stick toy offered the means to a fun and educational toy.

Charles thought of boring holes on the outer edge of the spool, as well as one through the center, thus allowing for the Pythagorean theory of the progressive right triangle.[22] By this means, a triangle composed of sticks and spools could become the side of an even bigger triangle, and a three-dimensional model could be built with infinite possibilities. Essentially, anything imaginable could be built from these simple components, then preserved or dismantled. Another advantage to this system was the lack of sharp metal parts, screws, or bolts to make the models. Young children could be given this toy without great safety concerns. The spools were smoothly finished, and the sticks were sanded smooth and blunt at the ends.

The pair of inventors were sure they had a winner in this toy, but there was one problem that seemed to defy solution. In order for the toy to be usable by young children, the sticks and spools needed to be easy to assemble and take apart. The partners found that if the openings in the spools were large enough to make the sticks easy to remove, then they were also too loose for the model to stay steady. Yet if the fit was tight enough to be steady, then the sticks were much too difficult for a child to remove. For months the partners spent their spare time wrestling with this difficulty, and at moments

Plate 5

1915 to 1923 style Tinkertoy canister with an outside screw top.

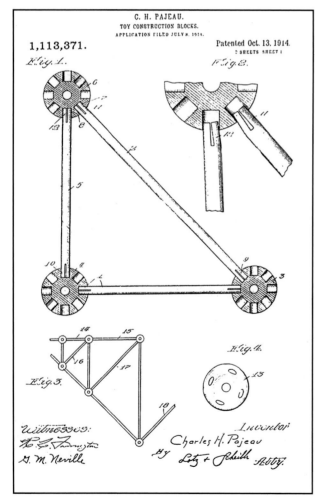

Plate 4

Patent application for the Tinkertoy, invented by Charles H. Pajeau, 1914.

talked of abandoning the whole thing; still, they persevered. Ultimately they arrived at the idea of slotting the ends of the dowel rod sticks, and the toy was able to perform as desired.

The next problems were to name and market the toy.[22] Charles fancied himself as quite the tinkerer. He set up a workshop in his basement at 325 Greenwood Street, Evanston, and turned out a line of toys for his daughter Grace. In the creative environment of Charles's presence, it is likely that Robert joined in on the notion. And if they were tinkering with toys in Evanston, then it was perfectly logical that the company should be "The Toy Tinkers of Evanston, Illinois." The name also lent itself to a playful, quaint sense which fit Charles perfectly, and helped to set the tone for the venture.

Since the product of this venture could be used to devise countless models and designs, making all who used it into tinkerers as well, then the name "Tinkertoy" was a logical choice.

With the name set, it was necessary to design a package and label, then market the toy. Pajeau and Pettit had come to their enterprise through years of business, and their share of hard lessons. They were savvy enough to know that proper packaging was a big part of promotion. They needed something that would make the product stand out in the very crowded field of toys, most of which were imported from Germany and Austria.

The idea of putting the Tinkertoy pieces into a can seemed to be an excellent solution on several fronts.[22] First, it was different. Next, it lent itself to ease of shipping, for it was basically a mailing tube. Finally, the container was very strong by its nature. Charles liked that the container was suitable for mailing in the U.S. Postal system. He learned from his experience with the "Yankee Doodle Sulky" that freight expenses could eat up a lot of money just getting the product to the customer. If that expense could be saved, it would make the product more competitive by being less costly to the customer.

The colors for the can needed to be eye catching, so the graphics were dark blue and bright orange on a white background. The can had the toy's name in large columns on two sides, and again in the center of a circle on the

A Tinkertoy Tank Line Car
One of a Thousand Motion Figures That Can
Be Made with One Set of

TINKERTOY
Pat. U. S. and Foreign Countries. Trade Mark Reg.

The 50c Wonder Builder

Made of wood rods and spools—73 pieces—in mathematical ratio—that can be taken apart and assembled to form an unlimited number of models of interest and delight to young and mature. A new toy for every day in the year—all for the cost of one.

Packed in the famous Tinkertoy tubular mailing case that travels around the world at one pound rates. Direction sheets in each package.

A window display of Tinkertoy moving figures operated by air from an electric fan will sell 25 to 250 toys a day at any season of the year.

MADE BY

THE TOY TINKERS of EVANSTON, ILL.

SELLING AGENTS

GEO. BORGFELDT & CO.　　　　　　CARDINELL-VINCENT CO.
NEW YORK　　　　　　　　　　　　　　　SAN FRANCISCO.

Plate 6

Trade advertisement for Tinkertoy, 1915.

front. The rest of the can showed the company name and several models which could be built. On the back of the can was a large mailing label, with space for postage to be affixed. The product was officially known as "Tinkertoy — The Wonder Builder," and a thousand different marvelous moving figures could be constructed with it. Inside the can were complete instructions for the toy, 73 spools and sticks of various lengths, plus wind blades — everything needed to make the models shown. They had a product and a package, and now they had to sell it to retailers.

It was not a very good time to enter the toy business.[22] The year 1914 had started out as usual, with toy buyers contracted for their typical supply of Christmas toys through German and Swiss suppliers. However, when World War I broke out, the shipments were held back by the British Navy. In a panic, the buyers made alternate arrangements by purchasing stocks of toys from American suppliers and Japanese toy makers. Just as the delivery date was to arrive, the European toys were released to the American market. So, in the middle of a financial downturn, American stores were stocked with double shipments of toys. As Charles H. Pajeau was quoted in *System Magazine* in 1918 as saying, "You couldn't have sold those buyers solid gold toys at five cents a pound."

Charles and Robert had devised and introduced the Tinkertoy to the world; unfortunately, no major buyer was at all interested in the product. The pair knew that they had something good, so they sought nontraditional outlets for the Tinkertoy sets. They found Chicago area magazine stands, cigar stores, and drug stores willing to carry the sets. The Toy Tinkers placed Ferris wheels made from the construction sets at all of the stores, and by means of an electric fan, kept the Ferris wheels in motion. The eye-catching displays did the trick, and soon the partners were unable to meet local demand for the sets. Charles and Robert had originally set up shop in a one-room alley space off Old Post Office Place (now Sherman Avenue halfway between Davis and Church Streets in Evanston).[8] The room measured 15 by 20 feet and served as the factory, design center, and sales showroom. They hired a young man to make the construction sets while the partners set off to expand their market. With Christmas of 1914 behind them, they made plans for the next holiday season.

An oddity of the time, the toy buyers were really the china buyers for major department stores and wholesalers.[35] Since toys were seen as a seasonal business in the early part of the century, and most came from Europe, the task of purchasing the Christmas stocks of toys fell to the china buyers. As they had to travel Europe to select dishwares, it was a logical but annoying additional job for these fellows to also buy toys. If an American toy manufacturer hoped to sell his goods, he had to catch these buyers before they left New York Harbor.

After the disaster of the preceding toy season, the buyers were so sick of toys and weary of novelty items, they would have nothing to do with the Tinkertoy in its odd can.[22] In February of 1915 Charles headed for New York City to start taking orders from the major toy buyers.[36] He set up his toys and displays at the Broadway Central Hotel on the fourth floor, with the other American toy sellers in the heart of the toy district, but he was not happy with the off-the-corridor room to which he was assigned.[37] After a couple of days sitting around and twiddling his thumbs, Pajeau decided to try what worked in Chicago. He identified the biggest drug stores on the most prominent corners

in New York City. He obtained permission from two of them to construct displays featuring his sets. These drug stores were located at Grand Central Station, and at Broadway and 34th Street across the street from Macy's Department Store.

The display models were propelled by means of a hidden electric fan. Charles hired two young men for each display and dressed them in Pierrot suits, demonstrating the toys. The sight of wooden windmills and Ferris wheels magically rotating in the store windows wowed the passing public. Police reserves were soon called to manage the crowds, and as a concession to the public peace Charles removed the demonstrators from the windows. For five days the Grand Central Station drug store sold over 300 sets a day, and the other location was not far behind.

The majority of the toy buyers were still in town, and soon they were looking for the man they had recently snubbed. Charles was stunned by the volume of orders he received, many of them for five gross and more of the Tinkertoy sets. The orders were sent back to the Evanston factory, where Robert Pettit must have gone from delight to near panic as the volume of orders hit home.

The Toy Tinkers were so overwhelmed with orders that a larger space was needed. They relocated to a former

Plate 7

Mabley and Carew Store window display, Cincinnati, Ohio.

June 1915 *Toys and Novelties* magazine.

public garage on Elmwood Avenue near Grove Street in Evanston.[8] Automated machinery was designed by a new employee of the Toy Tinkers, Henry Martin Svebilius.[38] Henry was a native of Alme, Sweden, who moved to Evanston in 1915. At 46 years of age, he was very good at designing machinery, and would go on to file several patents for Toy Tinkers and other firms. Henry also supervised the construction of automated machines that would cut and slot the sticks, and drill the spools. One of the machines was able to drill eight holes at once on the sides of the spools. The machinery was installed at the new location, and production began in earnest to fill all of those orders for Christmas delivery.

The Toy Tinkers signed up selling agent Cardinal-Vincent Company of San Francisco, to cover the West Coast, and George Borgfeldt and Company of New York to handle the East Coast.[36, 39] By June 1915, the Toy Tinkers began to offer advertising matter, window signs, and electrotypes to stores and dealers.[40]

The Toy Tinkers were kept busy making the sets until Christmas, and ultimately delivered 900,000 sets for 1915.[8, 22] The Tinkertoy was a sensation, a smash hit. The partners had seen it through, and proven yet again if you build a better toy, the world will beat a path to your door. 1915 was a heady year.

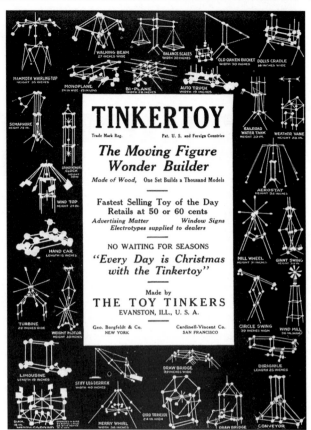

Plate 8

Trade advertisement for Tinkertoy, 1915.

TINKERPINS

"IT'S SKILL THAT WINS"

An unusually interesting and fascinating table game for family or club. Can be used at any season, time, or place where good, clean amusement is wanted.

Consists of a double track alley with ten pins at each end. A centrifugal governor that travels forward and back along the rails, automatically setting up the ten pins for the next player, and registering the count of the pins for the opponent's score. Spinner is returned by opponent's play from the opposite end. New principles, never before used in any game. Complete and easy instructions, showing how to play several games, are furnished with each set. Expert play comes with a little practice. "It's skill that wins in Tinkerpins." Every player becomes an enthusiast.

Wherever Tinkerpins is demonstrated, it is a big seller. We believe it to be one of the best games retailing at one dollar you could offer to your trade.

Packed flat in a 2 lb. box, wrapped ready to mail, express or deliver. Put together in a few moments. Size when set up 4 ft. 8 in. long.

Twelve Tinkerpins games are packed in a fibre shipping carton, weighing 26 lbs. complete.

Retails in the U.S.A. at One Dollar

Do Not Confuse This With Last Year's 50c Game Which Has Been Discontinued.

YOUR JOBBER IS NOW READY TO BOOK YOUR ORDERS.

Plate 9

Trade advertisement for Tinkerpins, 1917.

1916 – 1929
The Glory Years

After a blockbuster year like 1915, most people might be happy for a chance to relax a little, but Charles H. Pajeau was just getting started. He and Robert Pettit knew that in the volatile toy market of the time, today's hit could be tomorrow's memory. The Tinkertoy might only have a short life before losing its popular appeal, and the company would need more products to stay in business.[41] Charles was up to the task. He had been playing with toy ideas for quite some time, and was ready to invent more.

For 1916, the Toy Tinkers introduced one of Charles's inventions called Tinker Pins. This was a modified bowling game that used a gyrospinner on a set of rails to knock over sheet metal pins. The game sold for 50¢ that first year, but by 1917 it was priced at $1.00, after being improved.[42] Sales were so good in 1916 of both Tinker Pins and Tinkertoys that by early 1917 the business was overflowing the Elmwood location, with the installation of new production equipment for making Tinker Pins games.[43, 44]

A move to larger quarters was in order, so the Toy Tinkers took over a three-story brick and concrete build-

TINKERTOY 60c	TINKERPINS $1.00
TINKERBLOX 50c	TILLYTINKER 75c

Plate 10

Toy Tinkers Trade Advertisement, 1918.

ing at 721 Custer Avenue in Evanston. It was just in time, for 1917 saw the introduction of Miss Tilly Tinker, another Pajeau invention. This was an amazing balancing toy that proved a good seller.

The company recommended setting up twelve Tillys in a store window and keeping them moving by use of a concealed electric fan.[45] Other toys may have been introduced that year, but the evidence is sketchy with the

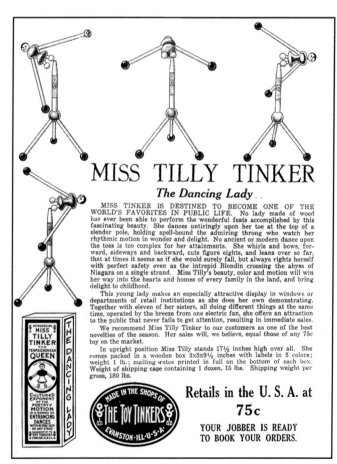

MISS TILLY TINKER

The Dancing Lady

MISS TINKER IS DESTINED TO BECOME ONE OF THE WORLD'S FAVORITES IN PUBLIC LIFE. No lady made of wood has ever been able to perform the wonderful feats accomplished by this fascinating beauty. She dances untiringly upon her toe at the top of a slender pole, holding spell-bound the admiring throng who watch her rhythmic motion in wonder and delight. No ancient or modern dance upon the toes is too complex for her attainments. She whirls and bows, forward, sideways and backward, cuts figure eights, and leans over so far, that at times it seems as if she would surely fall, but always rights herself with perfect safety even as the intrepid Blondin crossing the abyss of Niagara on a single strand. Miss Tilly's beauty, color and motion will win her way into the hearts and homes of every family in the land, and bring delight to childhood.

This young lady makes an especially attractive display in windows or departments of retail institutions as she does her own demonstrating. Together with eleven of her sisters, all doing different things at the same time, operated by the breeze from one electric fan, she offers an attraction to the public that never fails to get attention, resulting in immediate sales.

We recommend Miss Tilly Tinker to our customers as one of the best novelties of the season. Her sales will, we believe, equal those of any 75c toy on the market.

In upright position Miss Tilly stands 17½ inches high over all. She comes packed in a wooden box 3x3x9½ inches with labels in 5 colors; weight 1 lb.; mailing rates printed in full on the bottom of each box. Weight of shipping case containing 1 dozen, 15 lbs. Shipping weight per gross, 180 lbs.

Retails in the U.S.A. at 75c

YOUR JOBBER IS READY TO BOOK YOUR ORDERS.

The Dancing Lady Trade Advertisement, 1917.

Plate 11

Miss Tilly Tinker.

exception of Tinker Blox, which were in the new product line. This year purchasers of two or more cans of Tinkertoys were offered a free booklet, Book "B," showing models that could be built with more than one set.[46]

In addition to inventing toys and games, Charles also wrote the copy for the catalogs and verse about the toys for promotional pamphlets. He created the instruction booklets included with the toys, and the packaging. Tinker Blox being a case in point, he put together a twelve-page guide to the toy which featured an inspirational message for parents plus stories and games for the children.[41] He also quoted Mme. Montessori, the founder of the Montessori Method of child development, who in 1915 said, "When you have solved the problem of controlling the attention of the child, you have solved the entire problem of its education."[47] Pajeau went on to say of the quote, "That is the kernel of modern thought in regard to the best method of teaching the child. To combine instruction with play in such a way as to keep the child interested and enthusiastic is the theory endorsed by all authorities. This method finds its happiest expression, we believe, in Tinkerblox. With these little letter men, it is real fun for the child to learn the alphabet, make words, and use numbers."[47] This was a man who seriously believed in what he was doing.

World War I was still disrupting the supply lines between Europe and the United States, creating an ideal environment for the Toy Tinkers to expand. The company had seven toys in the product line listed in a 1918 promotional pamphlet.[22, 48] The toys included the Tinkertoy, Tinker Blox, Tilly Tinker, Flying Tinker, Jumpy Tinker, Tinker Pins, and Tinker Toss. The toys retailed from 10¢ to $1.00. The name Tinker was so famous that the company incorporated it into almost every product. In the early years, the Toy Tinkers encouraged the direct sale of toys from the factory.

Toys were offered in brochures for sale by mail, by adding a few cents to the listed price for postage.[49] Through its whole history, the company offered replace-

Plate 12

Toy Manufacturers dinner, January 15, 1917, Charles H. Pajeau is just left of center wearing a bow tie.

February 1917, *Toys and Novelties* magazine, p. 74.

ment parts by mail for the Tinkertoy sets. The instruction sheet would list the cost for different quantities of sticks and spools by mail. Through at least the 1930s, the parts were shipped in canvas bags imprinted with the company name and address with a guarantee of return postage.

In an effort to deal with a shortage of metal in 1918, Henry Martin Svebilius came up with a small metal clip which could be used to substitute wood or cardboard for a full metal lid or bottom of the Tinkertoy can.[50] The clip was patented and assigned to the Toy Tinkers by Mr. Svebilius, but it does not seem to have been used in actual production. The shortage of lids may have never materialized, and the war ended before this became a real problem.

The 721 Custer Avenue location provided the firm with 22,000 square feet of space, yet this was soon not enough.[8] They began to rent loft space and garages in the area to store the raw materials and finished goods. The product line was expanding and so was the demand for these goods. The problem of space as compounded by the fact that while orders were placed early in the year, deliveries were not made until closer to Christmas.[7] Thus the company needed to warehouse large stocks

of finished products until the wholesalers or department stores were ready to take delivery. This also made the toy business somewhat risky as the company spent money all year long, but only had a serious inflow of cash at the end of the year. A company had to be well managed to survive the usual economic problems which could arise.

Plate 14   *Systems* magazine, p. 834, December 1918.

Charles H. Pajeau in his workshop designing toys for the Toy Tinkers.

A problem which came up immediately for the Tinkertoy, due to the great and sudden success of the company, was patent infringement.[22] The toy being based upon the Pythagorean principle of the progressive right triangle

Pajeau of the Toy Tinkers Can Write Orders in Just the Grandest Manner You Ever Saw.

Plate 13   February 1917, pg. 80.

Caricature of Charles H. Pajeau as drawn by a staff artist for Toys and Novelties magazine.

required that the sticks be definite lengths relative to each other. The imitators did not grasp the importance of this fact. Charles Pajeau was quoted in a 1918 *System* magazine article explaining the situation, "We had dozens of imitators as soon as our toy became a success. We could have spent all out profits in patent-infringement litigation. But we smiled and let the infringers run along. And eventually they all discontinued the manufacture of wooden construction toys.

Because of the relative length of our sticks, a child is always able to make what he is constructing meet at both ends. The infringers selected haphazard lengths for their sticks, and so about half the time the youngster could not complete a job. That speedily put the other manufacturers up against it for a market." While many a copycat dropped by the way side, many more were waiting in the wings. Unfortunately, Pajeau himself may have enlightened many of them with his interview.

The year 1919 saw the addition of a toy called Tinkerblossoms, which appears to have been a whirly gig made to resemble a flower. The petals were angled to catch the wind. Also, the toy destined to become the company mascot was introduced in 1919. This was Tom Tinker, a bead doll made of wood. His sister Belle Tinker

---

GENERAL DESCRIPTION OF GOODS OFFERED FOR 1919

TOY BUILDING BLOCKS
DOLLS (TOM AND BELLE TINKER)
FIGURE TOYS (MAMMY TINKER)
BOWLING GAMES (TINKER PINS)
DUCK GAMES (TINKER DUX)
RATTLES (BABY DOLL TINKER)
SEESAWS
CONSTRUCTION TOYS (TINKERTOY)

Listed in company documents filed with the federal government in 1919.[53]

---

may have been introduced at the same time. She was made of bell-shaped wood pieces, comprising her body, legs, and arms. Other toys included a game called Tinker Dux, Bottle Tinker, Flying Tinker, Giant Tinker, Jumpy Tinker, Snappy Tinker, Target Tinker, Tilly Tinker, Tinkerpins, Tinkertoss, Tinkertoy, and Tinker Blox.[51, 52]

1920 had an impressive line-up of products, many of which would stay with Toy Tinkers a long time. Tom and Belle Tinker, The Wonder Builder Tinkertoy, Tinker Pins, Follo-Me-Tinker, Mammy Tinker, Whirley Tinker, Tinker Blox, Baby Doll Tinker, Tumble Tinker, Tilly Tinker, Flying Tinker, Tinker Dux, Noisy Tinker, and Jumpy Tinker made up the toy offerings. Sales for 1920 were the company's best to date.[41] By the end of 1920, they had sold over six million sets of Tinkertoy construction sets alone. The company noted in ads that 30 imitators had come and gone by that time.[54]

From the start, Charles Pajeau was concerned about making products which were not only fun and educational for children, but safe as well. One of his first inventions was the "Yankee Doodle Sulky," a non-capsizable cart used to transport children.[22] With safety in mind, Charles made all parts of the Tinkertoy smooth, rounded, and

Plate 15
Kaufman & Straus Window display featuring Tinker Toys.

January 1921, *Toys and Novelties* magazine, pg. 270.

GENERAL DESCRIPTION OF GOODS OFFERED FOR 1920

BUILDING BLOCKS
DOLLS (TOM AND BELLE TINKER)
FIGURE TOYS (MAMMY TINKER)
BOWLING GAMES (TINKER PINS)
DUCK GAMES (TINKER DUX)
RATTLES (BABY DOLL TINKER)
TOY ACROBATS
CONSTRUCTION TOYS (TINKERTOY)
FLYING TOYS (FLYING TINKER)
TABLE GAMES
TOY NOISEMAKERS (NOISY TINKER)
BALL TOSSING GAMES (TINKER TOSS)
CATAPULT & RING TABLE
    COURT GAMES (JUMPY TINKER)
WHEELED TOYS (TUMBLE TINKER,
    WHIRLY TINKER, FOLLOW-ME-TINKER)[55]

Listed in company documents filed with the federal government in 1920.

---

but he could not recall any being successful. Charles Pajeau was convinced that the paint they made was absolutely safe. After all, he helped develop the formula, and would often say, "I'll drink that paint and it won't hurt me!"[56]

Robert Pettit was also very safety conscious. He believed that making safe toys was good business. The Toy Tinkers' reputation was on the line every time a child received one of the company's toys.

1921 saw an economic downturn which cut sales by about 15% from the previous year.[41] Still, the Toy Tinkers were prospering in an economy which was hurting other companies. 1921 saw the following products added: Turtle Tinker, Siren Tinker, Rattle Box Tinker, and Bag Doll Tinker (blue eyes).[57–59] The choice of the name Siren Tinker is interesting in the light of a new company with which Charles and Robert would become involved in 1922.

Also in 1921, the Toy Tinkers sold the rights to "Tinker Blox," along with the machines to make the toy, to Halsam Products Company at 4114 - 4124 Ravenswood, Chicago, Illinois. It would appear that they were allowed to use the name "Tinker Blox," and the previously-produced instruction books. It is not clear how long Halsam produced Tinker Blox, although the means by which the deal was struck is very clear. Charles Pajeau and Harold H. Elliot, the president of Halsam Products, were both longtime members of the Sheridan Shore Yacht Club.[60–63]

without any paint or dyes that might be harmful.[8, 9] He was credited by those who knew him as a man with a great love and concern for children. This was a man who would give away toys to children he saw passing the factory. The late Fred Hiertz was emphatic in his belief that Charles Pajeau never wanted to see a child harmed by one of his toys.

Another former employee, Edgar Biemolt, told the story of how Pajeau had seen a child playing with a Tinker Toy called Rolo Polo.[9] It was a wheel and stick toy, likely modeled on the barrel hoop and stick that children had used for years. The wheel part got away from the child and rolled into the street. As children are apt to do, the youngster raced into the street after the toy. Charles hurried back to the factory and ordered a stop on production of the Rolo Polo, for he now felt it was not a safe toy.

Former long-time employee Larry J. Basting, who worked in the company paint shop for several years, talked about the paint that they custom mixed. He said that they never used lead in the paint. It was made of clay, pigment, and alcohol as a carrying agent. Later, the paint would be coated with shellac to seal it. Larry said of Charles, "I know Pajeau was awfully strict on the paint, so none of the kids would get hurt."[56]

Larry also mentioned that there had been some lawsuits against the company related to the safety of the toys,

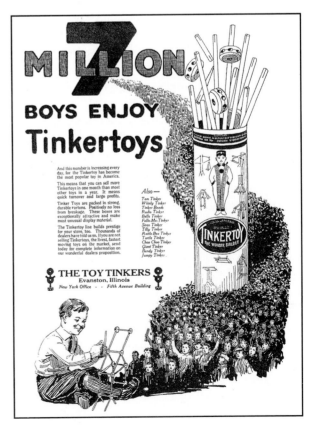

Plate 16

Tinker Toy trade advertisement, 1922.

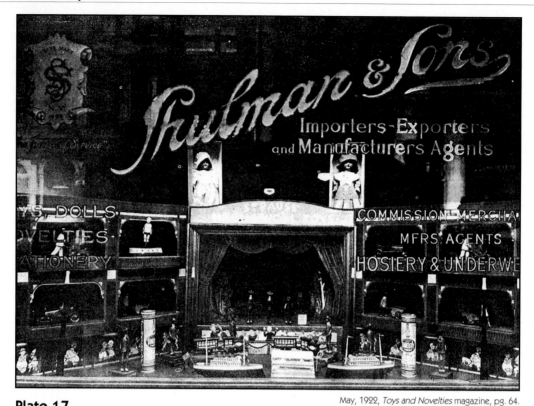

Plate 17

May, 1922, *Toys and Novelties* magazine, pg. 64.

Shulman & Sons Window Display featuring several Tinker Toys.

Several new items came to market in 1922, such as Radio Tinker, Tinker Beads (consisting of round beads) in a rectangular box, and Bendy Tinker. Bendy Tinker was a unique construction toy that could be used to create odd-looking animals.[64, 65] Choo Choo Tinker was introduced in 1922, but then withdrawn and reintroduced in a new form in 1924.

By 1922 the Toy Tinkers had added 826 Custer Avenue to their list of spaces, as the growth of the company demanded more room.[14] This haphazard arrangement could not last forever, but they were so busy, keeping up with orders was all they could manage. 1920 had been a great year for the Toy Tinkers, 1921 was even better, and in 1922 they did two and one-half times the business of 1921.[66]

On October 21, 1922, Albert S. Long, Samuel S. Holmes, and Alex Dushoff formed a business known as Siren Mills Corporation, located at 721 Custer Avenue in Evanston, Illinois.[67] What makes this of special interest is that the same address was also the location of the Toy Tinkers of Evanston, Illinois. Charles H. Pajeau, Robert Pettit, and Laurence D. Ely were the majority stockholders in the new venture. The corporation proposed to deal in "Chocolate powder and chemical food products of all kinds, and the raw materials from which they are made..."[67] (Plate 20).

After only a few years Charles's and Robert's names are no longer found in the corporate documents, and by 1928 they are not listed as stockholders. Laurence D. Ely was originally listed as the Toy Tinkers sales manager, and later as president of Siren Mills. Willis R. Brightmire held the posts of secretary and treasurer. He was very likely a good friend of Charles Pajeau, as his first residence in Evanston was listed as Charles's home at 1119 Michigan Avenue. In April of 1929 the company dealt in supplies used by soda fountains, and one of the four stockholders was listed as being the Walgreen Co., although it is not clear if this was the drug store chain. The business seems to have lost Mr. Ely between 1929 and 1933, and by 1943 the corporation was dissolved by the Secretary of State for failure to file reports and pay fees owed.

Mr. Brightmire stayed in Evanston and tried his hand in the restaurant business and insurance before becoming a manager for a Ford auto dealership. Charles initially appears to have had a keen interest in the business. Perhaps he created a chocolate syrup that he felt should be marketed, or he was just assisting several friends to get a new venture off the ground. The information available is not clear enough to answer those questions.

1923 saw several more winners incorporated into the product line of the Toy Tinkers. One was Tinker Beads, which consisted of round and oval wooden beads enameled in several colors, and sold in glass jars with a cord and pull needle for stringing. Another was Jump Rope Tinker. The jump rope had twenty enameled beads spaced on the rope and pinned in place. The idea was to

Plate 18

M.E. Smith Co. of Omaha, NE, Toy Display showing several of the Toy Tinkers products.

Toys and Novelties magazine, November 1923, pg. 49.

add weight to the rope to improve its swing. Tom Tinker Number Two was now offered in pastel colors for 75¢ retail, while Tom Tinker Number One was offered for 50¢ retail in primary colors.

By this time the company was very well established in department stores and with jobbers, who would resell to small retailers around the country.[41] Department stores would feature giant displays of the Tinker Toy line, and consequently sold large quantities of the products. Tinker Toys were prominently listed in store advertisements at Christmas time to help draw people into the establish-

ments. All the while, The Wonder Builder continued to be a consistent seller for the company.

After years of operating the company as a partnership, the Toy Tinkers reorganized as a corporation.[68] Attorney Joseph L. McNab of Plano, Illinois, filed the incorporation papers on December 15, 1923, in Cook County, Illinois. The declared purpose of the company was "to manufacture and sell toys and playthings of every kind and description."[68]

The company was capitalized with $200,000 worth of common stock, each share valued at $100. The stock was divided among the two partners and their wives, with each having 500 shares, except for Robert Pettit who was allotted 499 shares so that Joseph L. McNab could have one share. At some point in the company history, the executives of Toy Tinkers were allowed to receive stock in the corporation, which they later cashed-in when the company was sold. The only public indication of additional stock being created was in 1950, when 100 new shares were issued, but it did not specify who was to receive it.

The incorporation is noteworthy, in that it serves as a means of helping to date items sold by the company. After the incorporation, the abbreviation "Inc." was added to the company name. So a toy marked as "Toy Tinkers of Evanston, ILL." would likely be from 1923 or earlier, while one marked "Toy Tinkers Inc., Evanston, ILL." would be from 1924 or later.

Courtesy of the Evanston Historical Society.

Plate 19

Toy Tinker catalog page showing a 1923 store display of Tinker Toys.

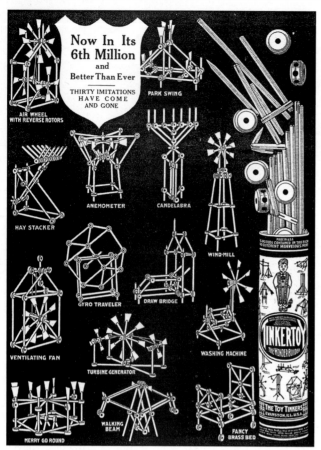

Plate 20

Tinkertoy Trade advertisement, 1921.

Charles Hamilton Pajeau was one of the founding members of the Sheridan Shore Yacht Club in Wilmette, Illinois. Lawrence Ely was also a member, and was in charge of the membership drive which ended in March of 1923. Charles was instrumental in helping the club to grow, and in the decision to utilize the Star Class sailboat for the club. He built at least two boats, one of which was constructed in the Tinker Toy factory. Charles was known for his sense of humor, which he showed off with a hard times party at the Tinker Toy factory in 1931. Games and frivolity were the order of the day for this party. Club member Walter Stockton recalled, in a December 16, 1971, *Wilmette Life* article, "Charlie was a good sailor, he was always kidding, and he always had something up his sleeve. A grand guy — wonderful guy."[60,69–71]

The Toy Tinkers expended a great deal of time, effort, and money promoting their goods with displays in stores, and advertising in national magazines.[41] They were rewarded with ever greater sales volume, and a reputation that excited children and got the attention of parents. 1924 saw Necklace Tinker, a ready-strung item intended for infants and toddlers, added to the inventory. Pony Tinker, Rowly Boat Tinker, Choo Choo Tinker, and Dragon Tinker were also added. 1924 seems to have been a good year for pull toys, as four of the five introductions were just that. By this

point the company was relying on sales to jobbers and department stores to move the product, and did not appear to solicit direct sales from the public, although replacement Tinkertoy parts were still available for a few cents.

The company was including little brochures with all their toys in 1924. These fold-out pamphlets listed several of the items offered by the Toy Tinkers, and for each there was a short poem written by Charles Pajeau. The poems told little stories about the toys from a make-believe land, or simply extolled the virtuous properties of the individual Tinker Toys.

Plate 21

Tinker Toys Trade advertisement, 1924.

Charming as they were to read, they amounted to advertising and seem to have been effective. 1924 also saw a go-together book called *Tinker Town Tom*, written by Esther Merriam Ames and illustrated by Arnold Lorne Hicks. The book, published by Rand McNally & Co. of Chicago, was a cloth-covered 96-page volume, with stories about Tom and Belle Tinker which included 43 color illustrations. A promotional pamphlet for *Tinker Town Tom* was enclosed in jars of Tinker Beads.

Books were not the only tie-in product for Tinker Toys. There was sheet music entitled "Dance of the Tinker-

Plate 22

A Giant Tom Tinker is featured in the window of R.H. Macy & Co. Store, December 1923.

Toys and Novelties magazine, pg. 166.

Courtesy of the Evanston Historical Society.

Plate 24

A Giant Tinker promotional photo from the early 1920s.

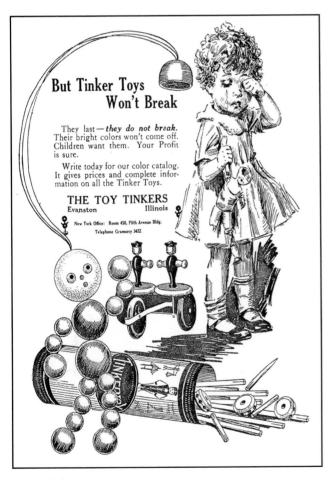

Plate 23

Tinker Toys trade advertisement, 1923.

toys" from 1927, and in 1944 came the "Parade of the Tinkertoys" for piano by Stanford King [72,73] There was also a Tinker Toy coloring book from 1939, which featured Tom and Belle Tinker, and others of the company line.[74]

In August of 1924 Fred Hiertz joined Toy Tinkers, and by the time he was ready to retire 50 years later, he was the plant superintendent.[9, 75] Fred would have been a good man to know, as he recommended a lot of friends and relatives for jobs with the Toy Tinkers over the next few years.

There were several changes to the company offerings for 1925. Topsy Tinker, a spinning doll in a metal frame, was added to the line. Clown Tinker, Surf Boat Tinker, Marathon Tinker, and Ten Pins Tinker were also new.[77] Items were typically kept in the inventory until sales started to fall off. When the fancy for a particular toy had passed, it would be removed and any remaining stock was sold at discount to department stores. The stores would usually offer the items in special sales, using the Toy Tinker name to draw people in while giving them a bargain. Occasionally, all a slow-selling toy needed was a modification to render it more salable, or make it more competitive.

The product mix must have been very good for 1926, as only three new items were listed in the company line. They were Seven-In-One Tinker, a construction toy for making vehicles, Lanky Tinker, and the New Tinker Pins.

The original Tinker Pins was withdrawn after 1920, and the new version had undergone several changes.

Courtesy of the Evanston Historical Society.

Plate 25

A Giant Tinker promotional photo from the early 1920s.

Where the original was mostly wood, the new form was mainly lithographed metal which would require much less hand finishing and assembly. Another advantage to this design was that there were less pieces for a child to lose. The original needed over twenty parts to assemble the game, and if you lost any of them the game might be unusable. The new game was preassembled.

Another difference was the size of the two toys. The original was almost 5 feet long when assembled, whereas the new form was only about 2 feet long. Both games used a gyrogovernor to ride the rails acting as a bowling ball, however the pin configuration was different.

Finally the Toy Tinkers took time to consider the untenable state of their manufacturing facilities, and in 1926 they announced plans to build a factory at 2012-20 Ridge Avenue in Evanston.[78] The *Evanston News Index* described the proposed structure as being fireproof, and noted that it would be built around an existing gas station which occupied the north-east corner of the lot. The gas station was later demolished. Robert Pettit was quoted in the same article as saying, "We are planning to occupy our new building by July 1. We are going to have a building which will not only be the latest word in factory construction, suitable to

TINKER TOY ASSORTMENT - B 1650

Carefully selected sure selling toys. Just the right quantity of each number. An easy way to buy these popular items.

Suggested retail price

12	B 1668 - Tinker Toys	$ .75	$9.00
6	B 1666 - Tom Tinker	$ .60	$3.60
6	B 1663 - Tinker Jar Beads	$1.00	$6.00
3	B 1670 - Marathon Tinker	$1.00	$3.00
6	B 1677 - Jump Rope Tinker	$ .50	$3.00
3	B 1680 - Pony Tinker	$1.25	$3.75
6	B 1672 - 50-cent Tinker Beads in Glass Jars	$ .50	$3.00
6	B 1676 - Clown Tinker	$ .60	$3.60
3	B 1674 - Rowly Boat Tinker	$1.00	$3.00
6	B 1671 - 25-cent Tinker Beads in Glass Jars	$ .25	$1.50
6	B 1682 - Follo-Me-Tinker	$ .60	$3.60
3	B 1669 - Ten Pin Tinker	$1.00	$3.00
3	B 1673 - Dragon Tinker	$1.00	$3.00
3	B 1684 - Whirly Tinker	$1.25	$3.75
3	B 1685 - Siren Tinker	$ .50	$1.50
3	B 1667 - Choo Choo Tinker	$1.00	$3.00
3	B 1665 - Necklace Tinker	$ .75	$2.25
2	B 1681 - Surf Boat Tinker	$1.50	$3.00

TOTAL RETAIL VALUE $62.55
COST TO DEALER $39.07
[76]   PROFIT, NEARLY 60% $23.48

our needs, but which will be an architectural credit to Evanston." (See Plate 28.)

The main building provided 65,000 square feet of daylight floor space, and would stand 52 feet high, with a tower rising 36 feet above that.[79] The building would have workshops, offices, assembly areas, recreational facilities, passenger and freight elevators, individual locker rooms, compressed air systems, and lots of storage space.[79] It would also have its own railroad siding at the loading dock. It was a remarkable building for its time, which even had a spiral metal chute for moving material from any floor to the basement for storage. The employees occasionally used the chute to get downstairs in a hurry. Finally the company was going to have a location suitable to their needs.

The Toy Tinkers seemed to be moving ever forward. Their sales continued to increase, and prosperity was a steady friend to them. The company added five new items to the 1927 line: Tinker Fish, Tinker Dogs, Steam Roller Tinker, Bunny Tinker, and Spinning Jack Tinker.[80, 81] Spinning Jack Tinker was a toy that operated on the governor principle. Once it was set in motion, you needed only give a slight occasional effort to keep it moving. The Toy Tinkers in 1927 were starting to feel the heat from competitors like Ted Toys and Hustler Toys, which were turning out a great variety of pull toys.[82]

Hustler Toys seemed to be mimicking the entire line of Tinker Toys right down to the three sizes of stringing beads in jars. But it was the pull toys in exotic designs that appeared to be the most competitive part of the market for

Toys and Novelties magazine, January 1925, pg. 257.

Plate 26

Selfridge's Christmas display showing several cans of Tinkertoys and a Tinkertoy model.

Toy Tinkers. Still, everyone was doing well, and the country had the money to spend. The company was well positioned as a high-quality American toy maker at competitive prices, with a name that people respected.

The promise of 1928 was of even better sales than the year before, and the promise was kept. The Tinkertoy had leveled off in sales at about 750,000 a year, although with the introduction just before Christmas 1927 of the Double Tinkertoy, sales had the potential to improve. The Double Tinkertoy contained twice the number of parts as The Wonder Builder, plus it had 4 wheels, 4 small pulleys, and 2 connecting rod bearings.

Up until this time, if you wished a larger model you were urged by the company to buy two or three sets, and that is often what people did. This helped to explain the continuing success of the Tinkertoy, as the next Christmas families would add another set to a child's collection. With the extra parts in Double Tinkertoy, people were encouraged by the store sales people to spend a little extra for greater flexibility in the toy.

New entries to the toy line for 1928 were Tinker Beads #4, Mule Tinker, Auto Racer #3, Lifeguard Tinker, Puppy Tinker, and Billy Goat Tinker. Puppy Tinker was a variation on Tom Tinker, and in fact the patent for Tom Tinker showed a four legged figure that resembled Puppy Tinker. Why Pajeau waited so long to introduce this form is open to speculation. The factory was turning out a tremendous array of products and shipping them all over the United States and the world.

Nearly every square inch of the plant was given over to production or storage. Over 100 people

Toys and Novelties magazine, December 1925, pg. 166.

Plate 27

John Wanamaker store window featuring a Giant Pony Tinker.

Courtesy of the Evanston Historical Society.

Plate 28

The New Toy Tinker Factory at 2012 Ridge, Evanston.

suit, and his attitude tended to match his attire. The formalities attended to, we would begin the tour of the plant. The first floor, aside from the offices, contains the loading dock, the paint room, and some storage. Stopping to gaze out of the loading dock bay gives us a view of the rail siding where all the spools, sticks, and miscellaneous materials are brought into the factory. As we watch, a boxcar is being off-loaded of its cargo of spools. One-hundred-pound burlap bags are hoisted over the backs of the employees and carried to the spiral metal chute to slide down to the basement for storage. Men in the basement are stacking the bags five and six high. The basement is packed with raw material, with every square inch utilized. Once emptied of the spools the burlap bags are cleaned and stacked about 25 high, rolled up, and sent back to the suppliers for re-use.

were directly employed in the factory in various stages of producing, stocking, or shipping the products of the Toy Tinkers.[38] Indirectly the company provided employment to many more people in wood shops, print shops, and such that produced the packaging and raw materials used to produce the toys in the Evanston factory.

Walking into the main entrance at the 2012 Ridge Avenue factory in 1929, we would find the main offices of the Toy Tinkers.[29,38,56,78,83–90] We would likely be greeted by the receptionist. Robert Pettit would probably be in his office arranging business details, and we might be allowed a brief audience. Mr. Pettit always dressed in a formal business

Plate 30

Tinker Toy trade advertisement, 1921.

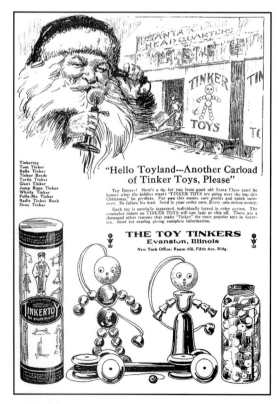

Plate 29

Tinker Toy trade advertisement, 1923.

Approaching the paint shop we see burlap bags stacked by its entrance. As we enter, raw wooden beads are being poured into one of several paint barrels. The beads have been cleaned of any wood dust so as not to foul the paint job. The paint used here was custom developed by the Toy Tinkers under Charles Pajeau's guidance. The paint is mixed in the shop to assure its safety and quality, which is why Charles has such great confidence in it. Each color has its own hexagonal shaped barrel, which could hold about 50 pounds of beads. There are some larger mixers as well. The beads being painted today will go into the Tinker Beads sets, sold in three sizes of glass jars. Five men are at work in the shop in various stages of the paint process. After the beads are painted, they are scooped out of the barrels with wire baskets and poured onto drying screens. Much the same process is used to paint the wood turnings that make up the other toys assembled by the Toy Tinkers. When the beads are finished they will be moved to storage, or to one of the assembly areas where they will be packed with stringing cord and a blunt needle in glass jars.

Stepping off the freight elevator on the second floor, we find assembly areas and some material stored ready to use. The assembly areas are made up of rows of tables, with chairs for the ladies to sit while they work. Here they are stringing together Belle Tinker. The arms and legs are expertly strung, and connected to the torso and head. Some foot pressure on the cord pulls it all tight, and then the knob is attached to the end of the cords. The finishing touch is the yellow metal label on the top of the knob, and another Belle is added to the ever-growing pile in front of the work tables. Supervisors regularly spot-check quality, though most of the women have worked here for years and know what is expected.

At the front of the building on the second floor, facing Ridge Avenue, is the lunchroom. Employees bring their own lunches, but are provided coffee and milk to drink.

Plate 32

Double Tinker Toy trade advertisement, 1927.

Courtesy of the Evanston Historical Society.

Plate 31

"The Portal of Progress," from the 1928 Toy Tinker Catalog.

Ella McKale takes off a few minutes early from her work to start the coffee for lunch. There are also offices on the second floor for the time keepers, and the Bench is also located there. The Bench is the canister assembly line, where the Tinkertoy sets are filled and packed for shipping. A man places the empty cans at the front of the line, and as they move down, the first lady rolls up the instruction book and shoots it into the can. The next woman drops the longest sticks into the can, and so on down the line until the last items to go in are the spools. Here, a handicapped gentleman is seated on a special chair, from which he operates the spool machine. He presses the can against a lever, and down drop a predetermined number of spools. The last man on the Bench picks up the can, snaps the lid on, and places it into a dozen-can shipping carton. When the carton is full, it is taped shut and shot down to the basement on the spiral chute. This last man is kept busy, as he is also responsible for keeping the Bench supplied with parts.

The third floor is wholly given over to assembly areas and packing. Here, they are snapping together the pull toy called Pony Tinker. The bright-colored wheels are put in place and the axles are crimped at the ends to hold the wheels on. On another part of the floor, Gym Tinker is being assembled. The ladies pull a spring through one of the half circles that make up his hands and feet, and using a cotter pin-like clip, secure it in place. The other turnings are then dropped in sequence on the spring, and the process is repeated until all limbs are connected within the torso. The spring tension then pulls Gym Tinker together. Rubber bands were tried for some of the flexible toys, but springs proved far superior as a backbone.

On the fourth floor we find the drill machine operation, where the men are turning out spools. One machine drills the center hole while another, known as the eight-hole machine, drills the side holes all in one operation, turning out 85 spools a minute.[23] The spools are poured into a hopper from which they roll down a little trail, fall into place, and the machine drills them. All the while, the compressed air system vacuums up the sawdust and funnels it to a tower, where it collects. The local farmers are given the sawdust to use for mulch, and it is popular with them. The ladies are operating the stick machines that cut the dowel rods to the proper lengths and slot the sticks at the same time. The sawdust has a tendency to build up under the horizontal blades on these machines, and the ladies brush it away with their hands. Cuts and nicked fingers are common.

The machine shop is also located on the fourth floor. This is where new machines are built and older ones maintained. Blades and drills are sharpened here, and standard twist drill bits are modified to drill a flat-bottomed hole for the spools' side holes. This modification is done by filing the bit top flat except for a pilot point in the very center.

Plate 34

A child's fascination with Tinker Toys. He is holding a Tom Tinker Doll.

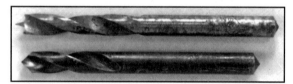

Plate 33

Author's collection.

Standard drill bit and modified drill bit used in the manufacture of Tinker Toys.

To the tower we go, where a conference room is located, and above that is Charles Pajeau's workshop. We find him working on a new type of rotary blotter, which he expects to patent any day now. The room is equipped with a drafting table and work benches. There are several toy posters and sketches hanging on the walls, all of which are his inventions. The boss needs to go back to work, so we head down to the rooftop recreation area. Here the employees can play tennis, basketball, or volleyball, on courts which are enclosed to prevent stray balls from creating havoc on the neighborhood.[79] This is a magnificent and busy place in 1929.

With the dawn of 1929, expectations grew like the numbers from the stock market, and the Toy Tinkers prepared for another record year. Stocks of toys were built up and the orders flowed in, for such new items as Auto Racer #2, Abacus Tinker, Go Round Tinker, Tip Toe Tinker, Gym Tinker, and the past winners.[91] Things were looking good for the Toy Tinkers and their customers. Then the stock market crashed, and so began a chain reaction that would have serious consequences for all concerned.

1929 ended with impressive sales gains for the American toy industry. Sales had been good for the Toy Tinkers.

Noisy Tinker—The new Tinker noise maker, two solid hardwood pieces, may be k. d., easily put together, improved construction, double usual noise, practically indestructible.

F3655—2 doz. in box .. Doz. **$1.20**
(Total **$2.40**)

1930 was proving to be much slower than 1929. Sales were seriously down. Worse yet, Charles Pajeau had personal financial problems with which to deal. He had invested in various ventures besides the Toy Tinkers, and now funds were tight for him.[56]

The company laid off the employees and shut down production. Larry J. Basting, a former employee, recalled that time. He had only recently come to work for the Toy Tinkers, and was happy when hired to work as a night watchman while the plant was closed down. Toy Tinkers needed to have a watchman to meet their insurance policy requirements for coverage of the giant building. Larry was earning $1.00 a night for a twelve-hour shift, where he walked all night punching a key clock as he made his rounds. The Toy Tinkers plant was awfully quiet those many months, waiting for the demand to recover.

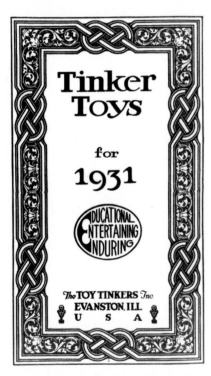

Courtesy of the Evanston Historical Society.

Plate 35

First page of the 1931 Toy Tinker Catalog.

Finally the orders began to eat through the backlog of toys, and the company started to call the workers back. Christmas 1930 was a lean affair, judged by the scarcity of toy advertisements in newspapers that heretofore were loaded with them. Still, the Toy Tinkers introduced Jockey Tinker to the line, as well as Jack and Jill Tinker, Tinker Kinderbeads, Tinkertoy Treasure Chest, Tinker Beads

Number 6, Tinker Dollhouse Furniture, and Casino Golf.[92] The word Tinker was not part of the name for Casino Golf, although the package indicates that it was from the Toy Tinkers of Evanston, Illinois. Casino Golf was a roulette wheel for golf balls, but required you to have a club and balls to use it.

Plate 36   Courtesy of the Evanston Historical Society.

1936 full page from the Toy Tinker Catalog, for Tom and Belle Tinker.

The adjustment was hard to make after so many good years. Pajeau was financially overextended, and by some reports, he had gone broke, which may have meant that he filed for bankruptcy.[9] By those same accounts, he was able to start over again. Back in about 1924, Charles and Grace Pajeau had moved to a lovely home in Glencoe, Illinois, a lakefront village north of Evanston. In about 1930 they moved back to an apartment in Evanston, which would fit with the reported financial difficulties.

As the shock waves of the great crash worked their way through the economy, toy companies were tightening to survive, and many did not. The Toy Tinkers began to feel intense competition in the area of pull toys, with many other makers producing them at lower prices.

The year 1931 found the Toy Tinkers introducing several new toys under the company name. There was Bunny

Boy Tinker, re-styled Bunny Tinker pull toy, Tinker Chicks, Tinker Rabbit, Tinker Tower, Tumble Bead Tinker, and Derby Tinker (re-stylized Jockey Tinker).[93] In all, the company was carrying a total of 26 items in the 1931 inventory. The company catalog sent to wholesalers and department stores had added the motto "Educational, Entertaining, Enduring" to the inside cover, presumably to quiet rumors of the company's demise. On the next page was a photo of the factory building, with an American flag flying over it. The caption told that the factory had over 65,000 square feet of floor space devoted to the manufacture of Tinker Toys. All of this was to lend an image of substantialness to the company.

The last two pages of the 1931 catalog were devoted to praising the quality of the company's products and explaining the service and publicity provided by Toy Tinkers. Among other things, they pointed out that the Toy Tinkers originated the idea of varnished toy packaging to prevent soiling during handling, that the company gave an unqualified guarantee with every toy they manufactured and they agreed to replace without charge any defective item brought to their attention. This was an attempt to reestablish their former position as a high-quality toy company, with reasonably priced goods, whose image was damaged by the Depression.

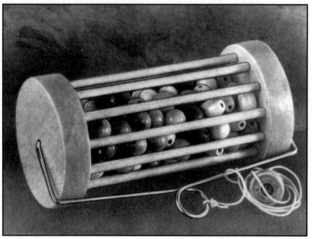

Plate 37

Courtesy of the Evanston Historical Society.

1936 catalog photo of Tumble Bead Tinker Toy.

In large part, a flood of cheap European toys and the price cutting by the surviving domestic manufacturers had made the image irrelevant.[94] Stores were also trying to stay afloat, and if they could sell cheap toys of minimal quality and make a better profit than by selling Tinker Toys, then so be it. Tinker Toys did not stop selling altogether, but demand was beginning to drop for all but the construction sets.

Motor Tinkertoy was introduced in 1932.[95] This construction set was the same as the Double Tinkertoy, with the addition of six new pieces and a wind-up spring motor. The Electric Tinkertoy introduced the same year was identical to Motor Tinkertoy, except that the motor was a 60-cycle, 110-volts, alternating current with a wall plug. Motor Tinkertoy was recommended for locations that did not have alternating current. Both motors were designed to be mounted on dowel rods and become integral parts of any model.

Plate 38

Tinker Toy Trade Advertisement, 1934.

The Toy Tinkers needed to cut costs to stay competitive, and no longer needed the same square footage.[96] So in 1933 they sold the 2012-20 Ridge building to Lady Ester, Inc., a fragrance manufacturer. The company moved next door to 1948 Ridge, which was about half the square footage of the property just sold. The new location was two stories high with a basement. The previous owner was a lamp manufacturer that specialized in marble lamp bases. As a result, marble dust still permeated the building. The basement endured a persistent water seepage problem. This was a step down from the heady days of the 1920s, but the Toy Tinkers were still a going concern.

They tightened their belts and got on with the business of making toys.

The motorized Tinkertoys were very successful in 1932, and the enthusiasm of customers over the new parts lead to another change. The Double Tinkertoy had 146 pieces plus 10 extra parts, but the motorized sets included six more pieces, or 162 altogether. For 1933 the Senior Tinkertoy was introduced to replace the Double Tinkertoy. The proportion of the parts were different in the Senior set, plus it had two large pulleys not available before. The 162 parts were all of wood, and the count did not include the windblades and belting cord to run the pulleys and gears. The extra parts allowed for greater flexibility in the design and variations of models which could be built.

Another new entry for 1933 was Junior Tinkertoy for Beginners, which was advertised as being the same as the Wonder Builder, without a few of the less-necessary parts. The less-necessary parts were the #6 sticks, 3 of the spools, two of the #B sticks (the short type with one pointed end), and #A sticks (the longer ones with one pointed end). The Junior set also used a hub identified as spool "J." The difference may be that it was not painted. The Junior set contained 59 wooden parts to The Wonder Builder's 73 pieces, while both sets had eight windblades. No other new items appeared to be introduced that year.

The trend moved toward concentrating on the sale of construction sets, and expanding the line in that direction. This was an area where the company was clearly better than their competitors. One change in the non-construction line was an effort to sell bags of Tinker Beads for 50¢ each. Since 1934 is the only year that any mention of the bags of Tinker Beads can be found, it is possible that they did not do well and were dropped in favor of the old standby, Tinker Beads in glass jars.[97] Added to the line for 1934 were two pull toys: Penguin Tinker and Dachshund Tinker. The wheels were set at odd angles to the axles, to create a waddle appropriate to the animals they mimicked.[98]

For 1935 one new game was introduced called the Peeza Game. Otherwise, the eighteen items that made up

the line were old tried and true toys, such as bead dolls, Tinker Beads in glass jars, Baby Doll Tinker, Tinker Necklace, Jack and Jill Tinker, and Tumble Bead Tinker. Tumble Bead Tinker was the only surviving pull toy in the company line. Of course, there were also the various Tinkertoy construction sets. The stock of toys available continued to reduce in number, with more emphasis being given to the Tinkertoy sets.

The 1935 catalog offered a special deal to promote the sale of Junior Tinkertoy. If six dozen of the Junior sets were ordered then the Toy Tinkers would loan the buyer a motorized display of the Junior Tinkertoy. They also offered several combinations of the Junior set with Wonder Builder, Senior, and motorized Tinkertoys. The display was also offered for outright sale at $1.50, if buyers preferred to own it. On the inside back cover of the same catalog was the notation, "1914 - Good then, 1935 - Good now, 2000 - Good always."

A look at the number 1948 Ridge Avenue factory shows a much more cramped space in 1936 than the previous building had been, but the move was necessary to keep the Toy Tinkers financially viable.[56, 83–90] Since 1932, The Wonder Builder and Senior Tinkertoy sets had red painted spools, keeping the paint shop busy. The paint shop was located on the first floor in the back. Here, Larry J. Basting and the rest of the paint crew used the process developed to produce large batches of painted spools. Larry J. Basting and Charles Pajeau spent almost a whole summer working out the process. The difficulty was to paint the wooden spools and prevent them from sticking together when they were done.

Usually, 250 pounds of spools were poured into a long cylindrical vat, with small doors on the top which could be sealed. A predetermined amount of paint was poured into the vat, the doors were secured, and the cylinder rotated to coat the spools. Compressed air was then forced through the ends of the vat until the spools were dry. At that point, a predetermined quantity of shellac was poured into the vat and it was rotated again. The air was forced through once more to dry the spools. Through careful experimentation, they learned how to process a

TINKERSAND PICTURES

For aspiring little artists, this new and original pastime created by The Toy Tinkers promises to fulfill a long felt need. The set as shown above consists of 12 outline pictures on 6¼ x 8¼ inch cards, 6 packages of finest sand in as many brilliant and fast colors, a jar of brushing cement, a brush and complete directions for making the pictures. With this outfit any child old enough to paint in an ordinary toy watercolor book can produce sand pictures that may really be classed as works of art. More mature students find the making of Tinkersand pictures both an inspiration and a pleasure. Finished subjects are suitable for framing and decoration. For weights and packing see price list.

Plate 39   Courtesy of the Evanston Historical Society.

1936 full page from the Toy Tinker catalog, for Tinkersand Pictures.

batch that would have only one or two sets of spools sticking together.

The paint shop also had another new task, the painting of sand for the Tinkersand picture sets, introduced in 1936. After painting the white sand, it was placed in small containers, then packaged with preprinted cards, glue, and brushes in attractive multicolored cardboard boxes.

```
TINKERTOYS 1936
3 BRAND NEW ORIGINALS
PYLON TINKER···TINKERSAND
BANDYBOARD TINKER
2 MAJOR IMPROVEMENTS
SPRING MOTOR TINKERTOY
NEW BEAD NECKLACE
AND ALL THE BEST OF
THE STAPLES INCLUDING
JUNIOR TINKERTOY
TINKERTOY
SENIOR TINKERTOY
ELECTRIC TINKERTOY
TOM TINKER···BELLE TINKER
BABY DOLL TINKER
BUNNY BOY TINKER
NECKLACE TINKER
TUMBLE BEAD TINKER
BEADS IN JARS···PEEZA
```

Plate 40

Tinker Toy Trade Advertisement, 1936.

The catalog for 1936 begins with "Tinker Toys in twenty-two years have made Fifty Million Friends, because they are Safe, Sane and Sure." The Toy Tinkers introduced four new items this year: Tinker Necklace #2, Bandy Board Tinker, Pylon Tinker, and Tinkersand. Tinker Necklace #2 would last for a while, but Tinkersand proved to be a hit and was offered for sale through at least 1940 in several different forms.[99] The idea was to paint the colored sand onto preprinted cards, to give a multi-dimensional appearance to them. The first set was scenes of ships, trains, children, and such. Later came Disney characters including Snow White, and Goofy and the gang, which were licensed by Walt Disney. Walt even came by the factory to inspect production of the sets.

Tinkersand was the last big hit for the Toy Tinkers for a non-construction toy. The other consistent sellers, like Tinker Beads and Tom and Belle Tinker, were being phased out by 1938. By 1939, the only product still listed for sale in store catalogs, besides Tinkertoy, was Tinkersand Pictures. After 1939, only the construction sets were

advertised, although company ads of that time included Tinkertoys, construction toys, beaded dolls, sand painting sets, coloring sets, and novelties.[100] 1939 saw the introduction of one last item, Tinker Craft Kits, priced at $1.00 each. This was a set intended to teach business skills to young children.[101]

Henry Martin Svebilius, the man who automated the plant and ran the machine shop for so many years at the Toy Tinkers, died one day before his 67th birthday.[102] His death came at his home in Wilmette, Illinois, on February 22, 1936. He had joined the company in 1915, and now his son Arnold took over the machine shop duties. Arnold would later be a member of the Evanston Draft Board during the Second World War and see many of the Toy Tinkers employees come before him.[56]

The exact date is not clear, but Charles Pajeau did try his hand at making and selling shaving cream. Larry J. Basting, a former long-time employee of the Toy Tinkers,

Plate 41   Courtesy of the Evanston Historical Society.

1936 full page from the Toy Tinker catalog, for Tinker Beads 1,2 & 3.

recalled the whole place stinking of the perfume. Charles gave the men tubes of his concoction to try out at home, and they dutifully shaved with it. There is no record of what became of this invention.

On June 21, 1938, Pajeau was almost killed in a plane crash in Glenview, Illinois.[103–111] The accident left him to spend many months recovering, and may have been the

Plate 42

Tinker Toy Trade Advertisement, 1939.

Plate 43

Tinker Toy Trade Advertisement, 1940.

final blow to the other toys in the company line. At this point he was 63 years old, and his partner was only a little younger. The company had expended a lot of money on developing and producing a series of toys and games that never found acceptance or profitability. Charles may not have had the energy to continue the chase for the next big blockbuster toy. The company had one product that had proven its staying power, and was even gaining sales in the late 1930s. It made sense to put all of their energies into producing the toy that was popular and very profitable, and forget the other toys.

In an interview with the *Evanston Review* in 1952, shortly before his death, Charles Pajeau said that the decision to phase out the other toys had been a wise one.[112] As a result, the company was able to buy top quality materials and retain their competitive edge. Of the 32 companies that had copied the Tinkertoy, only one was still in business at the time of the interview.

The Toy Tinkers of Evanston, Illinois, were ending one phase of their history, and were about to move into a new period.

Plate 44

Larry Basting driving the Toy Tinker truck, about 1940.

Courtesy of Larry Basting.

1940 saw the introduction of new style of graphics for the canisters that contained the construction sets. There are the cans known as the big "T" canisters. They were identified as such because of the long vertical line that runs from the bottom to the top of the can, and then meets a band running horizontally around the top. Viewed from the front this looks like the letter "T," thus the name. The sets available from 1940 to 1942 in the big "T" can were The Wonder Builder, Senior Tinkertoy, Junior Tinkertoy, Easy Tinkertoy, and Spring Motor and Electric Motor Tinkertoy. Somewhere in that time, red spools were phased out of production, replaced by natural wood spools for all sets, most likely another war casualty.

As the Second World War approached, the demand for Tinkertoy construction sets continued to grow, while the labor pool began to shrink. By 1941, high school students from Evanston were working the night shift at the Toy Tinkers factory. There would typically be about fifteen people working this 3 PM to 11 PM shift, most of whom were students. They worked Monday through Saturday, earning about 38¢ to 45¢ an hour. [86, 87]

In the summertime, the students entered a rotating shift with the regular factory employees. There was also an eleven to seven late shift, where two men were locked in by the night watchman to run the drill machines all night. The only way out was to have the watchman unlock the

Plate 45

Toy Tinkers Trade Advertisement for Tinkertoys, 1940.

— 36 —

Plate 46

Toy Tinker Trade Advertisement for Tinkertoys, 1943.

a new toy EVERY DAY

TINKERTOYS
EVANSTON ILLINOIS

Plate 47

Toy Tinker Trade Advertisement for Tinkertoys, 1943.

doors. At least one of the then students recalled working that shift.

The majority of the workers on the night shift were involved with the Bench, where canisters were filled with construction set pieces. Between 10 and 12 people worked the Bench, likely depending upon which set was being assembled. Junior or Easy Tinkertoy would require less people, as they contained less parts, while Senior and Electric sets had several items not included in the smaller sets. The salary varied depending upon which job was being done. If, for example, the employee running the drill machine met or exceeded the quota, pay was by a piece rate. But if the employee produced less than the quota, a lower regular hourly salary would be paid.

Julius Gardner, who worked on the Bench, recalled that if the quota was exceeded, the Bench workers would earn a bonus based on how many extra cans they filled.[88] So Julius would start feeding the cans a little faster to the line, so that people would have to pick up the pace. After a while, the others would realize that he was speeding things up and start to get annoyed at him. Of course, when there was extra money in their pay packets, they did not mind the extra pressure. Paul Gardner, the younger brother of Julius, recalled one evening when the crew working the Bench met their quota about an hour early, so

Plate 48

Author's collection.

Tinkertoy cans made of all cardboard, due to the metal shortage during World War II.

Plate 49

*Toy Tinker Trade Advertisement
for Tinkertoys, 1944.*

they decided to knock off and go home.[87] The supervisor would have none of that, and chased them back to the line.

Another former employee, Arlene R. Grewe, recalled that after 1942 the company was unable to obtain the metal lids for the containers, so the can was redesigned to be all cardboard.[85] The lid was a cardboard sleeve that fit over the top of the can. The can graphics again underwent a change, to what is known as the small "T" can. In this case, the vertical line runs from the bottom to the middle of the can, where a band runs horizontally around. This gives the appearance of a "T" that is about half the size of the previous style. The cardboard cans were marketed through 1944.

The employees had difficulty with the cardboard lids at first. These lids were tight, and when pushed onto the can, the air pressure within the can prevented the lids from sliding on. Soon the workers learned to push in the side of the can, allowing the air to escape, and the job became a little easier, although it was still hard on their hands. The schedule was rough on the high school students, who would go from school to work, get home in time to sleep, and then need to be up early for school again.[85-87] Yet, with the Toy Tinkers being such a part of their lives, they managed to have fun on the job.

The environment, while businesslike at the Toy Tinkers, also seems to have had room for some joking and fun in the course of work. It was common for related persons to work in the plant, as with the Gardner brothers, and Larry J. Basting's younger brother, Clarence Basting, was working there too. The work was mostly repetitive and needed some type of diversion to help break the monotony. Paul Gardner talked about the time during the summer when he was so badly sunburned that he was running the drill press without a shirt on. One of the girls

came up behind him and poured a bucket of sawdust on him. He was laughing when he told the story, so it appears that it was all in fun.[84]

Julius Gardner recalled the Toy Tinkers as being a fun place to work. He felt that the mix of ages added to that sense of fun. Arlene Grewe also had pleasant memories of the years at the company. She related one not-so-pleasant time, though, when she was running a drill press. Fred Hiertz was the night manager and he had a habit of creeping up behind the girls while they worked to make sure they were not goofing off. That evening he startled Arlene while she was drilling a piece, and she drilled her finger. It was not a serious injury, but she commented, "That got me off the drill machine for a while."[85]

At the time when cardboard lids were introduced for the Tinkertoy sets, the Electric and Spring Motor sets were discontinued. This was most likely a casualty of the war effort, with motors and metal suddenly being at a premium. This brought an end to a popular part of the line. The company was then offering Easy Tinkertoy, Junior Tinkertoy, Senior Tinkertoy, and The Wonder Builder.

1943 found one sad change at the Toy Tinkers of Evanston, Illinois.[113] One of the founders, Robert Pettit, died at Evanston Hospital on the evening of July 13. He was 62 years old. Robert was survived by his wife, Rachel Hazelhurst Pettit, and daughter, Mrs. Hollinshead T. Martin. The service was held at the family home at 1425 Ridge Avenue in Evanston, and was conducted by Reverend Robert Holmes of St. Marks Church in Evanston.

Charles had lost his long-time associate and friend. The post of vice president needed to be filled, and for the first time it would be held by a person who was not an original founder and owner of the Toy Tinkers. The job went to Albert J. Liescke, who had been with the company from early on in their history.[8]

Another change came at the end of 1943. The Toy Tinkers sold the factory building at 1948 Ridge to the Gray Mills Company of Chicago, who would be building portable pumps for the war effort.[96] The Toy Tinkers purchased buildings at 801 Greenwood Street and 1310 Sherman Avenue, both in Evanston. They moved their offices to the second floor of the Chandler Building, at the corner of Grove Street and Sherman Avenue. The Toy Tinkers proposed to spend about $5,000 on improvements to each of the buildings they purchased, and paid about $20,000 for each of the two properties. The Greenwood building was the manufacturing center, and Sherman Avenue served as the warehouse and shipping department. The locations totaled about 25,000 square feet of space for the Toy Tinkers' operations.

1944 found the company struggling to meet demands for the Tinkertoy line, with wood starting to be in short supply. The story was that the government had allowed the majority of lumberjacks to enlist, or be drafted, so suddenly no one was left to cut the lumber, and supplies dried up. A company ad for 1944 identified the lineup as Easy Tinkertoy, Junior Tinkertoy, Senior Tinkertoy, and The Tinkertoy (Wonder Builder).[114, 115]

Plate 50

Courtesy of the Evanston Historical Society.

Charles H. Pajeau at the Sheridan Shore Yacht Club, 1940s.

The war was clearly moving in the favor of the Allies as the year 1945 began, and metal for Tinkertoy lids again became available. Advertisements for 1945 show the cans in the small "T" style, using the metal screw-top lids. This style was used through 1949.[115, 116] The types of sets available varied by year. 1945 and 1946 continued to list Easy Tinkertoy, Junior Tinkertoy, The Wonder Builder (also known as Regular Tinkertoy), and Senior Tinkertoy. 1948 and 1949 sets included these plus Special Tinkertoy.

In 1947, Illinois was ranked third in the nation in the manufacture of toys.[19] Evanston was a leader in toy production for Illinois, with the Toy Tinkers taking the lion's share of the credit. That year the Toy Tinkers were producing 2,500,000 sets of Tinkertoys, and they held a record for production of a single product for several years. The baby boom was being felt by the Toy Tinkers, and they were benefiting handsomely from it. Copy from a March 1947 ad read: "33 years ago it all started with a stick and spool. Today 100 million sticks and 40 million spools are required annually to supply the world with Tinkertoys. Good Then. Good Now. Good Always."[118]

Plate 51

Tinkertoy Trade Advertisement, 1946.

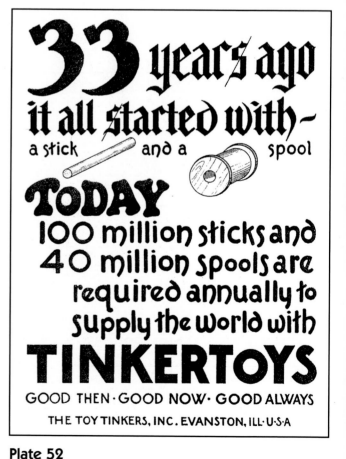

Plate 52

Tinkertoy Trade Advertisement, 1947.

The style of Tinkertoy cans changed again in 1950, with the use of a small "T" graphic in which the vertical line was made up of two thin blue stripes with white between them. The types available were the new Deluxe Tinkertoy, Junior Tinkertoy, Senior Tinkertoy, Special Tinkertoy, and The Wonder Builder.[119]

Charles H. Pajeau was 77 years of age in August of 1952. He was at the point where he was concerned about the future of the business. He had given over the day-to-day business decisions to Albert J. Liescke, vice president of Toy Tinkers, but Charles was still heavily involved in the creative decisions of the company. That included new product introductions, and design of the parts and artwork for all toys. Charles had an involved process to produce the model diagrams used in the instruction books that were packed with Tinkertoy sets.[90] He would take a photograph of a Tinkertoy model which he had put together, and then outline the subject, using a special pen. Next, he would place the photo in a special bleach bath which would completely remove the original photo image and leave only the penned outline. That penned outline was used in the instruction books. The process was repeated for all of the diagrams.

During this period a young man named John Wright arrived in the Chicago area, and made an appointment to see Charles Pajeau. John was a toy designer who was trying to interest toy manufacturers in some of his ideas. One was a plastic Humpty Dumpty toy which could be disassembled and reassembled by very young children. Charles was not interested in producing anything but Tinkertoy sets at this point in his life, but he was very

Plate 53

Tinkertoy Trade Advertisement, 1952.

impressed with young Mr. Wright. The two met several times, and Charles took the young man on a tour of the Toy Tinker facilities. He showed John how all of the design and creative functions were handled. John ended up selling his Humpty Dumpty toy to another manufacturer, but his encounter with Charles Pajeau would prove more significant.

Mrs. Muriel Biemolt, wife of former plant manager Edgar Biemolt, recalled Charles Pajeau as a sweet and charming man. She related the time in the early 1950s when she stopped by the plant to see her husband. Charles noticed that she was there, and came rushing down from high up in the factory to welcome her. "He was very cute," she noted.

The deal to sell the Toy Tinkers to A. G. Spalding Brothers was struck on a golf course during a game. Charles was persuaded that if the company was not sold before his death, that the ultimate disposition of the company may not be according to his wishes. He believed that Spalding would carry on the company in a fashion consistent with his philosophy, since several of the men involved in making the deal were native Evanstonians, who as boys had grown up near the Tinkertoy factory.[120] Charles felt that under Spalding the Tinkertoy would last for perhaps hundreds of years. In November of 1952 both he and the Spalding executives knew that they were buying a very profitable business, and all seemed very pleased with the terms.[112]

The stockholders of the Toy Tinkers at the time of sale were Mr. Charles and Mrs. Grace Pajeau, Mrs. Rachel Pettit, the widow of Robert Pettit, and some of the executives of the Toy Tinkers. The actual percentages held at the time of the sale were not available, although based upon other sources it could be guessed that Charles and his wife had 1,000 shares, Rachel Pettit controlled 999 shares, and the executives accounted for the remaining 101 shares. The sale price was $1,750,000 although it is not clear if that included the Canadian and other rights sold from Charles Pajeau's estate after his death.[121]

Muriel Biemolt felt that Charles regretted the sale of the company, that it had broken his heart to give up the Toy Tinkers. Had he been ten years younger, no one could have pried the business away from him, Charles had said.[112] The Toy Tinkers was his greatest business and creative achievement, and had been his constant concern for 38 years. The company was a reflection of Charles' spirit and dreams, and to sell it was an indication of how much he loved it and wished it to continue to thrive.

Charles put his affairs in order and arranged to have his will updated.[9] He also set about creating his famous Christmas cards for 1952, continuing this annual tradition for family and friends. He always designed the cards himself, and enclosed a dollar or two with each card, except for the young newlyweds to whom he would give as much as twenty dollars. Charles was always very generous, and for him Christmas was a very special time.

On December 16, 1952, Charles signed his will, and he had already mailed his Christmas cards. The next morning, December 17, 1952, Charles died of a heart attack in his penthouse apartment at the Orrington Hotel in Evanston, Illinois.[18, 122–124] Charles H. Pajeau, the son of a monument salesman, and a man who had started out in the same occupation, chose to be cremated like his father.[125]

When his will was read, it was learned that Charles had set up a trust to benefit children from poor and disadvantaged backgrounds.[126, 127] Half of Charles' estate went into the trust, and Grace Pajeau would later add to the fund upon her death. The trust is still very active today, providing money to make life better for children, as Charles had wished. Charles felt that he had lived a wonderful and exciting life, and been very successful. That success was due mainly to children, so he felt he owed them something. This trust would help to repay that debt in a small way.

Charles had created toys that have pleased and delighted generations, excited young imaginations, and expanded the creative possibilities of millions. At a recent exhibition of Tinker Toys participated in by the author, it seemed that almost all of the thousands of people who attended stopped to say that they remembered playing with the Tinkertoy. Men and women alike talked of how they created designs and models, and they all smiled with delight as they reminisced. People in their twenties to their seventies were included in that group. It was a reflection of a special man who, after already giving so much through his toys, felt that he owed still more.

The last of the founders had passed away, and now the preservation of the Tinkertoy was the responsibility of A. G. Spalding Brothers.

There was the time that Charles and Grace, his wife of many years, stopped by a friend's office to see him.[9] They seated themselves in the waiting area until the friend was available. When an assistant went in to advise the friend that the Pajeaus were there, the assistant also inquired as to whether the couple were newlyweds. The friend said "no," and asked why the question had come up. It seems that while they were waiting, Charles was reading poetry to Grace.

Plate 54

Advertisement to announce that Spalding owns the Toy Tinkers, 1953.

With his passing, the Toy Tinkers were in danger of losing the romance and wonderment that Charles had brought to the company. A transition in management can be difficult for a business when it goes from private control to corporate control. A. G. Spalding Bros. of Chicopee, MA, wished to make the transition as painless as possible.[112] They arranged to have Charles Pajeau stay on as a consultant, and to keep many of the company executives. Albert J. Liescke returned to the post of sales manager, making way for Walter B. Gerould to become the president of Toy Tinkers.[129] Mr. Gerould was a former Evanston-

ian, and was also a vice president and controller for Spalding Bros.[130] The vice president and treasurer posts went to Ernest Heilmann, also a Spalding executive. Mr. Gerould remained out east, while Mr. Heilmann moved to Evanston to run the day-to-day operations.

Photo by W. B. Nickerson.

Plate 55

Fred Hertz with employee at the stick machine, January 1964.

Spalding felt that Tinkertoys were a natural fit for the company's product line.[112] They were already heavily involved with sporting goods, and a toy line would be a good way to make youngsters familiar with the company name and their other products. Spalding planned a heavy promotion program for pre-school items, along with merchandising and advertising of the whole product line.

Spalding initially allowed the Toy Tinkers to continue as a wholly-owned subsidiary, but eventually it was made a division of Spalding Bros. John Wright was hired by Spalding to take over the creative and design work done previously by Charles Pajeau. Charles had recommended John for the job, as he was impressed by the young man's knowledge and abilities.

Spalding made some changes to the names of the stick-and-spool construction sets, and altered some of the parts. There were also new sets offered for sale. There was again a Motor Tinkertoy, Big Boy Tinkertoy, Grad Tinkertoy, and two familiar names, Easy and Junior Tinkertoy.

John Wright also designed several new items and reintroduced a couple of the older ones. These toys included Block and Roll pull toy, Color Coded Domino's, Count 'N Stack, Curtain Wall Builder, Design Blocks, Panel Builder, Pound A Block, Tinker Zoo, Tinkertown Trains, Tinker Fun Forms, Toy Maker, and a whole line of stacking toys.[121, 131–136] The stacking toys had names like Clown Stack, Jack Stack, Sally Stack, and Stack-Me-Sue.

Plate 56

Photo by W. B. Nickerson.

Tinkertoy assembly line, 1964.

The old veterans were Tinker Beads and Tom and Belle Tinker. Tinker Beads were offered in large and small sizes, but were shaped differently than the original style, with ridges cut into some of the beads. Tom and Belle Tinker appeared to be exactly the same as the Pajeau-period dolls, except that they had a round wooden ball at the end of the string instead of the half-circle handball with the company label.

The Spalding versions do not seem to have any marking to name the manufacturer. The 1950s Spalding Belle doll was the same style as produced after 1927, but with the round ball at the end of the string. Identification of the 1950s Tom could offer a little more trouble. The very early Tom Tinker dolls were sold with balls at the end of the string, though these dolls were labeled on the back of the torso beads. The labels were applied and then shellac was put on top of them, so some part of the label or evidence of it should still be apparent. So if the doll has a ball at the end and no label for the manufacturer, it is likely a Spalding-era product. Another indication of age would be the

colors of Tom Tinker, as the earlier dolls should look darker than the newer ones.

The Spalding Tom and Belle were introduced in 1954, and Tom was still for sale in 1959 as part of a "Treasure Trove for Tiny Tots." This "Treasure" also included Sally Stack, a Tinkertown Train engine and tender car, and a small can of Tinkertoys. It came packed in a cardboard display box with a treasure chest pictured on it.

The construction sets continued to be packed in the familiar cans, although at least one rectangular cardboard boxed Tinkertoy set was offered from 1959 to at least 1964, named set #179. The other toys were sold in clear plastic bags with cardboard labels, or in blister packs with cardboard backings, intended to be hung on peg boards. The Tinkertown Trains were packed in display boxes, and the construction sets like Tinker Zoo and Curtain Wall Builder were packed in cardboard canisters with metal lids, although Tinker Zoo was also sold in a box intended to be hung on a display rack.

Plate 57

Tinkertoy Trade advertisement, 1953.

The expansion of the product line required more space, so the warehouse at 547 Chicago Avenue was added to the company locations.

Starting in 1960 as a part of the company's ongoing advertising and promotion campaign, Spalding purchased ad time on the *Captain Kangaroo* television show. The

Plate 58   Author's collection.

Treasure Trove for Tiny Tots catalog ad, 1959.

ads were slated to run from September 27, 1960, up to Christmas, carried on 130 local CBS TV stations.[137, 138]

A similar campaign was used for 1961 as well, variously described as being carried on 140 and 150 CBS TV stations. In 1963 Jack White, the company sales manager, indicated that the Tinkertoy line would be advertised on national programs reaching an audience of 27,000,000 people.[139, 140] The shows identified included: *The Price Is Right*, *Queen For A Day*, *Say When*, and *Seven Keys*.

Additionally, the product line was to be promoted in three Sunday newspaper supplements across the United States. These were *Suburbia Today*, *Parade*, and *This Week*. Between the television and newspaper supplements, a potential audience of 95,000,000 people was expected. For the company's 50th anniversary, ads were placed in a number of magazines: *Jack and Jill*, *McCalls*, *Women's Day*, *Family Circle*, *Good Housekeeping*, *Readers Digest*, *Parade*, *This Week*, and *Ladies Home Journal*.[141]

The company provided point-of-sale help, advertising materials, and non-paid publicity to help customers. For suggesting new designs for Tinkertoys, Tinker Zoo, and Toy Maker, children could win a $1,000 saving bond and an expense-paid trip to New York City for themselves and their parents. The first winner was 12-year-old Ricky D. Fuhriman of Downey, Idaho, in 1966.[142]

Spalding also added a line of baseball gloves and assorted sports balls, called the Pace Setter line. This started in 1959, and ran through at least 1961.[143–146]

Plate 60   Photo by W. B. Nickerson.

John Wright working on Tinker Toys in his den, 1963.

Plate 59   Photo by W.B. Nickerson.

Jack White, sales manager, with bundles of white birch, 1964.

Charles Pajeau had always enjoyed being the life of the party. He was good at sleight-of-hand tricks, and seemed to constantly invent new jokes to tell. Grace Pajeau was the opposite of Charles, preferring the calm of a quiet corner to the spotlight of attention. Grace continued to live at the Orrington Hotel in Evanston after her husband's passing. She was 79 years old when she died on May 14, 1957.[147] There was no tombstone or monument for Grace Fuller Pajeau, as she was cremated like her late husband.

Sadly, the Pajeau bloodline ended with the death of Grace Pajeau Ross, nine months after her mothers death.[148] She died on February 8, 1958, from internal injuries suffered in an auto accident on an icy road nine miles north of South Haven, Michigan. Services were held in St. Joseph's, Michigan, and burial was at Mount Hope cemetery in Chicago. Grace was survived by her husband Donald Ross.

In 1964 Ernest F. Heilmann was the manager for the Toy Tinkers Division of Spalding Brothers, and Fred Hiertz was the plant superintendent.[121] John Wright continued his role as designer and developer, and Jack White served as the sales manager. That year the company had a team of five salespeople crisscrossing the United States. Spalding spent a modest $125,000 on promotion, advertising, and public relations each year. The basic patents for the Tinkertoy had since expired, and the company was concerned that they might need to make changes to the toy. However, after a product review by a consulting company, they were advised to not make any changes to the product, only to add more motion to the instruction booklets. The company was earning a higher-than-normal return on their over $2,000,000 in gross sales. The industry norm at the time was 2% to 4%, with Spalding earning possibly in the 8% to 10% range, but no exact figures were available.

In 1965, former Toy Tinker executive, William Powell, served as the office and credit manager. He reported that the other executives were General Manager Ernest Heil-

Plate 62   Photo by W.B. Nickerson.

Tinker Zoo display box, 1962.

mann, Assistant General Sales Manager R. A. Christofferson, Purchasing Agent Edgar Biemolt, Marketing Manager Robert A. Smallwood, and Toy Designer John Wright. The rest of the staff consisted of a secretary/receptionist, an order taker, an order writer, and a payroll bookkeeper. Mr. Powell also reported that due to the seasonal nature of the business, order typists were hired during the summer

Plate 61

Tinkertoy Trade Advertisement, 1959.

Plate 63   Photo by W.B. Nickerson.

Ernest F. Heilmann examining a Tinker Zoo creation, 1964.

Plate 64

Photo by W.B. Nickerson.

John Wright working on a Tinkertoy model at the company offices, 1964.

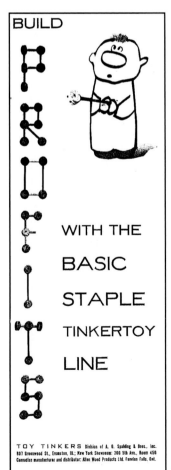

BUILD

WITH THE

BASIC

STAPLE

TINKERTOY

LINE

TOY TINKERS Division of A. G. Spalding & Bros., Inc.
807 Greenwood St., Evanston, Ill.; New York Showroom: 200 5th Ave., Room 450
Canadian manufacturer and distributor: Allen Wood Products Ltd. Fenelon Falls, Ont.

Plate 65

Tinkertoy Trade Advertisement, 1967.

months. Most of these typists were students at National College of Education in Evanston. Charles Pajeau had expressed in his will the hope that National College of Education would be a beneficiary of his trust.

Mr. Powell indicated that the production process was basically the same as when Mr. Pajeau had run the company. Mr. Powell also pointed out that Mr. Pajeau had a policy of employing handicapped persons at the Toy Tinkers factory.

In 1966, R. A. Christofferson was listed as president of the Toy Tinkers Division of Spalding. That same year Robert A. Smallwood, the marketing manager of Toy Tinkers, was promoted to vice president in charge of marketing.[149] Fred Hiertz was honored in August of 1966 for 42 years with Toy Tinkers.[75] He was the longest serving member of the staff of Toy Tinkers, having joined the company in August of 1924. He started out in the machine and paint shops, and had done every job in the plant. He was given a gold watch in honor of the occasion.

There was a minor disaster at the 1310 Sherman Avenue facility in February of 1967, when a heavy snowfall caused the roof to collapse on the warehouse building.[150] Repairs were made and the building was returned to service.

That same year, John Wright received two awards for the design of a package for Tinker Tools.[151] The set contained polyethylene tools with nuts and bolts for children from one to five years of age. John was also the man who introduced the idea of colored sticks to Tinkertoys.[90] He was approached by the advertising firm which represented Spalding and the Toy Tinkers. They wanted to jazz up the toy. John felt that the instructions were too complicated and confusing for young children to follow, with all the letter designations for various parts. Plus, many new pieces were added to the sets from 1927 on. To simplify this and to add some color, which was the trend at the time, he recommended color coding the sticks. This would allow a child who could not read to follow the instructions and build models. The instructions were also more colorful and visually interesting to young children with this change.

TOY MAKER
the best babysitter
any family ever had!"

Every day, we get letters from parents praising Toy Maker. And no wonder. Assorted wood and plastic parts snap together. Mobile push-pull toys assemble, take apart easily. Toy Maker teaches finger skills, color, assembly talent. Keeps girls and boys, ages 2 to 8, entertained for hours. Stock up now. Write for 1965 catalog today.

Quality Toys with a Purpose

THE TOY TINKERS Division of A. G. Spalding & Bros., Inc.
807 Greenwood St., Evanston, Ill. New York Showroom: 200 5th Ave., Room 450

Plate 66

Toy Maker Trade Advertisement, 1965.

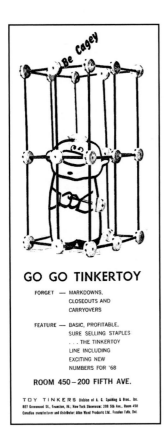

GO GO TINKERTOY

FORGET — MARKDOWNS,
CLOSEOUTS AND
CARRYOVERS

FEATURE — BASIC, PROFITABLE,
SURE SELLING STAPLES
. . . THE TINKERTOY
LINE INCLUDING
EXCITING NEW
NUMBERS FOR '68

ROOM 450–200 FIFTH AVE.

TOY TINKERS Division of A. G. Spalding & Bros., Inc.
807 Greenwood St., Evanston, Ill.; New York Showroom: 200 5th Ave., Room 450
Canadian manufacturer and Distributor: Allan Wood Products Ltd., Fenelon Falls, Ont.

Plate 68

Publicity photo of Big Boy Tinkertoy with young boy, 1962.

Plate 67

Tinkertoy Trade Advertisement, 1968.

Photo by W.B. Nickerson.

Some of John's other ideas were the Tinkertown Trains, which could be taken apart and reassembled in many different ways, and Tinker Zoo, which was a mix of flexible plastic parts and wooden sticks. There were several other items, such as stack toys and Curtain Wall Builder, which John also designed and developed.

Then there was the time when a Danish company was looking for an American firm to buy the U.S. rights to a plastic snap-together block.[90] John recommended the Spalding company should buy it, but nothing ever came of this, and eventually Samsonite Corporation secured the rights.[152] That toy became known as Lego.

Spalding Brothers carried on the creative spirit of Charles Pajeau, and added several new items to the toy line. In a sense, they recaptured something of the diversity of the products offered in the Toy Tinkers' prime under Charles Pajeau. Yet, as the sixties came to a close, the Toy Tinkers were feeling the effects of the passing of the Baby Boom. Sales of construction sets fell to below two million a year from their peak, close to three million, and soon would be closer to one million a year.[153] The employees were close to 50 in number as the production had fallen. In early 1969, Spalding Brothers Incorporated was acquired by Questor Corporation of Toledo, Ohio, and became part of their Child Guidance Line.[68]

Photo by W.B. Nickerson.

Plate 69

Publicity photo of Tinker Zoo can and two models, 1962.

Plate 70

Publicity photo for Giant Tinkertoy, 1971.

Questor Corporation, with the acquisition of Spalding Brothers, also took control of the Toy Tinkers Division of Spalding. Among the changes ahead for the Toy Tinkers was a change of name. Under Questor, the company name became "Tinkertoy Division of Questor Education Products Company, Evanston, Illinois." The Toy Tinkers of Evanston, Illinois, were no more, but the toys did live on.

In 1971 Questor introduced Giant Tinkertoy, which was literally a Tinkertoy set of giant size.[9] It was made of plastic tubing and mold-injection plastic spools several inches across. Questor began a heavy promotional campaign of the Giant Tinkertoy starting at the toy show in 1971. The company set up an elaborate display in the lobby of the First National City Bank. It consisted of several Giant models of Tinkertoys, in honor of City Parks Week.[154]

The promotion continued into 1974, when Questor Educational Products President William Crain appeared on the *What's My Line* television show. After his secret was revealed, the panel members (Soupy Sales, Lynn Redgrave, Gene Shalit, and Arlene Francis) participated in a race of one team against the other, to assemble models out of Giant Tinkertoys.[155]

New York City on February 14, 1977, marked the opening of the toy show with a renaming of Fifth Avenue to "Tinkertoy Lane" for the day. Aside from Giant Tinkertoy displays being set up, buttons were given out that said "Tinker Tim and Tina Love the Big Apple."[156] Additionally, a great deal of magazine advertising was conducted by the company to push Giant Tinkertoy.

The Giant set was not made at the Evanston facility, and this may have been a portent of things to come. In regular Tinkertoy sets the spools and sticks were made of wood, but most of the other parts were now plastic. The plastic pieces included the "B" or short pointed sticks, the "U" or end cap, the "L," the "ZP," the "TP," the crank

Plate 71

Questor Tinkertoy Trade advertisement, 1970.

handle or "CP," the Windblade, and a smaller pennant. But the biggest change of all was to come at the end of 1972, when it was announced that Questor would end all operations at its Evanston facilities by January 1, 1973.[157]

Questor termed the move a consolidation, and said that the production would be moved to a plant in the Bronx, New York. The original name was gone, and now the last physical evidence of its existence in Evanston, Illinois, would be gone as well. After 58 years in Evanston, the Tinkertoy was moving across the nation to a new home on the East Coast of the United States.

With that move, the Tinkertoy ceased to be a purely Evanston product. The Tinkertoy continued to be produced under the Questor name through January of 1978, when Questor sold the Child Guidance line to Gabriel Industries. The Tinkertoy passed with the rest of the line to Gabriel, which was itself acquired by CBS, Incorporated, in August of 1978. CBS, Inc., controlled the Child Guidance line until 1986, when certain parts of the company assets were sold to Hasbro, Incorporated, including the Tinkertoy.[158]

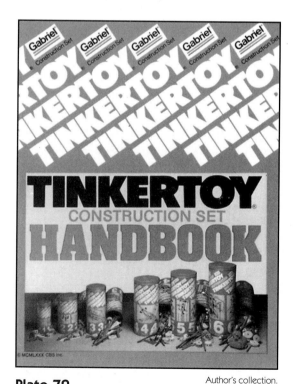

Plate 72 Author's collection.

Gabriel Tinkertoy Construction Set Handbook, a point of sale promotional piece.

Playskool®'s New-for-1992 Tinkertoys®

Courtesy of Hasbro/Playskool Incorporated.

Plate 73

Playskool Tinkertoy® publicity photo from 1992.

In 1984 Hasbro had acquired the Playskool and Milton Bradley companies. So when the Tinkertoy became an asset in 1986, it was made part of the Playskool line.[158]

For the first several years, Playskool offered wood stick and spool sets with plastic accessory parts, in cardboard cans with metal tops. The set progression began with the Beginners Set #840, next came the Basic Set #841, the Big Builder Set #842, and finally the Super Set #843.

In keeping with the times, instructions showed robots, droids, Delta spaceships, starfighters, helicopters, dinosaurs, and rockets. They also showed more traditional items, such as animals, cars, fire trucks, and the granddaddy of them all, the Ferris wheel.

In 1992, Playskool Division of Hasbro introduced a major change in the Tinkertoy. The Tinkertoy had been changing to more colorful plastic parts while retaining the wood sticks and spools. In 1992 that changed, too. The entire set was enlarged and made completely of plastic. The pieces were now twice as large as they had previously been. According to Edna Collette of Hasbro's public relations department, the change doubled demand in 1992 for the Playskool Tinkertoy sets.

Hasbro had taken its marketing skill and experience to reinvigorate the Tinkertoy, attracting a whole new generation of children. They are keeping this unique toy exciting and interesting after all these years. The January 16, 1995, *Rockford Register Star* newspaper's Life Style section ran a list of what was "in" and what was "out." On the "in" side was Tinkertoys.

According to Gary Serby, director of public relations for Hasbro, in 1995 the Tinkertoy continues to be manufactured at the Hasbro mold injection facilities in Central Falls, Rhode Island.

Fort Dearborn Magazine's December 1920 issue said, "The Toy Tinkers of Evanston rank as a Chicago industry, and their 'Tilly Tinker' and 'Tinker Pins,' etc., are making themselves a place in the world."[159]

The company was building a reputation and image as a maker of unusual and interesting toys of good quality at a reasonable price. Part of the secret was the demonstrators who were put into all the major cities' displays.[22,41] Another part was the sales staff, who actively worked with retailers and wholesalers to promote the product line and their customers' satisfaction.

Charles Pajeau was quoted in *System* magazine in December 1918 as saying, "If I had ever been in the toy business, we probably would not have given the dealer any help in selling our product. Many of the toy manufacturers seemed to consider a sale completed when the jobber had paid for the goods. But if I never got anything else from the monument business I learned that it takes more than a good product to make a satisfied customer. As a result we put out demonstrating crews which worked, one at a time, every big city in the country. The crews built up a demand: and in not one instance did the direct sales fail to pay the crew's expenses."[22]

The Toy Tinkers took great care to assist their customers, who were mostly jobbers (wholesalers) to businesses around the United States and the world.[41] About 15 percent of Toy Tinkers' sales were made directly to department stores, but otherwise they sold to jobbers, who in turn resold to stores and businesses.

Orders that came in to the Toy Tinkers' offices were sent out to the jobber from whose territory it had come. The company would suggest that the jobber might wish to reorder, if he was running low on stock to fill this new order. This strategy helped produce a lot of extra orders. After all, if someone is sending you business, you have to think well of them.

The reason why the Toy Tinkers directly handled department stores' business is especially interesting.[41] They discovered that building elaborate displays in the department stores of larger cities and towns served as hubs for the suburbs and surrounding communities. Business owners and managers in the outlying towns traveled in to the big city to see what were the latest trends. There, they would see the breathtaking Toy Tinker displays — some nine feet high with five shelves and electric motors that rotated them all the time. These displays were packed with the latest Tinker Toys.

Orders would start coming in to the local jobbers within a week or two of a new display being installed.[41] The Toy Tinkers also supplied displays with shelves which stood from four to six feet tall for smaller stores, such as dry goods or hardware stores which sold the toys at Christmas time. By 1922, the Toy Tinkers were successfully converting larger stores to the notion that Tinker Toys were a suitable year-round item. Many department stores had permanent Tinker Toy counters and/or displays. The jobbers were educated to the relationship which the Toy Tinkers had with the department stores, and understood the benefits of this arrangement.

The loyalty shown by the Toy Tinkers toward their wholesalers did not go unrewarded. Lawrence D. Ely, general sales manager for the company, wrote in the April 1922 *Printers Ink* magazine, "We get real cooperation all the way down the line from the jobber, his executives and his salesmen. We have our line in, I believe, practically every jobbing house in the country that handles toys; this includes toy jobbers, wholesale dry goods and hardware houses, and a great many others. We have good representation in their catalogues. To our way of thinking, the jobber's active cooperation is something that can be earned. Once earned, it is working for you all the time. Give the wholesaler outstanding assistance, and he will give you a loyal — yes, a militantly active — cooperation. But, like any other customer, he seldom will come around fighting for

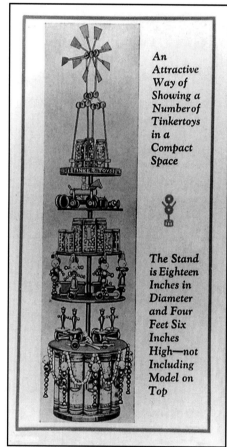

An Attractive Way of Showing a Number of Tinkertoys in a Compact Space

The Stand is Eighteen Inches in Diameter and Four Feet Six Inches High—not Including Model on Top

Plate 74   Courtesy of the Evanston Historical Society.

One of the display stands available from the Toy Tinkers, shown in the 1924 company catalog.

count it to move it out, or the company would modify the toy to improve its salability.

By 1947 the company was concerned solely with the sale of the construction sets, which had been helped along by the baby boom generation.[19] Sales were now approaching in excess of 2,500,000 sets a year. In fact, Toy Tinkers had set a record in the toy industry for the sale and production of a single product. They held the record for several years. The Tinkertoy had outpaced more than 30 competitors, and typically was sold out of their annual production by March. In the 33 years of production the company had sold in excess of 50 million toys, a good part of which were Tinker Toys, items other than the construction sets. Charles Pajeau estimated sales figures for 1952 to be about 2,800,000 construction sets. This was a world's record at the time for the sale of a single toy. Charles was finally getting used to the idea of the Tinekrtoys' success. He had originally thought that it would not last more than a few years, yet here the Tinkertoy had found a place in the hearts and minds of youth everywhere.

Plate 75

Printers Ink magazine. 1922.

Lawrence D. Ely, sales manager for the Toy Tinkers.

the opportunity to buy your line in large volume and push it of his own accord."

The Toy Tinkers of Evanston, Illinois, promoted their products through displays, demonstration crews, and advertising.[22] The demonstration crews were occasional hires, who seemed to be readily available, and willing to set up displays as needed. Other than the general sales manager, the only other full-time sales employee for the company was the manager of the New York City sales room.

Charles Pajeau turned over the job of sales manager after 1915 to other hands, as the demands of the business required more people to share the work. By 1922, Lawrence D. Ely had held the position for several years. In 1929 Albert J. Leiscke was the sales manager.

The product line continued to grow from one item in 1914 and 1915, to seven items in 1918, and about 15 products by 1922.[22, 41] The sales volume for 1929 of the construction sets was about 750,000, plus close to 500,000 other toys sold that year.[38] The factory was turning out about 4,200 construction sets a day, and approximately 2,600 assorted other toys a day. 1929 had 20 items listed in the wholesaler Toy Tinkers catalog. Former employee Larry J. Basting recalled Al Leiscke, "He was the best — he was good."[84] He noted that the sales staff was selling all the time and, "Must have been good because of the way they would empty that warehouse around May to November. They emptied that whole building. You could not believe it — but they did. Everybody knew the Tinker Toys!"[56] Larry also mentioned that when a toy did not sell, the sales manager would dis-

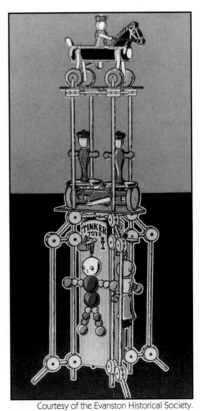

Courtesy of the Evanston Historical Society.

Plate 76

Small display stand as shown in the 1924 Toy Tinkers catalog.

Under Spalding Brothers, Tinkertoy sales for 1963 were about 2,000,000 sets a year.[121] The sets were selling at a gross sales price of approximately $1,600,000, while an additional

Plate 77

Printers Ink magazine, 1922.

The 1922 Toy Tinker catalog cover.

$500,000 in revenue came from other products such as Tinker Zoo. By 1971, sales had dropped to 1,000,000 sets a year.

Demographics and tastes were changing, and demand was not quite as strong. Yet there was a need that Tinkertoys filled, so they continued to be produced. By Christmas 1992 the Tinkertoy had undergone several changes, including the enlargement of the pieces, and they were completely made of plastic parts.[158] Playskool produced all of the parts at their molding facility in Central Falls, Rhode Island, and reported a doubling of demand since the enlargement of the toy pieces.

Back in 1922 when visiting department store buyers, or wholesales, Lawrence D. Ely would not talk Tinker Toys, "I talk turnover and bringing customers into the store, how toys help the children's store sell clothing, how they sell gift merchandise for the hardware dealer during the holidays, and all the rest of the facts which tend in that direction. We simply put ourselves in the retailer's place and talk about the things he is interested in. We do not probably, mention our products during the talk. They follow after the rest; when the dealer or wholesaler is sold on the idea, he quite naturally gives us his order."[41]

The Toy Tinkers supplied free samples to the salesmen of the jobbers, along with full-color drawings of the toys, and booklets containing all of the different products available. They also made available free artwork and glass printing slides for the different toys in the product line, so that wholesalers' catalogs and newspapers would be able to reproduce the artwork. The Toy Tinkers gladly sent out preassembled displays of construction sets, or stands on which to display the toys. Larry J. Basting recalled assembling, boxing, and shipping the displays out to the stores. Some of the displays were quite elaborate, as seen in the 1924 catalog.[160, 161] It identified the photo as, "a Tinkertoy Booth in one of the Large City Department Stores Christmas Season 1923." The photo shows two preassembled display towers interconnected with a spool and dowel bridge, a giant Tom Tinker doll, and the words, "Tinker Toys" spelled out in beads. Of course, every bit of the display is packed with Tinker Toys.

Tinker Toys were prominently mentioned in newspaper ads for department stores, hardware stores, and even automotive garages that would add a line of toys come Christmas time.[162] The toys were often listed by name, and were accompanied by one of the bits of artwork distributed by the company. The word "famous" was often associated with Tinker Toys in ads, something not seen with most of their contemporaries.[163] It was also common to find the phrase, "We have the whole line of Tinker Toys, come in and see them." Tinker Toys often served as a leader to get people into the store, and occasionally as a loss leader with ads trumpeting the Wonder Builder at prices well below those of other stores. These low prices were usually close to the cost paid by the stores to the wholesaler. The Toy Tinkers offered posters and signs to be used in store displays, all that a store needed to do was ask.

Lawrence D. Ely outlined the basic philosophy of the company as being, "Our whole philosophy of selling can be summed up briefly as: 'Be natural, friendly, and not too anxious to make a sale and a profit. For we know that bread cast upon the waters comes back buttered toast.'"[41] Proof of the reality of this philosophy was the time that a mail order house was hard pressed for cash, and was selling off inventory to a big department store. Not one Tinker Toy appeared in the lot of deeply-discounted merchandise that was sold to this store. Inquiries about why this was the case revealed that the mail order house had a full stock of Tinker Toys, with the 85¢ Tinker Toys being offered for prices so low, they could be resold for 35¢ and make a good profit. The department store buyer told Mr. Ely, "But I wouldn't buy. I told them, 'Those Toy Tinker folks are good friends of ours. They help us sell an awful lot of their goods ever year, and they spend a lot of money doing it. I don't want to cause them any trouble by putting on a price cut — and besides, if I did, they might stop helping us and then I'd lose more than I could gain the other way.'"[41]

The Toy Tinkers built a loyal sales network that held them in good stead for many years. But the trend was already away from the traditional jobber, and by the time Spalding took over, the wholesaler was replaced by a five-man sales force that was out in the field selling all of the time.[121] Spalding also continued the sales office in New York City.

The company's philosophy of fair dealing and extremely helpful service helped to make them into one of the major toy companies of their time. They were famous and sought after, a crowd pleaser that brought business into stores all over the United States.

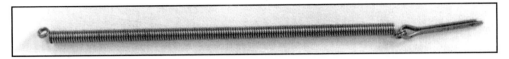

Plate 78

Author's collection.

Spring and cotter pin as used by the Toy Tinkers for toy asssembly, such as Gym Tinker.

To keep the Toy Tinkers factory in business required massive quantities of spools, dowel rods, beads, miscellaneous turnings, felt, leather, rubber bands, springs, cadmium-coated metal, cord, fringe, shipping cartons, canisters with lids, packages for the other toys, clay, pigment, shellac in 50-gallon barrels, alcohol, and various lubricants and solvents.[38, 56, 83–90] In 1937, company ads boasted that "25 million sticks and 10 million spools are required annually to supply the world with Tinkertoys."[164] Ten years later, in a similar ad, the numbers had increased to 100 million sticks and 40 million spools.[165] In its prime, the factory was located next to a railroad siding, so that train boxcars could be quickly and easily loaded and off loaded. All of the wood used in the construction sets was New England white birch.

In 1929, the factory was using ten boxcar loads of dowel rods a year. These rods arrived in bundles of 500, shipped from Maine. They were from 18 inches to 48 inches long, and a quarter inch across. The ten carloads represented the entire output of three woodworking shops for a year. The spools also came by boxcar, shipped in 100-pound burlap bags. Material arriving from local suppliers typically was delivered by truck, such as the canisters with the labels already on and the lids included.

Demand for the spools and sticks continued to grow, expanding the number of concerns required to produce them for the Toy Tinkers. By the late 1930s, the parts list for non-construction toys was shrinking as the factory concentrated on the construction sets. The only new item added to the list was the fine white sand used in Tinkersand sets. Larry J. Basting remembered processing and packing tons of it for these art sets. Yet even the sand was no longer called for after 1940, and the company began to focus on the construction sets alone. As demand for the Tinkertoy increased, the amount of sticks and spools required increased accordingly.

Working Conditions

Since the Toy Tinkers farmed out most of the wood turning operations to other vendors, that left only the dowel sizing and slotting, and spool drilling to be done in house.[38, 56, 78, 83–90] There were several operations done solely within the factory, such as paint manufacture, painting, drying, assembly, and packing.

When the new factory was constructed at 2012-20 Ridge Avenue in 1926, it was state of the art and then some. In addition to the machine shop that built and maintained all of the machines used in the factory, there were elevators and a metal spiral chute used to deliver materials to the basement for storage. As well, there were assembly rooms, the paint shop, offices, a lunchroom, rooftop recreation facilities, conference rooms, and Pajeau's workshop. The plant had a compressed air system that was used to keep sawdust out of the workers' eyes, and also played a key part in the drying operation in the paint room.

Yet with all of that to say for the Toy Tinkers building, by today's standards, conditions could be difficult for the employees. Working in the paint shop was one of the more stressful jobs, as the fumes could be very bad. Larry J. Basting, a former employee of the Toy Tinkers and longtime worker in the paint shop, wondered aloud, "How I ever lived through those fumes?" Larry went on to talk about the paint shop in summer, when if they were painting black or dark blue turnings, it was necessary to keep the room at a minimum of 80 degrees. Otherwise, the paint would not cure properly. It was a miserable job at that time of year.

The fumes from the paint also posed other dangers, as Larry learned one day when he reached into one of the small paint barrels, which could hold about 50 pounds of turnings. He was attempting to make an adjustment using small metal pliers, when he saw a spark and knew he was

Courtesy of the Evanston Historical Society.

Plate 79

The bloomer girls on lunch break. The outfits were designed not to snag in machinery at the Toy Tinker factory.

in a spot. He shut his eyes as tightly as he could, just as the spark ignited the contents of the barrel. The explosion caught Larry square in the face. It burned away his hair and his eyebrows, which were never quite right after that. Having his eyes closed was all that saved him from being blinded. It was a terrible experience, "But I got out of it!" Larry said.

After that day it was determined that brass pliers and hammers would be used, to prevent the arcing that had caused the explosion. Larry finally called it quits in 1941 when he developed stomach problems from the prolonged exposure to the paint fumes, after 12 years at the Toy Tinkers.

Women did most of the assembly work, and operated the dowel sizing and slotting machines, which could be dangerous as well. The ladies dropped the dowels into the sizing machine, which cut the sticks to the different lengths required for the construction sets.[9] As a result of the continuous cutting, sawdust would build up under the blade. The ladies were in the habit of brushing aside this sawdust with their hands. It was common for their hands to be nicked and cut by the spinning blade. This was seen as a normal hazard of the job.

The physical labor involved in loading and unloading the supplies and finished products of the factory was considerable, in the days before forklifts were commonly

used. Men had to unload boxcars full of spools, which were delivered in 100-pound burlap sacks. The sacks were tossed down the metal chute to the basement, where they were stacked six and seven high. Larry recounted how the regulars at the factory would have fun with the summer help. Northwestern University football players were hired to help with the unloading and stock work. Being young, big, and strong they were just a little bit cocky, so when it came to moving the bags of spools, the regulars were not too quick about explaining the trick of picking up the bags. When you repeat the same lifting movement hundreds of times in a day, it helps to know the right way. After the students had learned a little humility, seeing the regulars do the job without missing a beat or complaining, they were let in on what to do.

Then there was Harry Gennette, who worked at stenciling the faces on the toys. He sat the whole day at a turntable arrangement, which had about 25 doll heads on it. As the heads would go by, he would spray paint the faces using a stencil. Unfortunately, there was a constant splash back of the paint into Harry's face. As Larry put it, "Boy that will kill you. Harry finally just quit — just couldn't take it."[84]

There was a good side to working in the Toy Tinkers factory, however.[56, 83–90] In spite of hard work and discomforts, the workers enjoyed the time spent working for the

company. The Toy Tinkers made a point of hiring local people whenever possible. Often that meant that several related people worked together. Larry J. Basting recalled walking to work with several blood and marriage relations. They would stop and pick him up on the way to the factory in the morning. Fred Hiertz was a relation of Larry's, and was his connection to getting a job at the Toy Tinkers. The factory employed a wide range of age groups, and the environment was conducive to fun and camaraderie. There was a lot of good-natured fooling around and teasing. With the opening of the 2012-20 Ridge building in 1926, the employees had access to the rooftop recreation facilities, which included volleyball and tennis courts.[38, 78]

The company also made a ping pong table available for employee use after hours. Some men brought their own beer, and placed cardboard around this table to prevent the balls from rolling all over the factory.[56] The women who put the Tinker Toys together sat at rows of tables while they worked, which allowed them to socialize. The Bench was the most demanding assembly area in the factory, yet employees told of a sense of satisfaction when they beat the quota for the day. The lunchroom provided a place to catch up with other employees and friends, over hot coffee provided by the company.[38] In the early years the company was paying well for the type of work done in the factory, which was another plus to working there. When all the factors were balanced out, it was a good place to work in its time.

Plate 80   Courtesy of the Evanston Historical Society.

1936 Tinkertoys catalog back cover.

Exporting Tinker Toys

From early in the company history, the Toy Tinkers of Evanston, Illinois, exported their products. In 1929, Australia and New Zealand were the largest foreign markets.[8] Former employee Larry J. Basting recalled that, "We used to export and really put it in good boxes — good wooden boxes. We used shiplap boxes."[56] In 1953 the company was doing a worldwide business, trading with any country that could pay in American dollars. The business with Canada and other English-speaking countries comprised the bulk of the exports, although they did a nice business in South America as well. In 1953 the company was selling the construction sets only, although Spalding Brothers would start to add a revived Tom Tinker and some new items to the company line starting in 1954. In 1964, on the company's 50th anniversary, Toy Tinkers executive Jack White noted that the Tinkertoy had been exported to the Philippines, Venezuela, North Africa, and some parts of Europe.[121] England had been a good customer until after the Second World War, when they added a commodities tax to the already existing import duty, making it too

expensive to sell there. South Africa in 1964 was a good market for Tinkertoys. Sales in Central and South America, Canada, and some parts of Europe were still good. In addition, the company had United States military exchanges selling the Tinkertoy all over the world.

Over the years, the export of Tinker Toys was affected by war and financial depressions. However, when war prevented exports, the company often benefited by an expanded demand within the United States and Canada, as imports from European sources were limited, and in the Second World War from Japan as well. The First World War played a large role in the Toy Tinkers' rapid expansion, as it ultimately increased the demand for domestic toy production, and fostered competition. During that war, a great deal of shipping capacity was involved with moving and supplying the armies involved. The transport not tied up in such matters was hard pressed to meet normal shipping needs. Considering the loss of ships in military actions intended to disrupt the supply lines of one's enemy, it is easy to see that the laws of supply and demand would quickly make even cheap imports very expensive. Further, the early Tinker Toys were all or mostly wood, so it was easy to obtain production material, as wood did not tend to be seen as a limited resource in America. And finally, in any war the phrase "Made in America" holds far more importance than usual.

In the Second World War the facts were not much different, except metal became very scarce. After 1942, the company had difficulty obtaining metal for can lids and bottoms, so production switched to cardboard for that purpose. This had been considered in 1918, when Henry Sve-

bilius patented a small metal clip that could be used to replace the metal screw top for cans with cardboard or wood tops. But here again, since the toy was all wood, the Toy Tinkers had little trouble obtaining the material that they needed to maintain production, although with the shortages brought on by a lack of lumberjacks, they did not receive as much wood as they could have used. Since most of their competitors required various metals and rubber to produce their toys, many had their production restricted during the war, which only increased demand for those still in operation.

Advertising and Promotion

The Toy Tinkers of Evanston, Illinois, spent a great deal of time and money cultivating their image with the general public, and with retailers and wholesalers. For the public, Tinker Toys were safe, well made, economical, educational, and fun for children. For the business owner, they were well known, well made, popularly received by the public, heavily advertised, fast sellers, and a big draw in any a toy section.[41, 161–163] This was accomplished by the happy fact that the Tinkertoy had burst upon the scene and gained an instant reputation in 1915, so the company

only had to build upon and expand that positive perception. To that end, the Toy Tinkers advertised in children's magazines which were commonly read by both children and parents.

The ads stressed the wholesome nature of Tinker Toys, and the wisdom of purchasing them. The company also cultivated the idea of elves making Tinker Toys at the shop in Evanston, to help create a sense of fantasy and wonderment with the toys. To add to that sense of fantasy

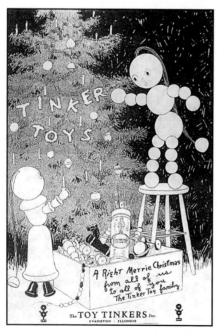

Plate 81

Author's collection.

Toy Tinker advertisement for the general public, mid-1920s.

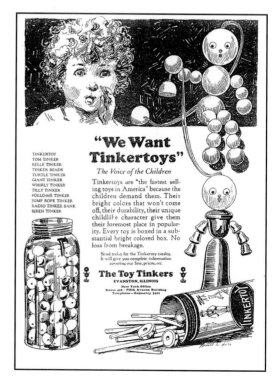

Plate 82

Tinker Toys trade advertisement, September 1923.

and wonderment, they distributed small fold-out brochures that showed all of the company's offerings with a verse for each. In fact, the Toy Tinkers specifically endeavored to maintain a quizzical tone to the promotional materials, so as to mimic the inquiring nature of a child's speech.[41] They would choose phrasing that was a little out of the ordinary to achieve this effect. This, they felt, was in keeping with the product line, and reinforced the overall message of Tinker Toys: playfulness, youthfulness, exploration, and education.

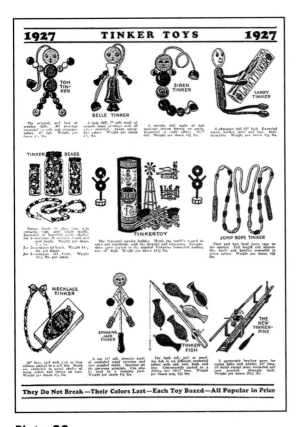

Plate 83

Tinker Toys advertisement, 1927.

The Toy Tinkers were strong believers in point-of-sale promotions.[161] Their store displays included brochures to be given out to anyone interested in the product line. Most of the time that would be a child, who could take the advertising home to reread it a thousand times, all the while pestering mom and dad for one or more of the Tinker Toys that the child really, really needed. Small stores would be offered display stands proportional to their orders and size, and these, too would have brochures included.

To interest businesses, the Toy Tinkers' wholesale catalogs were printed in multicolor form, and mailed out to jobbers and their salesmen, as well as department stores.[41, 161] In 1922, the company started to use government return postcards in a mailing sent to 25,000 toy retailers. These mailings included the name of the local jobber, and

an offer to send a free 32 page catalog to anyone replying by the enclosed postcard. The return portion was addressed:

> "Hurry home to
> The Toy Tinkers
> Evanston, Illinois."

After only three weeks the response rate was 12%, and cards were still being received by the company.[8, 22] It is possible that a lot of the other recipients simply contacted the jobbers. The catalogs offered all manner of promotional items to be used in stores by retailers, from posters and name banners to the displays mentioned earlier.

Plate 84

Tinker Toys advertisement, 1927.

Finding these gems today takes time and perseverance. Although the company sent out hundreds of thousands of printed pieces, only a fraction of them seem to be available now. Unfortunately, in the time when the Toy Tinkers promoted their goods, these pamphlets and catalogs held no more importance in people's minds than do the ads in today's Sunday paper. One would read it and use the information, then toss it away or use it to start up the fireplace.

A great many of the surviving paper items are likely in the collections of people who were not specifically collecting Tinker Toy materials. There are people who mainly

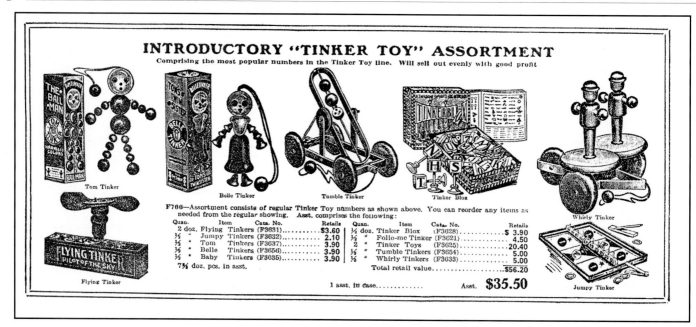

Plate 85

Introductory Tinker Toy assortment offered in 1920.

look for old catalogs or posters and such, who would be pleased to find a Toy Tinkers of Evanston, Illinois, catalog from 1922, for example. And there it will stay for a great many years. With time and information about the compa-ny, hopefully more of these paper goods will show up. The good news is that the Evanston Historical Society has a wonderful collection of original materials. With a little luck, that collection will grow even larger.

 Tinkertoy Models

From the very first set of Tinkertoys, the company offered an instruction booklet showing some of the models which could be built using the set.[8, 22] The nature of the models shown did change with the times, although the offerings never included guns or weapons of mass destruction. The progressive ratio of right triangles was the underlying principle of the Tinkertoy. The longer side of a triangle, whose other two sides were of equal length, would become the base of the next larger triangle, and so on. Thus the only limitations were the number of pieces available and the builder's imagination.

Early on, the instructions showed models of biplanes, windmills, haystackers, Ferris wheels, and railroad water tanks, to name a few. But as technology marched on, so did the variety of models listed. Later, monoplanes, printing presses, sprinklers, rockets with gantries, television broadcasting towers, and chemical mixers were shown. Whether one played in groups or alone, the Tinkertoy was a great choice. It swelled the imagination, and was a very satisfying toy.

AUTHOR'S NOTE:

I can recall building a rocket of Tinkertoys while watching one of the first U.S. manned space launches on

Plate 86

Tinkertoy Trade Advertisement, 1917.

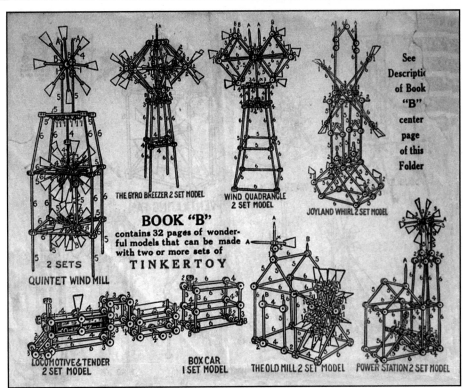

Plate 87

Models as shown in an early Tinkertoy instruction book.

television. In the course of play it was not uncommon for Tinkertoys to be incorporated with other toys, which served to broaden the experience and enlarge the scale of things. The use of Tinkertoy buildings with train sets, toy soldiers, or dolls was not unknown in my home. One of my many older brothers was studying engineering and would build elaborate bridges and structures with the accumulated Tinkertoy sets we had.

 # Mysteries of the Toy Tinkers

Toy Tinkers Sales Volume

The exact sales figures for the Toy Tinkers of Evanston, Illinois, are hard to come by, as only a few of the 58 years had actual numbers listed in articles or other sources. Actual sales figures would be very valuable in determining other information. Another problem is that for at least two years, the numbers listed appear to be understated by a substantial amount. In 1928 and 1929 the annual sales volume was put at 750,000 Tinkertoy construction sets and 465,000 other toys.[38] This does not seem to jibe with the success of the company, and the size of the work force.[56, 83–90]

The Toy Tinkers were working six-day weeks from January through to September or October, with warehouse staff being on duty through November and December, and most of the manufacturing curtailed in the last two months of the year. The given sales figures would mean that the factory was only in operation about 30 weeks out of the year, whereas they seemed to be fully functioning for at least 40 or 42 weeks out of the year, according to former employees. That being the case, the numbers should be more like, 1,058,000 Tinkertoy sets and 655,000 Tinker Toys, or 1,713,000 toys per year for 1928 and 1929. That would mean an understatement of about 500,000 toys per year.

The reason for such an understatement could be the hot competition between toy companies just before the Great Depression. A company might not want to let its real volume be known to other manufacturers. Locating the company records would answer questions such as this, but for now we are left to play detective and guess about exact figures.

The 1936 catalog states that the Toy Tinkers had made 50 million friends in the 22 years that they had been in business. Assuming that this meant they had sold 50 million toys, the average annual sales volume would need to be closer to 2,300,00 items a year. The Toy Tinkers did manufacture some non-toy items as well, and this could have helped to boost the sales figures to that level. The 50 million figure might also be based on the assumption that for every Tinktoy sold, perhaps two or three children would actually use it.

In the late 1940s the sales figures become clearer, with the company doing in the 2,500,000 range of sales of only the construction sets.[19] According to articles from the time,

the Toy Tinkers had been setting records in that level of sales for several years. By 1952 the sales volume was approaching 3,000,000 sets a year.[112] One of the reasons that the company discontinued the rest of the product line was that the quantity of Tinkertoy sets being sold made up for the volume of the other products. So, by the mid 1930s it is possible that the construction sets were selling close to 2,000,000 sets a year. No matter how you calculate the sales of the Toy Tinkers, by the time they left Evanston, the company had most probably sold 100,000,000 products around the world.

Pandora's Box

There is a story that has been passed around among Toy Tinker collectors, of something called Pandora's Box. The origin of the name is unclear, though it would not be a surprise if Pajeau coined the term himself. The tale involves the purported practice by Charles Pajeau of carefully adding to a box one of every toy the company ever produced. The toys were in the original packaging, and were to be preserved.

Rumors persist to this day regarding this magical box full of Tinker Toys. Some of the versions have the box being passed on to Spalding, in 1952 when the company was sold. Others say that Charles Pajeau moved the box to some mystery location that even now awaits discovery. When former employee Larry J. Basting was asked about the story, he could not recall such a box. However, he felt that it was possible that Mr. Pajeau would preserve one of each toy in such a box.

Muriel Bielmot, the wife of a past officer of Toy Tinkers, recalled a big display cabinet in the company offices. She said that it had one of each toy in it, but she could not remember if it was current production, or all of the toys ever produced. John Wright, who took over Mr. Pajeau's creative and artistic work after the sale to Spalding, noted that there was talk about a cedar chest full of toys. He felt that it must have gone with Mr. Pajeau, as it was not in the company's possession that he could recall.

If it did go with Charles Pajeau, then it would have passed on to his wife at his death. When his wife died in May of 1957, if she still had the cedar chest full of toys, it would have been turned over the the Pajeau's daughter. Assuming that it was not sold at the time of the mother's death, it may well have been disposed of in the aftermath of Grace Pajeau Ross's death in 1958. Perhaps it is sitting in storage, still waiting to be discovered.

The Big Swede

In the course of talking to former employees of the Toy Tinkers, there was recurrent mention of one man whom no one could recall by name. He was fondly remembered as the Big Swede. He was employed at the factory from the 1930s to at least the mid 1940s. He was impressively strong and well liked by the other employees, but no one could recall his name. The high school students remembered him as the only one that could stack

the bags of spools to the highest point by himself in the early 1940s. Larry J. Basting used to go to the Howard Street taverns with him in the 1930s. It was a rough area at the time, and because of the Big Swede's size and strength, other employees joked that he was Larry's bodyguard. The employee rolls were not available from the Toy Tinkers, and thus it cannot be said who this man was. Another Toy Tinkers mystery has yet to be solved.

The Company Records and Archives

From articles about the Toy Tinkers, and from conversations with past employees, it is clear that at least through the Spalding years, the company maintained ongoing records and an archive of products. Thus, in 1964 it was possible to line up samples of Tinkertoy cans dating back to 1914, for a publicity photo celebrating the 50th anniversary of the company.

At some point, these records and archives were relocated, discarded, or separated. The question is: which of those is the case? No one seems to know what happened to these valuable materials. The resolution of this mystery could answer a lot more questions about the Toy Tinkers.

The Pajeau Air Crash

It was to be a pleasant day of flying, but it ended in disaster.[104-111] The morning of June 21, 1938, Charley Pajeau and his friend and instructor Russell Stevenson, a 27-year-old pilot, planned to do some flying. Charley owned a Fairchild model 22 two-seater monoplane with dual controls. He wanted to show it off to Russ, and gain more instruction time in its use. Charley had logged about 80 hours of flight time up to this point.

Russ was a graduate of the Ryan School of Aviation in San Diego, and he held a commercial pilot's license. He lived at 7301 Sheridan Road in Chicago. Charley hangared his plane at Curtis Field in Glenview, Illinois (later to become Glenview Naval Air Station). The pair spent the morning flying, returning to Curtis Field for lunch and to have the aircraft refueled. After a leisurely lunch with Airport Manager Harold Darr, Charley and Russ made their way back to the Model 22 Fairchild to prepare for the afternoon flight.

Newspaper accounts have it that Charley had instructed the ground crew to refuel the plane while the pair were at lunch. What remains a mystery to this day is why the aircraft was not refueled. Russ Stevenson climbed into the pilot's seat and prepared to take the controls. This being the sixth week of instruction for Charley, he had deferred to his young friend for the second trip of the day.

The Fairchild model 22 monoplane moved to the runway, the engine revving in preparation for takeoff. The signal was given and they were off, speeding down the runway and airborne. The plane was headed fairly into the wind according to witness Ora Young, supervising inspector of the Bureau of Air Commerce. Ora was aloft at the time, and watched as the Pajeau monoplane's motor sputtered and Russ tried to turn the plane back toward the airport. The plane started to glide, and then nose dived with a roar to the ground. The aircraft dropped approximately 200 feet straight down before impact. The wreckage came to rest in a field of sweet clover and daisies. It was about 2:30 p.m. when the remains of the airship settled. Inside the mass of shattered metal and glass, one man lay dying and the other gravely hurt.

Harold Darr jumped aboard the field ambulance, riding out to the crash site. It was only about an hour since he had shared lunch with the two men who now lay in the wreck. Russ Stevenson was so badly crushed by the impact that he died before they could place him on a stretcher. Charley Pajeau was extricated from the wreckage and rushed to Evanston Hospital. In 1938 that would have been a long drive for a man in Pajeau's condition.

Charley had broken both his ankles, and his face was terribly cut up, particularly on the left side, leaving doctors to fear for his sight in one eye. Though he had no major internal injuries, he remained in a coma for six days before regaining consciousness. By July 14, 1938, the *Evanston Daily News Index* announced, "Pajeau Reported On Recovery Road." He had made a remarkable recovery which few had expected of a 63-year-old man. It would be almost another year before he would fully recover, but for Charley the crisis was over.

Ora Young landed immediately after witnessing the crash. It was determined that the tank was empty of gasoline. Russ Stenvson was at the pilot controls when the plane went down, and thus held responsibility for the crash. The plane was crumpled, with the engine having been driven into the cabin of the craft. By 4:30 p.m. the same day, ground crews had hacksawed the ship apart and hauled the pieces away. All that remained were the scars in the middle of the field.

Charley Pajeau never flew a plane again.

What Does It All Mean?

What is the underlying meaning of the story of the Toy Tinkers of Evanston, Illinois? This tale is of a man with a vision who was able to have fun, take risks, and achieve his desired goal. Toys are used to amuse children, but they also educate, inspire, and teach children about society and the world in which they live. Charles H. Pajeau sought to do all of this with his products. He wished to expand the world of his young customers, teach them how it worked, and in the process give them wonderment and an improved sense of themselves. He wished to teach the children to develop self reliance and problem solving skills. He not only wanted these things for his young customers, he was the embodiment of these values. Charles spent his years watching and learning from the world around him. He sought to find a balance between the needs of life and the pleasures that it offered. He and his company were a pure expression of the Tinkertoy, with all of its possibilities deriving from such simple materials.

Virtually everyone interviewed in the preparation of this history of the Toy Tinkers of Evanston, Illinois, had very definite and positive memories of the Tinkertoy. Whether they were 20 years old or 70, they recalled what fun and pleasure the Tinkertoy gave them. And most recog-

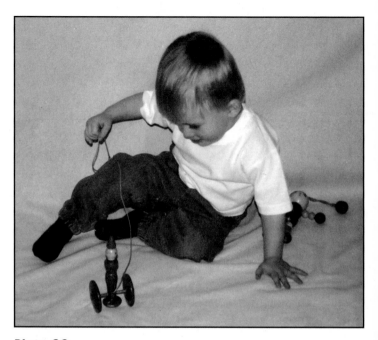

Plate 89

A young boy playing with Clown Tinker.

nized how valuable to their development it had been. This was the toy which trained the generation that went on to win the Second World War, rebuild the post-war world, and lay a foundation for the technological world of today.

In a sense the Tinkertoy was a product of its time, when technical skills were respected, and far more of the population was involved in manufacturing and production jobs than today. Yet even today the Tinkertoy continues to fascinate and delight young children with its ingenious simplicity.

Charles H. Pajeau saw a vision of the world yet to be realized, and he set about creating that vision through his ideas and deeds. Even he was amazed by its powerful nature and success. For a toy that should have lasted five years, the Tinkertoy had lived on and become the salvation of Charles himself. The Toy Tinkers had produced over 100 products under Charles's direction, and in the process provided hundreds of jobs all over the country, and, most importantly, touched children in a very positive way.

Finally, what this means is that we should not forget a special place and time in America, nor the powerful influence it had for generations of Americans. We should remember to have fun with what we do, and do it in a way that touches others and makes this world a better place than we found it. Charles achieved this, and the world was far better for his presence.

Plate 88

A young boy enjoying his Tom Tinker Doll.

The Story of the Little Tinker Men

"Once upon a time in a beautiful city on the shores of a bright blue lake lived two little tinker men.

They loved good little children and wanted to make them very happy, so they toiled and toiled and built a wonderful workshop where they could make playthings for these good little boys and girls.

It's pretty hard for even good little children to be careful of their toys all of the time, so these little tinker men decided to make their toys so sturdy and strong that they could not be easily broken.

They decided also to give their toys beautiful colors that wouldn't come off even if the toys should be left out doors in a hard rain.

Children liked the toys so well that these two little tinker men have had to get hundreds of other little tinker men to help them, and they are all just as busy as they can be, making beautiful toys for you to play with. In this little book you will see some of the things they make. The toy store man where you live has all of them, and maybe if you'll be real good, your mamma or daddy will get you the ones you want most. Look for the little tinker men on every package."

By Charles H. Pajeau

Plate 97 Courtesy of the Evanston Historical Society.

One of the panels for the Toys from Tinker Town three panel brochure.

From *The Story of the Little Tinker Men*

"To the parents and guardians of our little friends.

The Toys shown in this book are originated and made in the shops of the Toy Tinkers at Evanston, Illinois. The greatest care is used and all toys are subjected to rigid inspection before leaving the factory, with the intent that they shall reach you in perfect condition. We will gladly replace any toy which does not come to you in this way.

All these playthings are popularly priced and should be obtainable at any toy shop in your town. If you are unable to secure them please advise the factory who will see that you are promptly supplied.

If you and your children like these toys as fully as the Toy Tinkers enjoyed making them, then their purpose and mission will have been fully accomplished.

The Toy Tinkers, Evanston, Ill., U.S.A."

 **Action Toys**

Auto Racer No. 2 and No. 3

Plate 98

Auto Racer brochure plate, late 1920s. Auto Racer No. 2 and No.3, $30.00 – 40.00. Original box, add $20.00 – 40.00.

Author's collection.

Plate 99

Courtesy of the Evanston Historical Society.

Auto Racer No. 2 company catalog ad, 1931.

The first Auto Racer Tinker that I was able to locate advertising for was, oddly enough, No. 3. That was listed in the 1928 wholesale catalog put out by the Toy Tinkers. It was identified as being 10" long, made of wood and enameled in attractive colors. It came in its own box.

Auto Racer Tinker No. 2 was advertised for sale from 1929 through 1932. The description is essentially the same as No. 3, except that No. 2 measured 8¾" long. In 1929 it was wholesaling for $4.20 a dozen, so it was likely to be retailed for about 50¢. In 1931 it was wholesaling for $5.60 a dozen, so it was possibly retailing at about 70¢ to 75¢.

According to one former employee the Auto Racer Tinker was a push toy; it would roll across the floor with a good push. [56]

Flying Tinker

Flying Tinker was one of the early Tinker Toys. The advertising for it asked "Who can fly it highest!" It was available from about 1918 through 1921, and possibly a little after that. At 10¢, and later 15¢ each, it would not seem to be a high-profit item. Replacement blades were available at retailers for 10¢ a box of six. The Flying Tinker or replacement blades were 12¢ if ordered direct from the company by mail.

Flying Tinker was a propeller toy. It had a yellow metal blade that would fly off when you pulled a string wrapped around the handle. The handle was wood and had a moving piece on the top, where the blade rested. This is where the cord was wrapped around, so that when the cord was pulled, the top would rotate and generate enough speed to propel the blade skyward.

The brochure for Flying Tinker promised to teach young boys about aerodynamics by use of this toy. The brochure also claimed that the yellow metal blades would sail through the air for several hundred feet, which may explain why a child needed so many replacement blades on hand. Maybe this one was a big money maker after all.

Plate 100

Author's collection.

Flying Tinker panel from four-panel brochure, circa 1918.

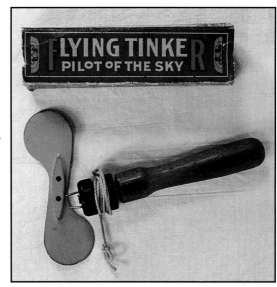

Plate 101

Flying Tinker with blade and original box, $20.00 – 25.00. Display box, $30.00 – 50.00.

Author's collection.

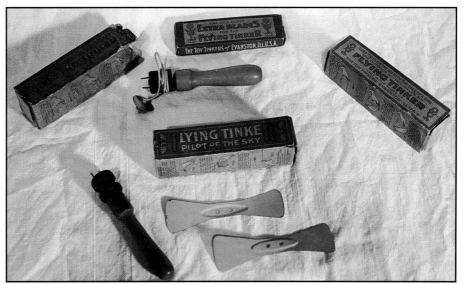

Courtesy of Frank Tolford.

Plate 102

Assortment of Flying Tinkers, boxes, and extra blades. Boxes of extra blades, $5.00 – 10.00.

Tinker Go-Round

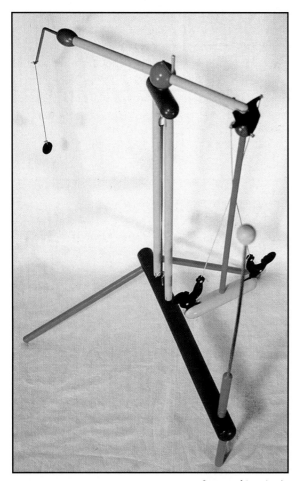

Plate 103

Tinker Go-Round toy fully assembled. Toy with box, $125.00 – 150.00.

Plate 104

Front and side view of Tinker Go-Round box.

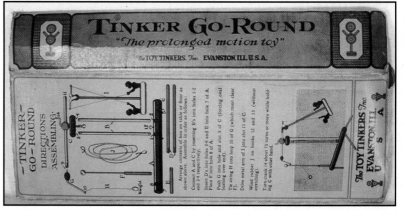

Plate 105

Back and side view of Tinker Go-Round box.

Tinker Go-Round was another short-lived toy by the Toy Tinkers. It was a rubber band propelled motion toy, that involved a rotating arm. This arm had two figures on a swinging element at one end and a weighted string at the other end. This string would wrap around a pole on one end of a platform, then unwrap and allow the rubber band to take over, all the while causing the figures on the swing to stay in motion. If it sounds complex, it is, and unless the rubber band is of just the right size, it will not work very well.

It is an interesting toy, yet I can see where it may not have been a big hit with its intended audience. The set is only listed in the 1929 catalog, and was retailing at $1.50. It is made of mostly wood dowel, enameled in yellow, blue, green, and red. The box size is 11¾" long by 3⅞" wide. The instructions for operating this toy are on the box, so it would be nice to find the two together.

Jump Rope Tinker

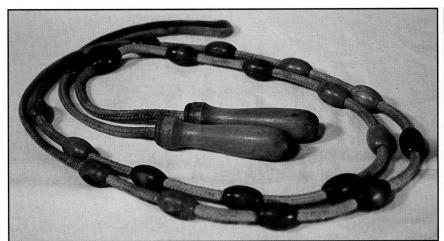

Plate 106

Courtesy of Kathy Trenter.

Jump Rope Tinker Toy, $15.00 – 25.00. With original box add $5.00 – 10.00.

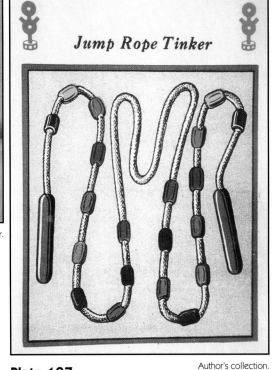

Plate 107

Author's collection.

Jump Rope Tinker catalog illustration, 1926 company catalog.

Plate 108

Author's collection.

Jump Rope Tinker brochure plate, mid-1920s.

"Jumping rope all the
live-long day is Betty's
favorite way to play.
She jumps, she skips, she
counts one, two, three;
A bead to count every jump, you see!"

C. Pajeau

Jump Rope Tinker was listed from at least 1923 to 1930 in newspaper ads and the company catalog. In 1923 it sold for 50¢ each, and by 1929 it retailed at about 75¢. Jump Rope Tinker had wooden handles painted red, and twenty beads pinned at intervals along the 90" rope. The beads were of alternating colors. For a jump rope, this was in the high-priced range, and even the ad copy acknowledges that Jump Rope Tinker cannot hope to compete with the garden-variety jump rope. The company contended that the Jump Rope Tinker was a higher class toy, and was weighted just right to give the proper momentum while skipping rope. I have never used a Jump Rope Tinker, but as people have commented, it must not have been fun if the rope hit you in the head. As with all Tinker Toys, Jump Rope Tinker came in its own box, and that would be a nice find.

Noisy Tinker

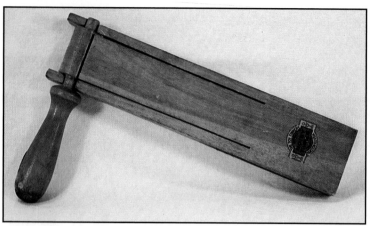

Plate 109

Noisy Tinker Toy, $15.00 – 25.00.

Noisy Tinker was listed as being a new item in the advertisements for 1920. Noisy consisted of two hardwood pieces that could be disassembled and reassembled easily. It promised to be twice as noisy as other, similar toys. There was a handle and a rectangular piece that fit on top. When rotating the handle, the top section would spin around and produce the sound. These were priced at $1.20 per dozen, which would give them a retail price of 15¢ each. The author's Noisy Tinker, when rotated fast, sounds like a very loud machine gun. It is very noisy! It measures 8" by 1¾" at the main body, from which the handle protrudes by 3".

Author's collection.

Radio Tinker Bank

This toy was available from 1922 to 1924 for certain, and it may have been available for a year or two longer, but so far there is no confirmation of this. This remarkable toy was a bank, and a make-believe radio that measured 8½" wide and 6" high. It combined a loud speaker that if spoken into would give the hollow sound of early radios, a telegraph key that would click when pressed, a coupler imitating static when turning the dial, a variometer which turned, and it also served as a coin depository. Instructions were glued to the bottom, and a decal on the front identified it as "Radio Tinker." In 1922, it was selling for $1.00 each.

Plate 110

Courtesy of Anne Lewis.

Radio Tinker Toy, front view, $75.00 – 100.00. Original box add $20.00 – 40.00.

Plate 111

Radio Tinker trade advertisement, 1922.

Plate 112

Radio Tinker brochure plate, early 1920s.

I'm a real Tinker Bank for your nickles and dimes;
I'm a make-believe Radio, up with the times;
I tune in on cities, and I 'code' Telegraph;
My 'talk' and my 'music' makes everyone laugh.

Author's collection.

Spinning Jack Tinker

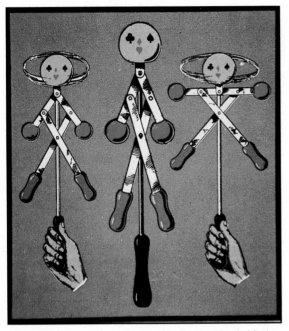

Plate 113
Spinning Jack Tinker company catalog ad, 1927.
Spinning Jack Tinker Toy, $80.00 – 100.00. Original
box add $20.00 – 40.00.

This Toy Top man whirls
fast as he can,
He's an acrobat dancer,
you see;
With feet off
the ground,
His arms wav-
ing 'round,
A SPINNING JACK
TINKER is he.

Plate 114
Spinning Jack Tinker brochure plate, 1927.

Spinning Jack Tinker is a spinning toy invented by Charles H. Pajeau. He assigned it to the Toy Tinkers of Evanston, Illinois, and it was filed on October 8, 1926. The patent was approved on March 1, 1927. Spinning Jack Tinker was only listed in the company catalog for one year, and the only store ads mentioning him were for the same year. He sold for 50¢.

Spinning Jack Tinker operated on the governor principle. By moving your hand, you could cause the figure to revolve and extend its arms. The arms could reach a 45- to 90-degree angle from this motion, and an occasional movement would keep him going. The toy could also be made to jump up and down, with the proper hand motion.

Spinning Jack Tinker was made of rustproof metal, and wood that was enameled. It measured 10" high. The eyes, nose, and mouth were represented by the card symbols of clubs, spades, hearts, and diamonds, thus the allusion to the "Jack" in a deck of cards.

Surf Boat Tinker

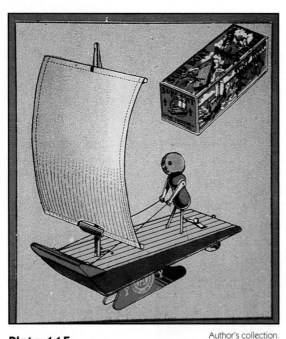

Plate 115
Surf Boat Tinker company catalog ad, 1926.

Plate 116
Surf Boat Tinker Toy without mast. As pictured, $90.00 – 120.00. With mast add $30.00. Original box add $20.00 – 40.00.

Surf Boat Tinker was invented by Anthon Morris Strom. He assigned the design to the Toy Tinkers of Evanston, Illinois, and it was filed for a design patent on October 20, 1924. The design patent was approved January 13, 1925. Surf Boat Tinker first appears in a 1925 wholesale catalog listing for Toy Tinkers products. It continued to appear until 1929. In 1925, its retail price was listed at $1.50, although it was selling for $1.25 in at least one store advertisement in 1925. By 1929, the wholesale price was still $12.00 a dozen, or retail of $1.50 each.

Surf Boat Tinker was advertised to be a real sailing model boat, although it looks more like a raft with a sail on it. Surf Boat Tinker was made of clear white pine that was enameled with celluloid waterproof paint. The rudder and keel had been enameled as well, and were made of steel.

When set up, it measured 11" high by 11" long. The mast and man could be removed to be packed into a box which measured 11" by 3¾" by 3¾". It was claimed to stay upright even when riding the waves, or in the bath tub.

This is a nice toy to find, but the fact that it came apart could reduce the chance of finding it complete. A further problem would be that it was intended for use in water, which may have resulted in a lot of them being severely damaged along the way.

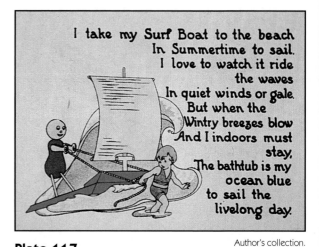

I take my Surf Boat to the beach
In Summertime to sail.
I love to watch it ride
the waves
In quiet winds or gale.
But when the
Wintry breezes blow
And I indoors must
stay,
The bathtub is my
ocean blue
to sail the
livelong day.

Plate 117
Surf Boat Tinker brochure plate, late 1920s.

Tilly Tinker

Plate 118

*Tilly Tinker Toy shown with wooden boxes. Tilly Tinker
with box, $80.00 – 125.00.*

Tilly Tinker was a balancing toy invented by Charles
H. Pajeau. He filed for the application February 1, 1917,
and it was approved July 31, 1917. Tilly Tinker was
weighted so that she would balance on one foot and
would not fall off her stand, no matter how animatedly she
was spun. The toy was made of wood, except for the
weights at the ends of her long arms and the nail in her
foot on which she balanced.

If you like variations in a toy, you will love Tilly Tinker. Almost everything about this toy has variations, from
the tripod on which she balances to Tilly herself. To start
with, the original package for Tilly Tinker was a wooden
box with tongue-and-groove joints, paper labels on the
front and back, and the words "The Dancing Lady" painted
on the sides. One side of the box was designed to allow it

to slide out. The 1924 catalog shows Tilly being sold in a
cardboard box. Tilly was priced at 75¢ continuously from
1917 to 1924, which may explain why the modifications
were made: to keep Tilly competitively priced.

The tripod early on was made completely of wood,
with several variations in the column on which Tilly balances. Some columns are one piece of wood tapering to a
point with a recessed top for the nail to rest in; others are
made up of different sized dowel pieces. The legs of the
tripod are later switched from wood to metal, and are
placed at a more gradual angle to increase the platform's
stability.

The style of Tilly varies, with some being larger than
others, and cut differently in the shape of the skirt and
upper body. Then there are the feet, which early on are

Plate 119 & 120 Courtesy of the Evanston Historical Society.

Tilly Tinker Cardboard box front and back views,
$20.00 – 40.00.

Plate 121 Author's collection.

Tilly Tinker brochure plate, circa 1918.

two balls attached to the body by dowel legs, with one of
the feet having a nail in it. Later versions have no wooden
feet at all, just two nails to serve as the feet. Finally, there is
the curl controversy. Some collectors claim that there is a
variation in the curl that hangs down between Tilly's eyes.

A problem with Tilly Tinker is her arm holes. When
the arms are inserted, the angle seems prone to damage of
the opening. The only version that I have seen without
this damage is a larger Tilly which may be a very early edi-
tion. Since this version's shoulders are larger, this may
make the openings less prone to damage.

A direction sheet from the collection of Anne Lewis
tells how to assemble Tilly, and then lists some of her
many accomplishments: the Forward Dip, the Side Step,
the Dignified Whirl, the Revolutionary Glide, the Figure
Eight, the Whirling Dervish, and the Dance of the Wind.
The sheet also explains how to achieve them.

The paper label on the wooden Tilly Tinker box reads:
"Introducing Miss Tilly Tinker the Terpsichorean Queen,
cultured exponent of the poetry of motion in a series of
entrancing dances never before seen on any stage. Management of the Toy Tinkers Evanston, Ill. U.S.A."

Tip-Toe Tinker

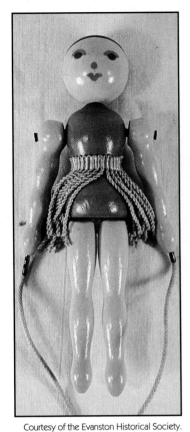

Plate 122

Tip-Toe Tinker Toy shown without handle. Complete and with box, $80.00 – 125.00.

Plate 123 & 124

Tip-Toe Tinker box, front view (left) and back view (right).

Tip-Toe Tinker was introduced in 1929. She was a doll that you made jump rope by connecting a handle to her shoulder joint, then rotating your wrist. She had a fringed skirt that would move, as well. She stood 7⅛" high, and in 1929 was wholesaling at $7.80 a dozen, or retail of $1.00 each. By 1931, there is no sign of her, and she may not have made it to 1930. This is a very nice toy, if you can come across one.

Topsy Tinker

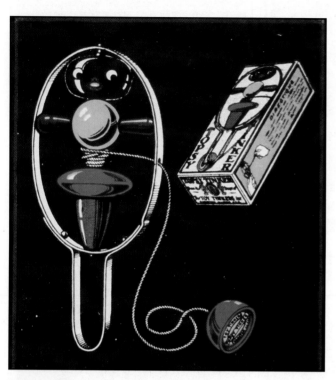

Plate 125

Topsy Tinker Toy advertising panel, 1925. Topsy Tinker Toy, $80.00 – 125.00. Original box, add $20.00 – 40.00.

A Topsy Tinker dollie
In a little oval cage,
She whirls to right,
She whirls to left
Like dancers on the
stage;
She's only made of wood,
of course,
But still she's all
the rage.

Author's collection.

Plate 126

Topsy Tinker brochure plate, 1925. Poem by C. Pajeau was included with Topsy Tinker.

Topsy Tinker was a gyroscopic type toy. It consisted of an oval frame on top of a handle. Inside of the frame, a doll rotated from pivots at her base and from the center of her head. The doll had a black head, white eyes, and red lips. The arms were painted green, the upper body was yellow, a skirt-like piece was red, and her legs were blue. There was a spot in her mid-section to wrap a cord around, which you could pull to cause her to spin. Topsy Tinker was illustrated in a promotional pamphlet which was given away with other Tinker Toys. Topsy Tinker was also shown in company ads for 1925. Topsy does not seem to have lasted beyond that year.

Art Sets

Bandy Board Tinker

Bandy Board Tinker was listed in the 1936 catalog. It was a design toy that reminds me of the square frame my sisters used in the 1960s to make potholders with flexible fabric bands. Bandy Board Tinker had ten flanges on each of its four inside surfaces. The toy included thirty-six 3" by ⅛" rubber bands. The rubber bands were intended to make patterns on the frame by stretching the bands of four different colors across the frame. The board was made of hardwood veneer and was lacquered.

The only year in which it seems to have been advertised was 1936, but time will tell.

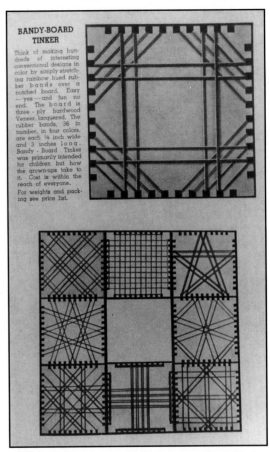

Courtesy of the Evanston Historical Society.

Plate 127

Bandy Board Tinker company catalog page. With box, $40.00 – 50.00.

Little Artist Tinker

"A box of shadow pictures,
No two are the same;
A dozen pretty subjects
To color up and frame."

C. Pajeau

Little Artist Tinker was shown in the 1928 catalog for the Toy Tinkers of Evanston, Illinois. It was a set of cards, one dozen in all, with silhouettes printed on them. The cards are each 7" by 9", and have a large area of undecorated space for the child to fill in. It is suggested by the catalog commentary that after a child has applied watercolors to one of the silhouettes, she or he will feel a sense of accomplishment.

The card subjects are: a child releasing a bird, a boy walking followed by a duck, a little girl teaching a dog to sit up, a child holding a birthday cake, a boy ice skating, a little girl with her doll, what appears to be an elf on a large toadstool, a boy running with several packages, a girl carrying a roll of fabric, a girl carrying flowers, a woman wearing a bonnet, and a little girl running with a stick in her hand rolling a rim. Perhaps the last one is a Rolo Polo Tinker. This is identified as "series one," and there may well be other series out there, but so far I have not heard of such.

The set was boxed in a cardboard package with the front showing a little girl's silhouette and the name "Little Artist Tinker, Twelve Silhouettes To Color." The back shows the twelve scenes enclosed, and has room for postage plus mailing and return address.

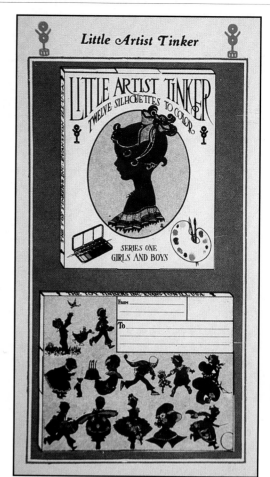

Plate 128   Courtesy of the Evanston Historical Society.

Little Artist Tinker company catalog page. With box, $50.00 – 70.00.

Tinkersand Pictures

Tinkersand Pictures were introduced in 1936. The first set featured a dozen cards with outlines to be filled in. The novel approach of this toy was that you put glue on the card, then poured colored sand on it to help decorate the card. The glue, sand, and a paint brush for applying the glue were all included. Directions were listed on the inside of the box lid. The cards were 6¼" by 8¼" and had the following scenes: an ocean liner being moved by a tug boat, a farm landscape, an airplane landing, a gondola in Venice, a little girl walking in front of a wood fence, a clown with a tiny umbrella, a dog in front of his doghouse, a chef flipping pancakes, a streamlined train, a Mexican scene, a sailor climbing a net, and a penguin with its baby. The set sold for about $1.00.

Tinkersand Pictures must have proven a big hit for it was sold until at least 1940, and spawned several variations as well. One was a Snow White series of Tinkersand

Pictures with scenes from the Disney movie of the same name. Another Disney theme set had Mickey Mouse and several other regular Disney characters. There is also a report of a jungle scene set of Tinkersand Pictures, although no hard evidence yet. The sets were offered in several sizes, including a set of ten cards measuring 6¼" by 4¾" each, which came with three boxes of colored sand. The larger sets came with six boxes of colored sand. In 1939 Sears was offering the large set for 89¢ and the small set for 43¢.

Company ads of 1937 also listed a third size set, that retailed for $2.00. The sixteen cards measured 10⅞" by 8⅜" each. The twelve tubes of colored sand were named red, blue, yellow, green, brown, flesh, purple, magenta, orange, robin's egg, gray, and black. Two jars of cement, two brushes (large and small), four sand trays, complete color schemes, and directions were also included.

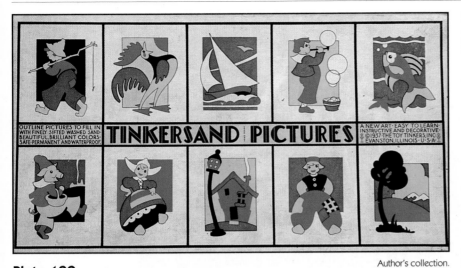

Plate 129

Generic Tinkersand Pictures ten card set, $55.00 – 70.00.

Author's collection.

THERE are twelve subjects in the Tinkersand set, on cards 6½ x 8½ inches. The finished pictures in sand relief are more beautiful and effective than flat illustration such as the above, can show.

Plate 130

Courtesy of the Evanston Historical Society.

Tinkersand company catalog illustration, 1936.

Plate 131

Tinkersand Pictures Snow White Series twelve card set, $100.00 – 150.00.

Courtesy of Anne Lewis.

Plate 132

Tinkersand Pictures Mickey Mouse Series ten card set, $100.00 – 150.00.

Author's collection.

Tinkerprints

Plate 133

Tinkerprints art set, $40.00 – 60.00.

Courtesy of Kathy Ade.

Tinkerprints was copyrighted in 1938 by the Toy Tinkers. Most likely, it was an attempt to follow up on the success of the Tinkersand Art sets.

Tinkerprints was comprised of 18 pre-printed cards for children to color with crayons. The scenes shown on the box cover, provided by Kathy Ade, consisted of: a Dutch girl carrying buckets on a bar across her shoulders, a turtle and a rabbit, fish swimming, a Japanese woman holding an umbrella while examining a flower, a marching band drummer playing, a rabbit with two carrots, a clown, an Eskimo on snow shoes, a dog dressed like a hobo hitchhiking, a dog looking at a beetle, a pelican wearing a top hat, an ocean liner at sea, an elephant under the circus big top, a gondola in front of a city scene, two chicks fighting over a worm, a goat leaping in front of a farm, two butterflies flying, and a country scene with a road and houses.

The box cover tells us "TINKERPRINTS with magic lines and crayon tints easy for pictures for children to make." The meaning of magic lines and crayon tints is not clear; perhaps when you colored with crayons, the pre-printed lines may have faded away. This is only a guess, however.

From the company advertisements listing the Toy Tinkers offerings for 1939 in general terms, it is reasonable to surmise that Tinkerprints were offered that year. They may also have been available in 1938, and possibly as late as 1940. At this time no evidence supports these dates.

Tinker Spots

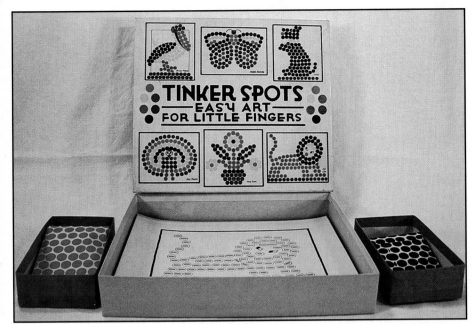

Plate 134

Tinker Spots art set, $40.00 – 60.00.

Plate 135

Tinker Spots art set box cover.

This is a very interesting and unusual art set. The box cover announces "Tinker Spots, Easy Art For Little Fingers." It contained six pre-printed cards, showing: Penny Pelican, Madam Butterfly, Scottie (dog), Peter Peacock, Saucy Susans (brown-eyed Susans), and Leo Lion. Six bags of colored spots were included, each spot measuring 7/16". The colors were red, blue, green, black, brown, and yellow. Metal tweezers, a wooden stick with a rubber tip, and two boxes for holding the spots were also part of this set. The instructions were printed on the inside of the lid, and a loose note was included to explain how to prepare the glue spots for sticking on the dots.

The cards each had outline circles that made up the pictures. Each circle contained the color name to be used, and a dried circle of glue. Using the rubber-tipped applicator, a small amount of water was applied to the glue spot, then rubbed with the applicator until sticky. Then the tweezers were used to apply and press down the color spot onto the card. If a child could not read the color names, then the box lid graphics served as a guide for which color went where. The box measures 11" by 9½" by 1¾".

There is no clear indication as to the manufacture date for this set, although an educated guess would be the late 1930s. This was during the period of the very successful Tinkersand art set, when Pajeau also introduced Tinkerprints. Having perceived this niche as wide open, Pajeau may have pushed to take it over.

The dealer, David Katz, who found this set noted that the instructions say to use paste or mucilage, should the glue spots not become sticky with water. He suggested that any toy mentioning "mucilage" must be old. He was right.

Baby Doll Tinker

Courtesy of the Evanston Historical Society.

Plate 136

Baby Tinker rattle, $40.00 – 60.00.

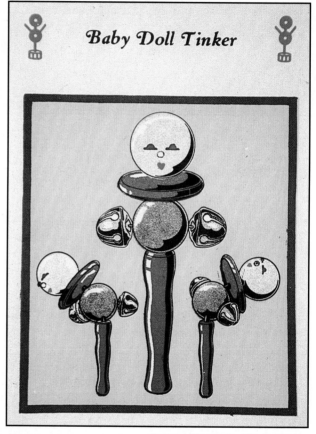

Baby Doll Tinker

Courtesy of the Evanston Historical Society.

Plate 137

Baby Doll Tinker rattle company catalog ad. Baby Doll Tinker, $40.00 – 60.00.

Baby Doll Tinker lead a double life, from what I have found. The first advertisement for her shows up in 1920, when she was called Baby Tinker. She seems to have faded away in about 1923 or so. Then, starting in 1928, she reappears as Baby Doll Tinker, lasting until about 1936 in newspapers and catalogs.

Baby Tinker was a rattle with two wooden balls for hands attached by a string. Baby Doll Tinker had bells in place of the balls. Her head and mid-section were flexible by means of a rubber backbone, as the copy said. Both Baby and Baby Doll Tinker were intended for infants, and the ad copy notes that they were ideally suited to gift and infants shops. Baby Doll Tinker was listed as being 5½" high up until 1929. After that she was listed as being 6⅛" high. If these dimensions are accurate, it is a useful means of dating the rattles. In 1929 she was wholesaling for $4.20 a dozen, so most likely the retail price was about 50¢. In 1931 the wholesale price was $8.00 a dozen, so retail was probably about $1.00 each. A promotional piece in the 1931 *Toys and Novelties* magazine identifies her as a new item.

Another difference is in the eyes. In 1920 Baby Tinker was sold in a canister with her name and picture on it, and it likely had a mailing label on the back. The 1920 ad shows her with wide open eyes. In ad copy for 1928 and 1929 her eyes are half circles on a straight line, the line being on the bottom. The 1931 and later ads show her eyes wide open and looking to the left.

Plate 138

Baby Doll Tinker brochure plate, late 1920s. Written by Charles H. Pajeau.

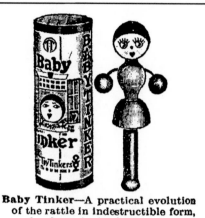

Plate 139

Baby Tinker 1920 wholesale ad showing the mailing tube style package.

Author's collection.

Belle Tinker

Plate 140

Three Belle Tinker (older) dolls, showing decals on back and color variations. Good to excellent condition, $40.00 – 60.00.

Author's collection.

Belle Tinker and her brother Tom Tinker had very long lives. The first listing for Belle Tinker was in the 1920 Sears catalog, where she was priced at 59¢. In 1924 she was wholesale priced at $4.00 per dozen and retailed at 50¢ each. The original Belle Tinker had an inverted bell for her upper body, and a larger bell that served as her skirt/lower body. She had one bell for each foot, and three bells for each arm. There are many color variations for Belle Tinker.

The configuration of Belle was changed in 1928, when the inverted bell was done away with and the skirt-like bell was moved up to become the torso of the doll. She still had three bells for each arm, but now she had three bells for her legs with a ball for each foot. By 1929 Belle's wholesale price was $6.00 a dozen, putting her at about 75¢ retail. In 1931 she was retailing for $1.00 each. The early Belle was listed as being 7" tall, which is the same as the later Belle. The last listing for

Plate 141

Author's collection.

Belle Tinker (newer) doll, showing hand ball with medallion, $25.00 – 45.00. With original box, add $20.00 – 40.00.

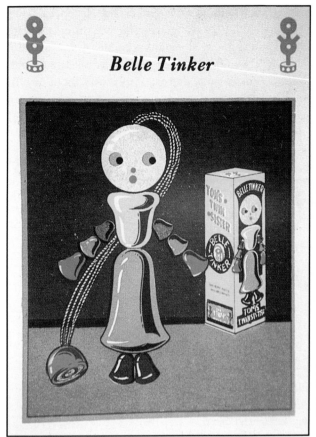

Belle Tinker

Plate 142

Author's collection.

Belle Tinker company catalog page, 1926.

Belle Tinker was 1939 in the company advertisements.

Then, in 1954 under Spalding, Belle was resurrected and listed as still 7" tall, and selling for $1.00. A difference between the Spalding Belle and the older redesigned Belle seems to be in the piece at the end of the cord. The Toy Tinkers ads all show the half circle wooden knob which had a yellow metal disk with the Toy Tinkers name on it. The Spalding ad shows a white ball at the end of the cord. I am not certain of how long Spalding sold their Belle Tinker; she seems to have vanished from company ads by 1958.

Here are two different verses written by Charles Pajeau for Belle Tinker. The first (Plate 143) was for the early form of Belle, and the second for the later variation.

"Tom Tinker's sister belle
is a very winsome miss;
and in her brand new costume
looks sweet enough to kiss."

Belle Tinker is this fair lady's name;
When first to "Toy-Tinker Town" she came
The children from East, the children
From West said, "Belle is the One I
Love the Best."

Plate 143

Author's collection.

Belle Tinker brochure plate, mid-1920s.

Bunny Boy Tinker

Plate 144   Courtesy of the Evanston Historical Society.

Bunny Boy Tinker company catalog page, 1931.
Bunny Boy Tinker, $40.00 – 60.00.

Courtesy of the Evanston Historical Society.

Plate 145

Bunny Boy Tinker photo from 1936
company catalog.

Bunny Boy Tinker is Tom Tinker with an egg-shaped head and long felt ears attached by rivets that also serve as his eyes. The egg-shaped wood is positioned so that the small end acts as the Bunny's nose and mouth. Bunny Boy Tinker is painted in pastel shades, and was intended as an Easter toy. He was listed as being 7" tall. He was part of the Toy Tinker catalog listing from 1931 to 1936. He also may have been available in 1930.

Gym Tinker

Gym Tinker is a really neat Tinker Toy. He is an adjustable figure that can balance on his hand, foot, head, or any combination thereof. He is held together by a series of strong springs, run through his limbs and torso to his head. At 8½" tall, and colored in red, green, light peach, yellow, and black or blue, he made quite an eye-catching figure. He was made of white birch from Maine, which was enameled in five of the above colors, with black and blue being variable. Gym Tinker the acrobatic clown was available from at least 1929 to 1933, and must have been a reasonable success in those years. He was wholesaling in 1929 for $12.00 a dozen, and retailing for about $1.50 each. In 1931 his wholesale price had gone up to $16.00 a dozen, so he would be retailing at $2.00 in most stores.

> "On his head or feet or hands;
> in any funny pose he stands —
> Gym Tinker is the jointed clown,
> who brings the laughs to Tinker Town."
>
> Charles Pajeau

Plate 146
Gym Tinker dolls in various poses, $75.00 – 100.00.

Author's collection.

Plate 147 Courtesy of the Evanston Historical Society.
Gym Tinker company catalog page, 1931.

Lanky Tinker

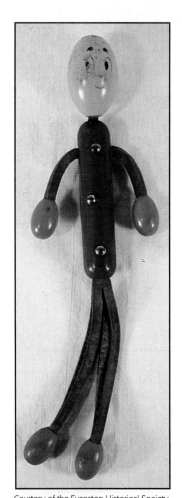

Courtesy of the Evanston Historical Society.
Plate 148
Lanky Tinker Doll, $40.00 – 60.00.

Plate 149 Author's collection.
Lanky Tinker company catalog ad, 1926.

Plate 150
Lanky Tinker brochure plate, 1926 or 1927.

Lanky Tinker is found in the 1926 and 1927 company catalogs. He is a wood doll painted red, yellow, blue, green, and black, with a highly-polished finish. His arms and legs are made of laminated pigskin, according to the 1927 catalog, while the 1926 catalog simply says strong leather belting. He is 12" high. Store ads for 1927 have him selling for 50¢. According to the ad copy from 1926, Lanky Tinker is, "tall, thin and handsome, so strong that no amount of tumbling around or rough abuse can hurt him in the least. He will grow up with the baby and be handed down to the next generation. Lanky has no brains because his head is made of wood, so, of course, he's never cross but always smiling."

Author's collection.

Mammy Tinker

Plate 151 & 152

Author's collection.

Mammy Tinker doll front and back views showing decal, $90.00 – 125.00. Original box add $20.00 – 40.00.

Mammy Tinker—A new and attractive Tinker novelty hardwood, no sharp corners, permanent colors, each in attractively colored round mailing carton, 2¾x8 in.
F3653—½ doz. in pkg..Doz. **$5.20**

Plate 153

Author's collection.

Mammy Tinker 1920 wholesale ad showing the mailing tube style package.

Mammy Tinker is an interesting toy from the early years of the Toy Tinkers. Mammy Tinker came in a 2¾" by 8" can with her name and picture on the cover. The advertisements show her selling for 59¢ to 65¢ in 1920. She was listed as a knockabout doll with no sharp corners. Her can was suitable for mailing, which most probably means that it had a mailing label printed on the back. She is a toy version of the stereotyped Mammy character.

She stands 7½" high. Her feet and skirt are black, her upper torso is caramel brown, and her face and arms are black. She is wearing a bandanna on her head. Each arm consists of a single large black bead, attached to the upper torso by cord. It is certain that Mammy Tinker was sold in 1920, that being her first year, but how long after that is not clear. I suspect that she was short lived, and may be in short supply today. Examples tend to show up in good shape, but some are missing the feet. A Mammy Tinker doll will likely still have the Toy Tinker decal on its back, so identifying it should be simple. Good luck!

Puppy Tinker

Plate 154   Author's collection.

Puppy Tinker brochure plate, late 1920s. Poem by Charles Pajeau.

Plate 155   Author's collection.

Puppy Tinker with original box. Puppy Tinker, $40.00 — 60.00. With box, add $20.00 – 40.00.

Puppy Tinker was based on the same patent as Tom Tinker, which was granted in 1919. The first catalog listing for Puppy Tinker is 1928, and continues until 1931 when it was no longer shown. Puppy Tinker's legs are nailed to the main body to allow it to stand up, while it has a flexible torso and head. The flexibility is made possible by a spring that holds the upper body together. The eyes are rivets or tacks that hold the ears in place.

The catalog touted Puppy Tinker as "the Circus Dog, is an acrobatic canine that assumes many unusual and unique postures at the whim of the owner." The colors were bright enamel in red, green, blue, and yellow. The catalog listed him as measuring 6½" long, and shipped in his own box. In 1929 Puppy Tinker was selling for 75¢ each, and in 1931 for $1.00 each.

Tinker Rabbit

Plate 156   Courtesy of Larry Basting.

Tinker Rabbit Toy, $50.00 – 75.00.

This is another Easter-theme toy in pastel enamel paint. Tinker Rabbit is Puppy Tinker with an egg-shaped head, and rabbit-like ears attached to the head with rivets or tacks that act as the eyes. As with Puppy Tinker, Tinker Rabbit relies on a spring backbone to make it flexible, and the legs are nailed to the main body so that it can stand up. It measures 6⅛" long, and was packed in its own box. The catalog recommended that this toy would see year 'round demand. It was available in the company catalog from 1931 to 1935. In 1931 the wholesale cost per dozen was $8.00, with it retailing at $1.00 each.

Plate 157
Tinker Rabbit company catalog ad, 1931.

Courtesy of the Evanston Historical Society.

Siren Tinker

Siren Tinker was for sale from 1921 until 1932. This is another bead doll like Tom and Belle Tinker. Siren Tinker is a series of balls that gives a snake-like appearance. With the head being the largest, the balls get progressively smaller toward the end. The head has two balls as earrings.

Siren Tinker is marked with the Toy Tinkers yellow metal label, affixed to the handball at the top of the string.

A unique feature of Siren Tinker is that the balls are not secured in place, so that they may be moved up and down the length of the cord. In 1924, Siren Tinker was selling retail for 50¢, in 1929 it cost 75¢ retail, and in 1931 the price was $1.00. Siren was 8¼" high and enameled in multiple colors.

Courtesy of the Evanston Historical Society.

Plate 158
Siren Tinker Doll, $40.00 – 60.00.

This fascinating "Siren"
Has come to love and bless
With happy smiles
and fairest wiles
And songs of
happiness.

Author's collection.

Plate 159
Siren Tinker brochure plate, mid-1920s. Poem by C. Pajeau from The Story of the Little Tinker Men.

Plate 160

Author's collection.

Siren Tinker company catalog ad, 1926.

Verse for Siren Tinker

"A fascinating siren doll
To take where e'er you go;
She's made of balls, both large and small
That slide both to and fro."

Tom Tinker

Plate 161

Courtesy of Anne Lewis.

Three Tom Tinker dolls, center older style, left and right newer style. Older style, $40.00 – 60.00. Newer style, $25.00 – 45.00.

Tom Tinker was available starting in 1919, until at least 1939. The Sears 1920 catalog lists him alongside his twin sister, Belle Tinker, and Mammy Tinker. He was described as being 7½" high, made of nice smooth balls of wood, with four cords strung together and extending about one foot above his head. The balls were colored black, purple,

Plate 162
Tom Tinker II company advertisement, 1923.

Author's collection.
Plate 163
Two views of Tom Tinker box, $20.00 – 40.00.

Author's collection.
Plate 164
Tom Tinker doll with hand ball and medallion in mint condition, $65.00.

pink, red, and green, although Tom is found in many color variations. The dyes used were said to be harmless. Sears was charging 59¢ for Tom.

The patent for Tom Tinker was filed on March 31, 1919, and was approved on December 23, 1919. The patent also allowed for a four-legged doll that looked just like Puppy Tinker except for the head. Due to all the imitators of Tom Tinker which came out after his introduction, Pajeau filed a design patent on December 21, 1921. It was approved on May 22, 1923. This protected the appearance of Tom from copycats for 14 years.

Interestingly, the year 1923 saw two variations of Tom Tinker being manufactured by the company. One version was less expensive, for large customers like Sears. This less expensive version was promoted as Tom Tinker the Ball Man, and was done in primary colors for 50¢ retail. The other, more expensive version was done in pastel colors, and retailed for 75¢. The latter version came in a more detailed and colorful box. In 1924, the company announced that only the best features of the two were being kept, and the price would be in the middle of the last year's Toms.

Sears was selling Tom Tinker the Ball Man for 42¢ in 1923, while in other retail establishments he sold for 50¢. In 1924 and 1925, stores were charging 60¢ for him, yet by 1927 Tom was back to 50¢ again. Then, in 1929, he was priced at 75¢ retail, and $1.00 in 1931.

Tom Tinker was listed as being 8" tall in the 1927 cata-

log, while Spalding listed a reissued Tom Tinker as being 7" tall, the same size as his reissued sister, Belle Tinker. This information may prove useful if these measurements are accurate, although the Tom Tinker dolls with the Toy Tinker labels that I measured are 7" as well.

The Spalding ad mentions that Tom and Belle Tinker are made with ten fascinating colors. The Spalding Tom has a white ball at the end of the cord, rather than the typical half-circle knob. The earliest Tom Tinker dolls are shown with a ball in place of the knob, and an early Tom Tinker label glued on the doll's back, coated with shellac.

Once from the Land of "I-Dont-Know-Where," there came the "King of The Toys" so fair. Can you guess His name by his color bright? Tom Tinker!-yes-you guessed it right.

Author's collection.
Plate 165
Tom Tinker brochure plate, mid-1920s. Poem by C. Pajeau.

Plate 166

Courtesy of Larry Basting.

Custom painted Tom Tinker doll in black, $100.00.

The Tinker Twins
Tom and Belle

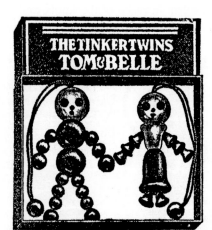

The Tinker Twins, Tom and Belle
—The famous Tom and Belle
Tinker combined in a single pkg.
F3620—¼ doz. sets in pkg.
Doz. sets, **$10.00**

Tom and Belle came packaged in a box together as the Tinker Twins, according to ads from 1920. The wholesale price was $10.00 per dozen, which would put the retail at about $1.25 for the set. The bead dolls were promoted as being for "the period of a baby's life between the rattle and the real doll, no sharp corners." Finding one of these original boxes would be your lucky day.

Plate 167

Tom and Belle Tinker — The Tinker Twins 1920 wholesale ad showing them in their package. With box, $120.00 – 165.00.

Author's collection.

Bead Toys

Tinker Beads
(round in a box)

Plate 168

Courtesy of the Evanston Historical Society.

Tinker Beads in a rectangular box, $50.00 – 75.00.

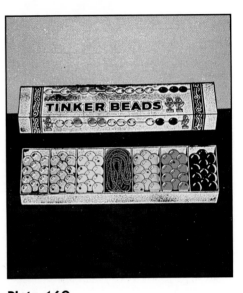

Plate 169

Tinker Beads company advertisement.

Tinker Beads were listed from 1922 to 1924, in company advertisements and catalogs. They came in a cardboard box, and were decorated in strong primary colors. These beads were all ⅝" round, and divided by color into six compartments. There were 144 beads to a set, with a length of cord and a blunt needle. The beads were made of white birch.

Tinker Beads No. 1, No. 2, No. 3

Tinker Beads appeared in 1923 in the company listings. They were advertised at 25¢, 50¢, and $1.00. In the 1924 Toy Tinkers catalog, they were listed as consisting of beads in seven pastel colors, in oval and round shapes. The seven colors found in the jar of Tinker Beads which I bought from a dealer were: light pink, bright pink, light blue, dark blue, purple, green, and yellow. The enameled beads were ⅝" round and 1" oval.

The jars were glass with a metal lithographed lid in white, pink, and dark blue. The lid shows two little Tinkermen side by side, and announces that the beads are made of harmless enameled colors and are waterproof. The 50¢ jar (No. 2) contained 63 beads; 28 were oval with four in each of the above colors, and 35 were round with

In jars of glass all showing thru
Are Tinker Beads for Sis and you;
Their dainty colors always last,
And here's a cord to
string them fast.

Plate 170

Author's collection.

Tinker Beads No. 1, 2 & 3 brochure plate, mid 1920s. Poem by Charles Pajeau.

Plate 171

Author's collection.

*Tinker Beads No. 2 and No. 1 jars with beads, etc. No. 1,
$10.00 – 25.00. No. 2, $15.00 – 30.00.*

Courtesy of Lonnie and Joanne Litwiller.

Plate 172

*Tinker Beads No. 3 jar with
beads, etc., $20.00 – 40.00.*

five in each of the colors. The No. 1 jar had 28 beads, reported to be enough to make a necklace that would go over the head easily. Tinker Beads No. 3 contained 133 beads, which was more than twice as many as the No. 2 set.

All sets included polished cord with a celluloid bead at one end to keep the wood beads from sliding off, and a safety needle to help string the beads. After about 1927 the polished cord was replaced by stringing tape, which appears to be a fabric-like flat material. Another change occurred after 1926, when the oval beads were listed as being ⅞" long instead of 1" long, as they were in 1924. This size information could be useful in dating the age of one of these sets. The Tinker Beads No. 1, 2 & 3 were listed in newspaper ads and company catalogs until 1939.

Tinker Beads in a Bag

Tinker Beads in a Bag were listed in newspaper advertisements for the year 1934. There are no other listings, photos, or drawings known at this time to indicate the type of bag, or how many beads were included. I would speculate that the set which retailed for 50¢, was the same set sold in the glass jars for 50¢ and contained 63 beads, string, and a bodkin. Switching to a bag was likely an attempt to cut the cost of the beads and keep them prof-itable for the Toy Tinkers. The glass jar with its lithographed top must have been more expensive to purchase for the Toy Tinkers. Another consideration would be the shipping weight for the set in the jar. The jar made up the largest part of the product's weight, and eliminating that would have made it cheaper to transport.

Tinker Beads in a Bag value ranges from $20.00 for good to $40.00 for excellent.

Tinker Beads No. 4

This set of Tinker Beads came in a round metal box, which was lithographed. It contained 168 beads, eighty-four ⅝" round and eighty-four ⅝" oval. They were painted in seven pastel shades, and included stringing tape and a bodkin (blunt needle). The box was 8" in diameter by 1⅜" deep. The No. 4 set was intended for customers looking for a larger set than the No. 3 Tinker Beads, which only contained 133 beads. Of course, No. 4 was also appealing to people looking for a nicer presentation, such as grandparents. Tinker Beads No. 4 were listed in the company catalogs from 1928 to 1930. In 1929 the beads were listed wholesale at $15.00 a dozen, so that they would be selling for about $2.00 each.

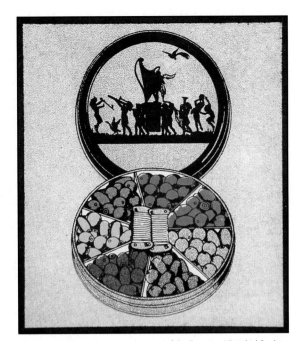

Plate 173   Courtesy of the Evanston Historical Society.

Tinker Beads No. 4 company catalog ad, 1928.
Tinker Beads No. 4 with tin box, $60.00 – 80.00.

Tinker Beads No. 6

Plate 174   Courtesy of the Evanston Historical Society.

Tinker Beads No. 6 company catalog page, 1931.
Jar with beads, $30.00 – 60.00.

This was a greatly enlarged set of beads. The set included thirty-six ⅞" balls and ⅞" by 1³⁄₁₆" ovals, packed with tape and a bodkin for stringing. The set came in a safety-glass jar with a screw top. The jar lid was lithographed metal. The beads were enameled in six safe, brilliant, glossy primary colors. The set was recommended for use in kindergarten. The Toy Tinkers catalog listed Tinker Beads No. 6 from 1930 to 1935.

Tinker Kinderbeads

Plate 175

Tinker Kinder Beads.

Courtesy of Lonnie and Joanne Litwiller.

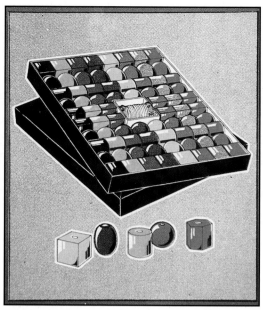

Plate 176   Courtesy of the Evanston Historical Society.

Tinker Kinder Beads company catalog ad, 1931. Beads and string with box, $60.00 – 80.00.

The 1930 through 1932 Toy Tinkers catalogs listed Tinker Kinderbeads. The set consisted of 76 wooden beads, made up of 1" cubes, 1" hexagons, 1" cylinders, 1" balls, and 1⅛" ovals. The beads were enameled by the Tinker Toy safety process in eight brilliant primary colors. The set also included a bodkin and five yards of stringing tape. The set came in a box that measured 10¾" by 8¼" by 1⅛".

Necklace Tinker No. 1

The Toy Tinkers introduced a pre-strung necklace of Tinker Beads that was 30" long. The first listing for it that I have found was 1924, although it may have been available earlier than that. In 1924 it was retailing for 75¢, and in 1929 it was going for the same price. Necklace Tinker was listed in company catalogs until at least 1936. In the early years of its production it was simply known as Necklace Tinker, yet when a shorter version was introduced the number was assigned. Necklace Tinker came in a nice display box with a ribbon attached to the necklace in your choice of pink or blue. This was considered a baby toy much like Tom and Belle Tinker, and was suggested for infant's wear departments and gift shops.

Plate 177

Tinker necklace No. 1 box. Box alone, $5.00 – 10.00.

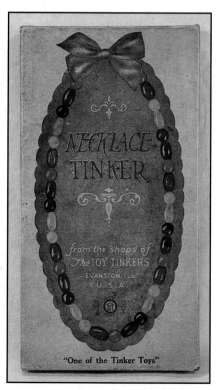

Author's collection.

Plate 178

Author's collection.

Tinker Necklace No. 1 company catalog ad, 1926. Necklace, $15.00 – 30.00.

A "Necklace"
with a silken bow
And beads in
wonder shades;
It never fails
to bring delight
To tiny men
and maids.

Plate 179

Author's collection.

Tinker Necklace brochure plate, mid-1920s. Poem by Charles Pajeau.

Necklace Tinker No. 2

Tinker Necklace No. 2 was introduced in 1936, as an economical version of No. 1. It measured only 24" instead of the 30" for Necklace Tinker No. 1. It came in a long narrow box with a clear plastic cover, so the necklace could be seen. There seems to have been listings for No. 2 up through 1938. It was made with the same type beads as No. 1, and included the choice of ribbon color; No. 2 was just shorter.

Plate 180

Courtesy of the Evanston Historical Sociey.

Tinker Necklace No. 1 and No. 2 company catalog photo, 1936. Necklace No. 2, $15.00 – 30.00. With box, add $5.00 – 10.00.

♟ Construction Sets ♟

Introduction

The Toy Tinkers of Evanston began with the Tinkertoy construction set in 1914, and sold only this one style until 1927, when they introduced Double Tinkertoy. In 1932 the company began to expand the product line with the introduction of electric and spring motor sets, and in 1933 replaced Double Tinkertoy with Senior Tinkertoy. Also in 1933, the company offered Junior Tinkertoy. In 1941 the Easy Tinkertoy was brought out, and 1943 saw Special Tinkertoy introduced to replace the motor and electric sets that were dropped due to the war. In 1950, Deluxe Tinkertoy was offered for sale, and was the last product introduced under Pajeau's guidance.

Within a couple of years after Spalding Bros. took over the Toy Tinkers, the line was undergoing multiple changes. The canister sets now had painted sticks, and the sets began to take on new names. The addition of new items also followed.

If you like variations, hold onto your hat, because there are many when you get into the sets of Tinkertoys. If you wish to collect one of every variation, you could easily be talking 50 or more cans. Not just the types of sets varied but items within the sets as well. Spools are beveled and not, natural wood and painted, windblades are different colors, parts change within a given Tinkertoy set. What follows are descriptions of each set and information about the variations, but is by no means a final word on those variations.

Charles H. Pajeau loved magic tricks; he often performed them for friends and family. In the 1940s through 1952 construction sets, an instruction booklet and small pamphlet entitled "Tinkertoy Tricks" were often included. The pamphlet showed several tricks, games, and puzzles that the young magician could learn to do by using the various parts of a Tinkertoy set.

Plate 181　　　　　　　　　　　Author's collection.
Wonder Builder brochure plate, mid-1920s.

> "I build a thousand wondrous things
> That teach both girl and boy;
> I bring content and happiness;
> My name is Tinkertoy."
>
> C. Pajeau

The Thousand Wonder Builder
(also known as "The Wonder Builder")

The Thousand Wonder Builder was the first product of the Toy Tinkers of Evanston, Illinois. The set contained 73 wooden parts and eight cardboard windblades. The set sold for 50¢ in 1914. Even the earliest set included an instruction booklet, which listed the parts and showed several models that could be constructed. The set remained unchanged for several years, but there were variations over time. While the parts list was constant, the container varied.

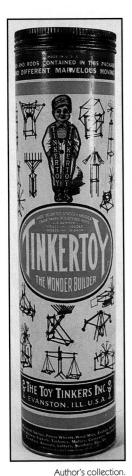

Plate 182

Tinkertoy Wonder Builder can. Can with lid, instructions, and all parts, $20.00 – 35.00.

Author's collection.

The Wonder Builder can was 12" tall and 3" in diameter. From a publicity photo taken in 1964 with general manager E. W. Heilmann, the earliest can appears to have a cardboard top, and does not have the little man above the round logo. The caption credits this can as being from 1914. That was the first year of production, when the cans were distributed only in the Chicago area.

The Toy Tinkers seemed to realize after that first year that a metal lid would be necessary, if the toy's lid was to be more durable. By 1915, the lids were metal, an inside-threading type, with a pencil slot to facilitate removal of the lid. These cans were red and blue with white background. The 1916 instruction books showed cans with the next step in inside-threading lids. This version had a small cardboard handle bisecting the lid top. The metal-top cans have the little man wearing a pillbox-type hat and coveralls with the word "Tinkertoy" running from each shoulder to each pant cuff. The outside screw top was introduced in about 1920, and replaced the previous recessed lids. The outside screw top is the style of lid used for the Tinkertoy company from then on, with the exception of a brief period during the Second World War.

Plate 183

Author's collection.

Tinkertoy brochure panel, circa 1918.

Another variation involved the spools included with the set. This had to do with the lack of grooves on the outside edge, and with the mysterious-sounding spool "X," The grooves allowed the spool to be a pulley or a guide for string, when a model called for such. The directions in some of the sets before 1916 suggested that you can cut the groove yourself. This must have gone over like a lead balloon, for by 1916 the grooves were being cut into the spools.

Spool "X" was also being provided with the set. The purpose of spool "X" was to serve as a bearing for an axle, since the center hole was drilled to a larger diameter than the typical spool, designated spool "Z." The "X" spool could also serve as a wheel for vehicles. Before the "X" spool was included in the set, Toy Tinkers offered 5 of them for 10¢ by mail. By 1923, these were no longer shown in the parts list for The Wonder Builder; only the standard spool was identified.

Plate 184

Author's collection.

Variations in Tinkertoy Wonder Builder can lids. The lid to the right screws down into the can and has a cardboard handle. The lid to the left is an outside screw top type.

Continuing with variations, the earliest spools were not beveled on the edges, and the windblades were red, white, and blue. These were in the pencil-slot cans. The cardboard-handled cans had spools with beveled edges, and the windblades were red with the Tinkertoy logo printed on them. The screw-top cans had spools that were

not beveled, and the fan blades were red or blue. The spools were painted red in some of the Tinekrtoy sets starting in 1932. This included The Wonder Builder, and continued through 1942.

Plate 185

Courtesy of the Evanston Historical Society.

Tinkertoy Wonder Builder company catalog ad, 1924.

In December of 1923, the Toy Tinkers reorganized the partnership into a corporation. This is significant, as after that date the cans were marked "Toy Tinkers Inc., Evanston, ILL." A can so marked must be from 1924 or later. The can colors continued to be red and blue with white background.

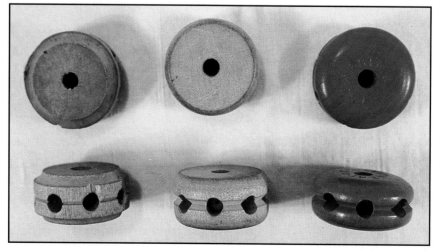

Plate 186

Author's collection.

Variations in Tinkertoy spools. Left is early beveled style spool. Center is mid-1920s style spool. Right is 1930s painted style spool.

In 1940 the Big "T" can was introduced. The little man was gone, and the can had a dark line running the length of the can with a horizontal band around the top. From the front, this gives the appearance of a large "T," This can had a metal outside screw-top lid, and was sold from 1940 to 1942. 1940 also found The Wonder Builder enlarged to 116 pieces from the previous 73. In addition to spools, it now came with Disk "D," loose pulley "Y," long bearing "L," cross bearing "C," windblade holder "H," and button "U." The 116 parts do not include eight windblades, which also came with the set. In 1943, the metal shortages brought on by the Second World War changed the can to what is known as the small "T" can. The horizontal band is located at the midsection of the canister with the vertical line traveling from the bottom to the middle of the can. From 1943 to 1944, these cans had cardboard tops and bottoms. The spools were stamped "Tinkertoy," and the windblades were blue.

Things had improved by 1945, for the small "T" cans had metal tops and bottoms. The spools were not marked "Tinkertoy," and the blades were blue and purple. This style of can continued through 1949.

In 1950 the small "T" can showed another change. The vertical band now consisted of two thin blue lines with white in between. The spools were marked "Tinker-toy" and the windblades were red. This style of can continued through 1952.

With the sale of the company in November of 1952, the cans for 1953 took on the name of A. G. Spalding Bros., and the sticks shown on the can were red. The sticks inside of the can were also red, and the windblades were green. Later, Spalding would color code the dowel rods, with each size being a different color. This allowed for easier use of the instructions by even very young children. Spalding Bros. continued to make changes, adding new variations of construction sets. After 1954, The Wonder Builder was no longer listed for sale, being retired after 40 long years.

Plate 187 Courtesy of the Evanston Historical Society.

Wonder Builder full page ad from 1936 company catalog.

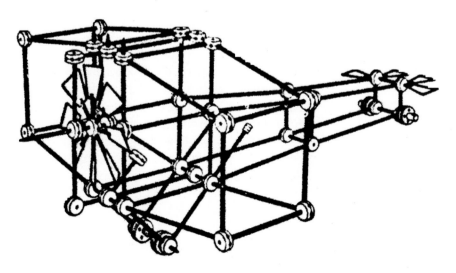

Giant Tinker

"The highest point to which a construction toy for children has been developed." So reads an ad for Giant Tinker, the multi-motion model maker for young mechanics, architects, and engineers. This set was offered from at least 1919 through 1926. With it, you could build models from one foot to nine feet high. It was intended for older children as an advancement over The Wonder Builder set.

It used no screws, blots, or nuts to connect the over 200 parts. The pieces were made of wood and metal, and were advertised as "designed on a principle of exact mathematical ratios, radiating from universal joint centers, by which means structural rods of correct length are always at hand to properly connect and build any given figure." All of the Giant Tinker girders, or connecting rods, were made of white hardwood. The hub, or universal joints, were steel. The wood pulleys and wheels were coated with brilliant red color. The set also included cord belting and fiber propellers for power-driven and wind-operating models. The ad copy promised that with the instructions and diagrams included with the set, "boys and girls of average intelligence can proceed without help."

The set weighed in at just over 8 pounds, and came in a compartment box that measured 21½" by 17" by 1⅜". It was the most expensive of the Tinker Toys, with a retail price of $5.00 from 1922 to 1924.

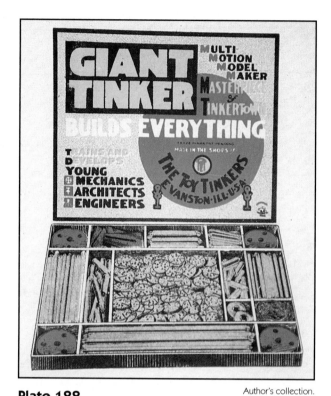

Plate 188   Author's collection.

Giant Tinker company catalog plate, 1926. Giant Tinker, $175.00 – 225.00.

Bendy Tinker

This toy was for sale in 1922, and does not seem to have been made after that year. A 1922 *Elgin Daily Courier* newspaper had Bendy Tinker in a Theo. F. Swan Store ad, with a selling price of 69¢. Bendy was a construction set in a canister that consisted of several sets of 18 different parts made of hard, natural finished wood. They could be arranged to make odd-looking animals. One description listed the following possibilities: ostrich, reindeer, lobster, boxer, acrobat, stork, camel, peacock, dachshund, kangaroo, and sixteen other animals.[115] Each set came equipped with a pair of pliers, which would suggest the difficulty of pulling the pieces apart. Value $75.00 good to $100.00 excellent, with original can and lid.

Double Tinkertoy

In 1927 Double Tinkertoy was introduced. This included twice the parts of The Wonder Builder, as well as 4 wheels (W), 4 small pulleys (P), and 2 connecting rod bearings (C) to increase the flexibility of the toy. Up until that time, if you wanted a bigger set you simply bought more of The Wonder Builder sets. With the change to Double Tinkertoy you now had parts not available before. Double Tinkertoy continued to be sold through 1932. Double Tinkertoy listed for $1.50 in 1927, and $2.00 in Canada.

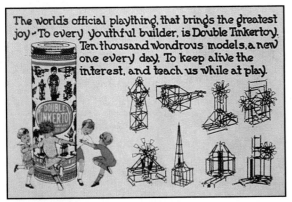

Plate 189

Author's collection.

Double Tinkertoy brochure plate, late-1920s.

Plate 190

Courtesy of Anne Lewis.

Double Tinkertoy along side a Wonder Builder set. Double Tinkertoy, $25.00 – 40.00.

Treasure Chest Tinkertoy

The name tells it like it is. The set contained 108 sticks, spools, and other motion pieces found in the Double Tinkertoy, as well as 12 windblades and a directions sheet. This set fell between the Wonder Builder and the Double Tinkertoy in the number of parts. It came packed in a treasure chest that appears to have been made of wood. The chest may have been made from cardboard or fiber board on which the design was painted. The set was available for 1930 only, from all indications.

Plate 191

Treasure Chest Tinkertoy, drawing. Treasure Chest Tinkertoy, $40.00 – 60.00.

Electric Tinkertoy &
Spring Motor Tinkertoy

In 1932 the Toy Tinkers introduced Motor Tinkertoy and Electric Tinkertoy. These were reformulated sets that had two new large pulleys and a larger proportion of pulleys and connecting bearing rods than in the Double Tinkertoy. Altogether there were six more wooden parts in this set, allowing for greater flexibility in motion models. This set proved to be so popular that it was offered the following year without the motor as Senior Tinkertoy. The motorized units were offered through 1942, when war demands forced their discontinuation.

The Spring Motor set was offered for locations where alternating current was not available, although it may have also sold to parents who did not want their children playing with electricity. The Spring and Electric sets were identical, except for the style of motor. In 1932 the Toy Tinkers began to paint the spools red, a practice that went on until 1942, presumably another casualty of the war effort.

Courtesy of the Evanston Historical Society.

Plate 192

Electric Tinkertoy full-page company catalog ad, 1935. Complete can with motor, $40.00 – 60.00.

Author's collection.

Plate 193

Electric Tinkertoy can, Big-T style. Complete can with motor, $40.00 – 60.00.

Courtesy of the Evanston Historical Society.

Plate 194

Motor Tinkertoy full-page company catalog ad, 1932. Complete can with motor, $40.00 – 60.00.

Plate 195

Electric motor, $15.00 – 25.00.

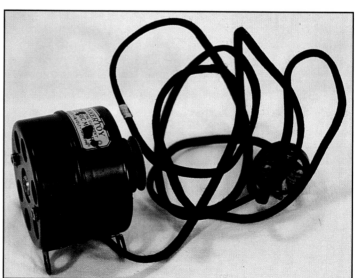

Author's collection.

Plate 196

Spring Motor Tinker Toys, two variations, $15.00 – 25.00 each.

Senior Tinkertoy

Courtesy of Anne Lewis.

Plate 197

Three Styles of Senior Tinker-toy cans. Early style, Big-T style, and Small-T style. Complete can, all parts, and instructions, $20.00 – 40.00.

Plate 198

Senior Tinkertoy in the later Small-T style can. Complete, $20.00 – 40.00.

Author's collection.

Senior Tinkertoy was introduced in 1933 to replace the Double Tinkertoy. The Senior set had 36 spools, as opposed to 40 in the Double set, and 20 No. 1 dowel rods instead of the 16 in Double Tinkertoy. There were only 12 of the No. 6 rods in the Senior, whereas the Double had 16 of these. Senior had six part "C" connector bearings, while Double had four. Finally, Senior had two of part "S," which was a large pulley. In 1933 the parts list was 163 which included the ball of string, and in addition the set had 16 windblades or a total of 179 parts.

By 1948, Senior Tinkertoy had evolved to 187 parts. The catalog listing says 189 parts but my count of the parts list showed only 187. Included were an oversized crank shaft, two spools identified as "BG," and "SP," a piece

designed to fit on the oversized shaft. This was the heart of the Windlass Drive, replacing the Motor Tinkertoy sets during the Second World War. There were also medium-sized pulleys "Z," and a crank handle "CH," and parts "P" and "J."

Another set of Senior Tinkertoys from the early 1940s shows the Windlass Drive, and included two lengths of oversized shafts, and two "PG" pegs to fit into the holes at the ends of these shafts. There is also Crank Wheel "CW," to fit on the shaft's end. This Crank Wheel has an offset hole in which a piece of dowel is placed, to use as a handle. This turns the shaft by hand. Later, a metal handle was added that could be placed at the end of the shaft without part CW." "CW" and the two "PG" parts were thus eliminated, reducing the parts list from 190 to 187.

Junior Tinkertoy

Plate 199

Courtesy of Anne Lewis.

Four Styles of Junior Tinkertoys. From Left the early style, Big-T style, World War II Small-T style, and the later Small-T style can. Complete can with all parts and instructions, $15.00 – 25.00.

Introduced in 1933 was Junior Tinkertoy. This set was billed as being for beginners, and contained only 59 wooden parts and eight windblades. Its 9" can was green and red with a white background. The spools in this set were not painted, and were identified for reordering purposes as "J2." The windblades were light blue.

By 1942, Junior Tinkertoy had undergone some changes. The set now contained 73 wooden parts and eight windblades. Among the new parts were four button "U" pieces, four windblade holders "HC," and four windblade holders "H."

Junior Tinkertoy had undergone another change for 1950, resulting in only 48 wooden parts and four windblades. Junior Tinkertoy was obviously an effort to offer a competitive product that might also engage a young child, and lead to the sale of larger sets.

Courtesy of Lonnie and Joanne Litwiller.

Easy Tinkertoy

Plate 200

Easy Tinkertoy, two variations of Big-T can. Complete set with instructions, $10.00 – 20.00.

Easy Tinkertoy was introduced in 1941. It was listed as having 42 pieces: eight spools, four windblades, two points "B," four windblade holders "HC," four buttons "U," and eight No. 1 dowel rods, four No. 2, four No. 3, and four No. 4. This was another attempt to offer a product at a competitive price marketed for younger children.

Pylon Tinker

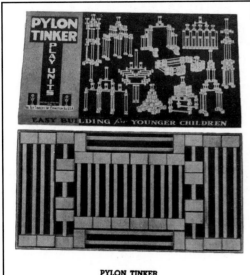

Courtesy of the Evanston Historical Society.

Plate 201

Pylon Tinker full-page company catalog ad, 1936. Complete set in box, $85.00 – 125.00.

Plate 202

Pylon Tinker model as shown in 1935 company catalog.

Courtesy of the Evanston Historical Society.

Pylon Tinker is first listed in 1936. It was a pile up and knock down building set. It consisted of wood blocks and dowels pre-assembled into pylons. The blocks measured approximately 1⅜" by 1⅜" by 1¼", and were connected by different length dowel rods which were approximately ⅜" in diameter. The pylons were therefore different lengths, with six being about 11" long, six being just under 4" long, and six of just under 8" long. The wood was identified as clear, natural, and unfinished, as there was no paint or varnish used.

The box listed it as "Easy Building for Younger Children," and called the set "Pylon Tinker Play Units." The box was 2" by 11" by 21½" in size. In 1936, Butler Bros. listed the Pylon Tinker for $8.00 a dozen, which would translate to $1.00 each retail.

Regular Tinkertoy

Regular Tinkertoy has been something of an enigma. What type of a set was it, and did it even exist? The answer to the latter question is yes, it did exist. The former's answer seems to be that Regular Tinkertoy was the same as The Wonder Builder. Collector David Lewis found the evidence that seems to confirm this. In 1947 Sears catalog advertisements, there was a listing for Junior Tinkertoy and the Wonder Builder. The accompanying photographs were of a Junior Tinkertoy can and a Regular Tinkertoy can. The year 1948 listed Regular Tinkertoy and showed its can, with no mention of the Wonder Builder. Then, in 1949, the Wonder Builder was again listed and shown in the Sears catalog.

Since the other construction sets had names like Junior, Easy, Standard, and Senior, the name of the Wonder Builder may have sounded awkward, so the title Regular was attempt at uniformity. I suspect that the name Regular failed to survive when parents came looking for the Wonder Builder set that they knew from childhood, and could not find it. Most toy clerks were not likely aware that it was the same toy. So, by 1949 the Wonder Builder name was back. Value ranges from $20.00 for good to $30.00 for excellent, with original can and lid.

Plate 203

Courtesy of the Evanston Historical Society.

Tinker Towers advertisement from 1931 company catalog. Complete set in box, $85.00 – 125.00.

Plate 204

Special Tinkertoy in the Small-T style can. Complete can with instruction, $20.00 – 30.00.

Author's collection.

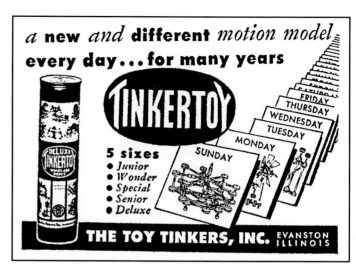

Plate 205

DeLuxe Tinkertoy advertisement, 1952. Complete can with instructions, $20.00 – 30.00.

Tinker Towers

Tinker Towers appears in the 1931 company catalog, and by 1932 it is absent. This is a building set including sixty ⅜" dowel rods of clear birch wood, that were each 3¾" long. There were also twelve blocks measuring 3¾" square by 1¼" thick, four triangular 3¾" blocks, and eight 3¾" by 1¼" blocks. All were of smooth-sanded white wood. The blocks had been drilled, to accept the dowel rods on the ends and on the corners. The cover of the box listed several models which could be built using the set, and of course, the possibilities were even greater. The box measured 11¾" by 11¾" by 2½", and weighed in at six pounds.

Special Tinkertoy

Introduced in 1943, Special Tinkertoy with Windlass Drive had 135 parts, although the advertisements listed it as being 137. In 1950, the set was changed so that it had only 128 parts. It lost some of the dowel pieces and part "C" connecting bearing, although it did have a cotter pin not found in the earlier sets.

DeLuxe Tinkertoy

DeLuxe Tinkertoy was introduced in 1950. This was the last construction set under Charles H. Pajeau's guidance. It contained 202 pieces, and featured the windlass drive for models. For the years 1950 to 1953, the DeLuxe was the largest set offered by the Toy Tinkers. The DeLuxe set was available until 1954.

♟ Games ♟

Abacus Tinker

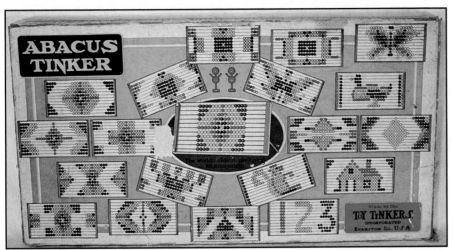

Plate 206

Abascus Tinker box cover.

Abacus Tinker is just what its name says. It was an abacus, the ancient counting devise that utilized several rows of beads. Since it had the word Tinker as part of the name, it is not surprising that the beads could be removed from the metal rods and rearranged in different ways. There were 165 colored wooden beads. The abacus measured 18" long, and 9¼" high. The toy wholesaled for $24.00 a dozen, which would indicate from other listings I have seen that a retail price of $3.00 was expected. Abacus Tinker was offered for sale in 1929 and 1930. It came packed in a printed cardboard box.

Plate 207

Abascus Tinker brochure plate, late 1920s. Poem by Charles Pajeau.

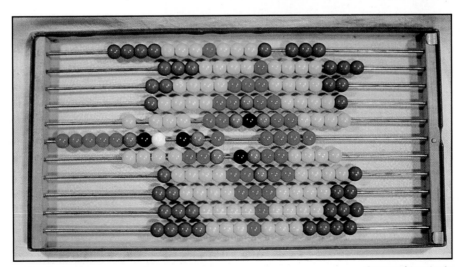

Plate 208

Abascus Tinker Toy. With box, $80.00 – 110.00.

Tinkerblox

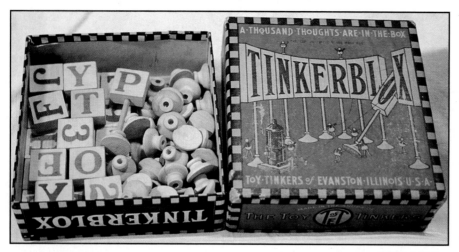

Plate 209

Author's collection.

Tinkerblox cardboard box and parts. Complete toy with box, $40.00 – 60.00.

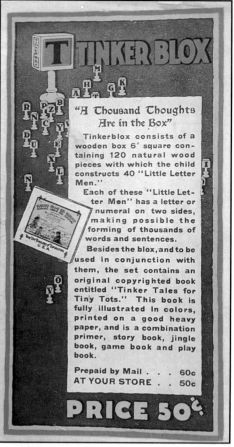

Plate 210

Author's collection.

Tinkerblox brochure plate, circa 1918.

Plate 211

Author's collection.

Variations in box type. On the left is the cardboard box and the right is a wooden early style box. Complete toy with box, $40.00 – 60.00.

Tinkerblox was a spelling game. The patent for this toy was filed February 1, 1917, and approved on September 25, 1917. Tinkerblox was introduced in 1917, and according to the sources I have located was available through 1920. For a year or two after that, they were manufactured and sold by Halsam Products Company, who had bought the rights and equipment from the Toy Tinkers.

Tinkerblox contained 120 wood pieces that made up forty letter men, each having a letter or number on two sides. It also included a booklet entitled "Tinker Tales For Tiny Tots." The book was fully illustrated in colors, and was reported to be a combination primer, story book, game book, and play book. The set was sold in wooden as well as cardboard boxes. The wooden box denotes an earlier age. The cardboard boxes were used later to cut the cost of the sets, keeping them competitively priced. From 1918 to 1920, the Tinkerblox sets retailed for 50¢ a set. Or, if you ordered it direct from the Toy Tinkers, the cost was 60¢ to have it mailed to your home.

Recently, while talking with Anne and David Lewis, fellow collectors of Tinker Toys, we realized that the early wooden boxes of Tinkerblox were designed to be used as display pieces. They each had a paper letter pasted to the back of the box, and a hole drilled in the bottom of the box. They could then have a stand inserted, and be used like the little lettermen which they contained.

Casino Golf

Casino Golf was one of the Tinker Toys. It was available from 1930 to 1932. Casino Golf had a raised platform with numbers on it that would spin like a roulette wheel. There were two metal approaches or ramps and a dozen embossed distance markers. All were intended to be used with a regular golf ball and putter. The box was 5" by 8" by 10", the metal approaches were 10" long, and the spinner was 8" and made of enameled wood. The embossed markers were numbered 1 through 6, with two of each. Casino Golf was recommended for the parlor or lawn.

Courtesy of the Evanston Historical Society.

Plate 212

Casino Golf company catalog advertisement, 1932.

Author's collection.

Plate 213

Casino Golf game with all parts shown. Complete set with box and instructions, $80.00 – 120.00.

Tinkerdux

Tinkerdux is a game that promises to be "Speedy – Hilarious – Rollicking – Rattling Fun." The set includes a cardboard box that is about 8" square, with game instructions on the inside of the lid. There are two hammer-like devises with ends resembling clothes pins, although the gap between the prongs is wide enough for a nail to be secured there. There are also 21 short sections of painted dowel and two containers for use during the game.

The hammers are called dux, and you use the clothes pin end to capture the pieces of dowel, which are worms. The object is to capture as many of the worms as possible, preferable more than the other player. The containers are for holding your worms until the end of the game, when you count to see who won. The worms are captured with a fast hammering motion, so the pace would be very fast. The color of the worm determines its value.

The dowels or worms are about ⅜" in diameter, and came in red, yellow, green, blue, and purple. The hammers are of natural wood. Tinkerdux was available in 1919 and 1920, and perhaps other years, as well. In 1919, it was selling in the Sears catalog for 45¢. Most likely it had a suggested retail price of 50¢.

This is a nice find, when complete.

Plate 214

Tinkerdux box.

Plate 215

Tinkerdux box and parts. Complete game with box, $40.00 – 60.00.

Tinker Fish

Plate 216

Tinker Fish game with box, $30.00 – 50.00.

This was only listed in the company catalog for the year 1927, and the only newspaper advertisement I have found was also for 1927. Tinker Fish was listed for 50¢ each. The set had six fish, each in a different enameled color. Each fish had a metal eye into which a hook could be snagged, so that it could be caught. The set also included a rod, reel, hook, and line. It all came packed in a box with a sliding lid that measured 10½" long. The set was intended to be used in water, in a bath tub, pail, or pond. It seems like a nice little set for 50¢, but it must not have been a winner.

Plate 217

Tinker Fish brochure plate, 1927.

Jumpy Tinker

Plate 218

Jumpy Tinker brochure plate, circa 1918.

Author's collection.

Plate 219

Jumpy Tinker box cover.

Author's collection.

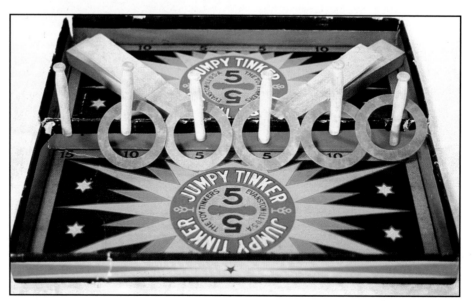

Courtesy of Anne Lewis.

Plate 220

Later style Jumpy Tinker game using cloths pins to hold the box lids together. Complete, $30.00 – 50.00.

Plate 221

Author's collection.

Jumpy Tinker game, early production, using a single piece fence to join the box lids, $30.00 – 50.00.

Jumpy Tinker is a game that involves tossing fiber rings using wooden catapults, in an attempt to catch them on wooden pegs. In some versions of the game, the pegs are dowel rods fit into a long piece of wood with numbers on it. This slides down over the lip of the overturned box top and bottom, which are put together. The inside of the box then becomes the playing field. This would seem to be the early version of the game, with a large number two in the middle of each box, and equally large number ones on either side of it.

Jumpy Tinker sold for 25¢ in 1918 at the store, or 30¢ by mail from the Toy Tinkers. To keep Jumpy Tinkers competitive, modifications were made. The long wooden piece and dowels were replaced by clothes pins, and the numbers were printed at intervals along the edge of the overturned box top and bottom. This kept the cost of production down, allowing the Toy Tinkers to continue to sell Jumpy Tinkers for 25¢. If it was wholesaling at about 16¢ to 17¢, then the Toy Tinkers were selling to jobbers at about 12½¢ a set. This would require them to produce it very cheaply to show a profit, for they still had to pay for promotion, salaries, insurance, etc. Jumpy Tinkers was being advertised as late as 1923, and might have been available after that.

Marathon Tinker

Marathan Tinker was the invention of Charles H. Pajeau. He filed for a patent on January 2, 1925, and had it approved on July 14, 1925. Marathon Tinker continued to be sold from 1925 through 1927. In 1929, a store ad listed Marathon Tinker as being discounted from 98¢ to 15¢, with a group of shop-worn toys in an odd lot sale. That may represent the final sale of this toy from the Toy Tinkers' inventory. Marathon Tinker was a race game, involving two figures attached to a metal platform by rails. By moving the rails back and forth, you would cause the figures to move from one end of the platform to the other, and so could have them race against each other. In 1925 they were selling for $1.00 each at retail.

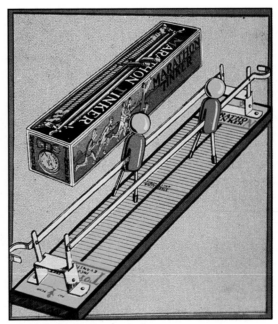

Plate 222

Author's collection.

Marathon Tinker company catalog ad, 1926.

Plate 223
*Marathon Tinker game,
$90.00 – 130.00. Original
box, add $20.00 – 40.00.*

Courtesy of the Evanston Historical Society.

Plate 224   Author's collection.
Marathon Tinker brochure plate, mid-1920s. Poem by C. Pajeau.

Peeza Game

The Peeza Game was introduced in 1935, and reappeared again in 1936. It involved piling up round building blocks until someone made them topple over. The player preceding the one causing the fall takes the pot, represented by the fallen pieces. There are seven balls of seven different colors, which each can represent a different player. Playing order is determined by how the balls come out of the mixer. There are fifty round building blocks, seven player markers, seven balls, a mixer, and a flat-top cone as a balance piece, on which the building blocks are placed when in play. Due to its late introduction, it was not a long lived game.

Plate 225   Courtesy of the Evanston Historical Society.
Peeza game advertisement, 1936 company catalog.

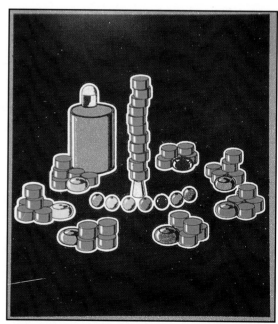

Plate 226   Courtesy of the Evanston Historical Society.
*Peeza game advertisement, 1936 company catalog.
Complete game with box, $40.00 – 60.00.*

Ten Pin Tinker

Plate 228

Ten Pin Tinker brochure plate, mid-1920s.

Plate 227

Ten Pin Tinker game. Complete game with box, $50.00 – 75.00.

Plate 229

Ten Pin Tinker box.

Ten Pin Tinker was first listed in 1925 in a wholesaler's listing for Toy Tinkers items. It was a bowling game with ten pins that resembled little men of turned wood. The set included three balls, and was enameled in bright colors. In 1925 the wholesale price was $8.00 a dozen, with a retail price of $1.00 each. In 1927, one store was selling Ten Pin Tinker at 75¢ each. 1927 was the last year that Ten Pin Tinker was listed for sale.

Tinkerpins (old)

Plate 230

Two styles of Tinkerpins boxes with a view of contents. Complete with box, $75.00 – 100.00.

Plate 231

Tinkerpins brochure plate, circa 1918.

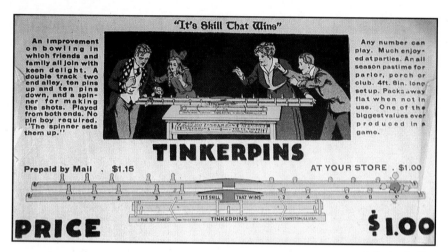

Plate 232

1917 Tinkerpins advertisement.

The original Tinkerpins game was patented on June 20, 1916, with the application being filed March 1, 1916. It was first offered for sale in 1916, and was listed for sale until at least 1920. The old Tinkerpins was quite a game. It measured 4' 8" long when assembled, so a dining room table or a lot of floor space was needed to play this one. A gyro-spinner was rolled along a set of rails, with the object of knocking down sheet-metal bowling pins incorporated into the rails on pivots.

The game was designed so that on your turn you would set up the pins for your opponents turn by rolling the spinner. You, of course, were to try to knock down as many pins as possible on your turn. In the first year, Tin-

kerpins sold for 50¢ a set, the same price as the Wonder Builder.

Tinkerpins was the second entry to the product line for the Toy Tinkers. By 1917 Tinkerpins was retailing at $1.00 a set, or could be had for $1.15 prepaid by mail from the company. The game was constructed out of all wood, except for the metal pins and rods in the spinner. Some versions came with spring metal clips to keep the game snug when assembled. These clips, and some other refinements, are the cause of the price increase of 1917. In response to the shaky nature of the 50¢ version, the company strengthened and improved the toy for 1917, and raised the price.

The New Tinkerpins

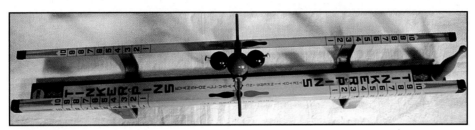

Plate 233

Courtesy of Frank Tolford.

New Tinkerpins game. Complete, $75.00 – 100.00.

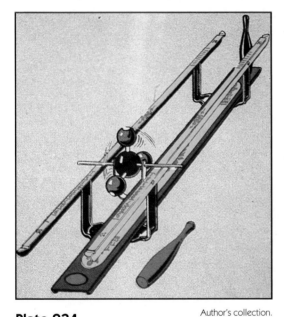

Plate 234

Author's collection.

New Tinkerpins company catalog ad, 1926.

"No idle hours on rainy days
No parties stiff or tame,
With tinkerpins, 'it's skill that wins;'
A fascinating game."

C. Pajeau

A modified version of the old Tinkerpins, this version was introduced in 1926. It measured only 24" long, and was made of metal except for the pins. The gryo-spinner was a combination of wood and metal. The box listed the playing information on its side. Tinkerpins were available until 1929, at which time the wholesale price was $12.00 a dozen, or $1.50 each at retail. It may have been offered in 1930, but was no longer listed in the company catalog in 1931.

Tinker Toss

Plate 235

Courtesy of Frank Tolford.

Tinker Toss game and box, $40.00 – 60.00.

Plate 236

Author's collection.

Tinker Toss brochure plate, circa 1918.

Tinker Toss: "For out door fun it is the Boss," so goes a brochure listing seven of the Toy Tinkers items, circa 1918. This game involved the tossing of two painted wooden balls connected by string, between two players with catching foils. The game came complete with instructions and scoring information, all for only 25¢ at the store, or 30¢ by mail from the Toy Tinkers.

The hype on the brochure is so good, that I include it here: "Not since the invention of lawn tennis has there been such fascinating sport as Tinker Toss. No court is required. Two balls connected by a strong cord are passed back and forth, being served and caught on foils in the hands of the players. Expert play results from a little practice. Scoring rules and instructions are furnished with each set. Tinker Toss makes men boys and boys men. The girls, too, come in for their share of the fun."

Rolo Polo Tinker

This was described as a wheel-and-stick affair by one of the former long-time employees of the Toy Tinkers. It may well be just like the barrel hoop and a stick that was often a plaything for children in the 1800s and early 1900s. It was described as a wheel independent of the stick, with the stick used to propel the wheel along. No year is available as to when this may have been produced, nor information on how it was marked. For that matter, what it actually looked like is not available, so good luck identifying it. Value ranges from $30.00 for good to $40.00 for excellent.

Bag Doll Tinker

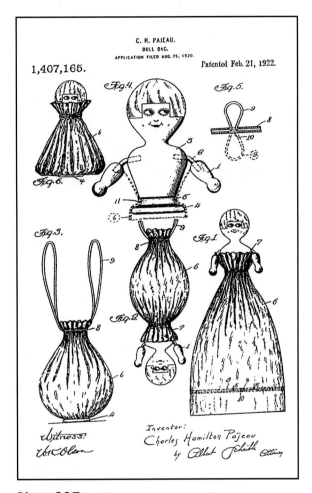

Plate 237

Bag Doll Tinker patent application drawings. Bag Doll Tinker, $40.00 – 60.00. Original box, $20.00 – 40.00.

This toy was available in 1921 for certain. Identified in editorial copy of *Toys and Novelties* magazine, February 1921, page 148 as: "Strictly for the little girl is Blue Eyes Doll Bag. Which looks like an ordinary little colored bag, until turned inside out, it makes a doll. It can also be used as a handbag, with doll head hanging down outside, or as a dressing table ornament."

Charles H. Pajeau applied for a patent for a bag doll on August 25, 1920. On February 27, 1922, he was granted a patent. Bag Doll Tinker consisted of a rubber head and torso with flexible arms. Just below the arms, a dress was attached. The dress could serve as a bag by either pulling the dress up over the doll's head or simply inverting the whole doll and using the purse string incorporated in the dress as handles. When the dress was pulled up over the doll's head, the bottom of the torso served as a base, allowing the bag to stand upright.

Tinkerblossoms

Plate 238

Systems magazine, 1918.

Charles H. Pajeau in his workshop with what is likely a prototype of Tinker Blossoms, to his left. Tinker Blossoms, $25.00 – 30.00.

Listed in the Tinkerblox instruction booklet from about 1919 were several offerings of the Toy Tinkers. One of them was Tinkerblossoms. There is no indication of what it was. I suspect that the answer can be found in the 1918 *Systems* magazine photo of Charles H. Pajeau in his workshop. On the table to Charles's left sits a whirly gig made to resemble a flower. I believe that this is Tinkerblossoms. Time will tell if my guess is correct.

Tinkercraft Kit No. 1

Plate 239

Tinkercraft Kit No. 1 — For Junior Manufacturers, box and contents. Complete with box, $40.00 – 60.00.

Tinkercraft kits were a whole new category of Tinker products. This was a set of wood parts that included everything needed to build twelve identical items, which could then be offered for sale. When sold for the suggested price of 25¢ each by young entrepreneurs a profit of two times the original investment would be realized. The company ads touted that a third dimension had

Courtesy of Gale Bailey.

been added to toy utility. The first was recreation, the second was education, and the third was compensation.

Junior manufacturers could absorb many of the principles of production and sales by the use of Tinkercraft Kit No. 1. The No. 1 set contained all the parts necessary to build twelve "Safety First Dog Houses." These were intended as receptacles for used razor blades. The packaging was a rectangular cardboard box with black and white print, red background, and a yellow drawing of a finished doghouse with the decal in place. The box featured two large black and white photographs that showed all the parts included and a young boy in a workshop assembling the doghouses. 1939 is the only year that ads for this item are found. The No. 1 set is the only one identified thus far; though possibly others were offered.

Tinker Doll House Furniture

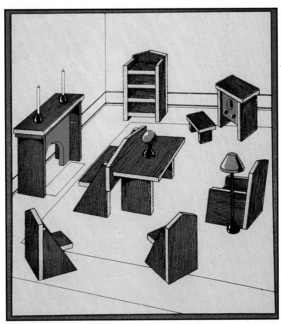

Courtesy of the Evanston Historical Society.

Plate 240

Tinker Doll House Furniture company catalog ad, 1931. Complete set, $75.00 – 100.00. Original box, $20.00 – 40.00.

The 1930 company advertisements show Tinker Doll House Furniture. The set consisted of 13 pieces finished in walnut, ranging in size from 2" to 4". The pieces were: a fireplace mantel, a floor lamp, a table lamp, a bench, a dining table with two chairs, an arm chair, a bookshelf, a small stool, a radio set, and two candleholders with candles. This was not promoted very long, and may have been a very poor seller. I have no price list for this, so I can only guess that it was too expensive or otherwise undesirable. 1931 is the last year for which this item appears in company advertising.

Jack and Jill Tinker

Plate 241   Author's collection.

Jack and Jill Tinker company catalog ad, 1926.

Plate 242   Courtesy of Lonnie and Joanne Litwiller.

Jack and Jill Tinker can and some parts. Complete, $40.00 – 65.00.

Courtesy of the
Evanston Historical Society.

Plate 243

Rear view of Jack and Jill Tinker can.

Jack and Jill Tinker was a set of stacking pieces packed in a small canister of the type used for Tinkertoys. The parts were of wood and fiber, enameled in several colors. The bases and center poles allowed the dolls to be varied in countless possible configurations. The top and bottom pieces were designed to lock all intervening parts in place. With the 36 parts included in the set, you could construct two to three dolls at one time.

Jack and Jill Tinker was introduced in 1930 and appeared in the company catalog until 1935.

Tinker Table

This was a play table made by the Toy Tinkers. It stood approximately two feet high, and had legs made of dowel rods. It was stained and had a decal and shellac applied. This description comes from a former employee who recalled making these tables. How many were made and for how long is not known. Since the Toy Tinkers seemed to mark all of their products, there is a chance that if you find a Tinker Table, it will be identifiable. Value ranges from $30.00 for good to $50.00 for excellent.

Bead Doll Pull Toy Tinker

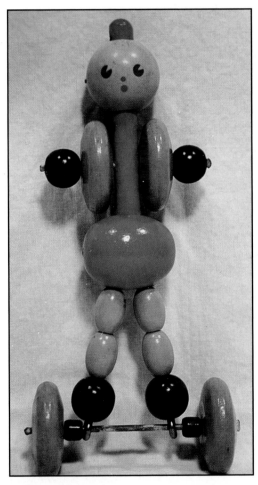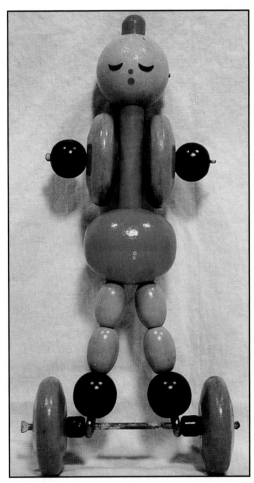

Plate 244 & 245

Courtesy of Larry Basting.

Bead doll pull toy . Left, eyes open, right, eyes closed. Each, $35.00 – 60.00. Original box, $20.00 – 40.00.

This toy was shown to me by Larry J. Basting, a former long-time Toy Tinkers employee. He could not recall what it was named, but he was certain that it was in production for a time at the factory. This pull toy is a doll on wheels. She has two faces. Depending on which side is facing up, she has her eyes open or her eyes closed. The face is light peach, the main body is pink and red, the legs are green beads, and the feet and hands are black beads. The four wheels are bright blue and are on axles that are crimped at the ends. As with other Tinker Toys, the colors may vary.

Billy Goat Tinker

Plate 246

Author's collection.

Billy Goat Tinker pull toy, $90.00 – 120.00. Original box, $20.00 – 40.00.

"Billy Goat Tinker, true to his instincts, is always butting in. Being young, he is unusually full of this sort of energy, to the extreme delight of his juvenile audience." So reads the catalog copy for this neat toy. It was made of enameled wood, rustproof metal, and hard fiber. It measures ten inches long. The fiber parts are the tail, legs, and head. The main body and wheels are wood, and the frame and mechanism are made of metal. When you pull it along the floor it imitates the movements of a billy goat.

This toy was listed in the catalogs from 1928 to 1930. It was also advertised in newspapers for those years. In 1929, the wholesale price was $12.00 a dozen, meaning that it would retail for $1.50 each.

Plate 247

Courtesy of the Evanston Historical Society.

Billy Goat Tinker company ad, 1928.

Billy Goat Tinker leaps and plays,
With little tots through happy days;
He chases you, and when you run
Just pull the string and watch the fun.

Plate 248

Author's collection.

Billy Goat Tinker brochure plate, late 1920s.

Bunny Tinker

Plate 249

Courtesy of the Evanston Historical Society.

Bunny Tinker pull toys. Wooden version on left, $80.00 – 100.00. Metal version on right, $60.00 – 80.00. Original box, $20.00 – 40.00.

Plate 250

Author's collection.

Bunny Tinker brochure plate, late 1920s.

Bunny Tinker was patented on April 19, 1927, after the application was filed on October 6, 1926. It was advertised in the 1927 company catalog, retailing for 50¢, and appeared until at least 1931. Bunny Tinker was a pull toy that mimicked the motion of a rabbit leaping, as it had an offset axle.

This is one of many toys that underwent changes during their production lives. For the first several years, the main body was of rustproof metal with wooden wheels and head. In 1931, Bunny Tinker was revised so that the head, body, wheels, and tail were all made of wood lacquered in pastel colors. The ad copy promoted Bunny Tinker as a year-round item, but said it was of extra appeal for Christmas and Easter.

The 1929 wholesaler ads listed Bunny Tinker at $6.00 a dozen, which would put it at 75¢ retail. The metal Bunny Tinker was listed as being 9" long, and was said to be enameled in baby colors. In contrast, the 1931 revised wood Bunny Tinker was 8¾" long, and retailed at $1.00 each. Judging from what is shown in the advertisements, all versions of Bunny Tinker are equipped with the Toy Tinker pull knob.

Plate 251

Courtesy of the Evanston Historical Society.

Bunny Tinker company catalog ad, 1931.

Plate 252

Courtesy of the Evanston Historical Society.

Bunny Tinker company catalog ad, 1927, showing original box.

Tinker Chicks

Plate 253
Courtesy of Larry Basting.

Tinker Chick.

Plate 254
Courtesy of the Evanston Historical Society.

Tinker Chicks pull toy company ad, 1931. Complete set, $90.00 – 120.00. With original box, add $20.00 – 40.00.

Tinker Chicks are a little different than most of the other toys turned out by the Toy Tinkers. This one involved a wooden platform that was 14" long with four wooden wheels. The platform was painted white and the wheels were painted green. There were three baby chicks and a mother hen, all painted bright yellow with red and light blue trim. The chicks could be set in depressions on the platform or removed from it. They would stand by themselves, and their heads could swivel.

Although they were indicated to be an Easter toy, they were recommended by the ad copy to have a spot on the toy display year 'round. The chicks measured $2\frac{7}{8}$" high, and the mother hen measured $3\frac{5}{8}$" high. In 1931, Tinker Chicks wholesaled at $16.00 a dozen, which would put them in the $2.00 range for retail. They were available in 1931 and 1932.

This is a very nice toy, but the fact that the chicks could be separated from the platform makes it less likely that Tinker Chicks will be found all together.

Choo Choo Tinker

Plate 255

Two styles of Choo Choo Tinker. Above: metal version, $75.00 – 120.00; below: early wood version, $100.00 – 150.00. Original box, $20.00 – 40.00.

Author's collection.

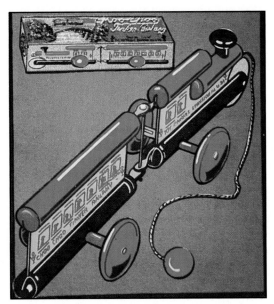

Plate 256   Author's collection.
Choo Choo Tinker company catalog, 1926.

Plate 257   Author's collection.
Choo Choo Tinker brochure plate, mid 1920s.

Choo Choo Tinker was a popular toy, with at least two variations in its history. From company advertisements and catalogs, we know that Choo Choo Tinker was sold in 1922, and then not sold in 1923. It was reintroduced in 1924 in a new form, patented on October 21, 1924, which was available until 1930.

The original Choo Choo Tinker had a metal base divided into two sections connected with a single joint. Attached to the bases were wood blocks shaped like a train engine and a passenger car. Both blocks had half-round wood attached to their tops, and the engine also had a pull knob-shaped piece of wood for a stack. There were two large red wheels in the mid-section of each block.

The bodies of the engine and passenger car were painted yellow, with decals of engineers and passengers on the sides. There were also decals that read "Choo Choo Tinker Railway," and "The Toy Tinkers — Evanston, ILL U.S.A. — Pat. Pend."

There were problems with the early version. It was prone to bending at the one coupling, and it may have violated another party's patent, as no patent was ever issued on this design.

After being redesigned, the train had a double coupler and a main body of lithographed metal. The bottom and top of the metal were covered with wooden dowel. The engine now had three wheels, a flat metal wheel at the very front and two wooden ones that were moved back toward the end. The resulting passenger car had only two wheels in its middle. The pull knob for Choo Choo Tinker was a ball. The redesigned version was listed in the catalog as being 14" long.

In 1925, Choo Choo Tinker was selling for $1.00 at most outlets, although Sears was listing it at 83¢ that year. By 1929, Choo Choo Tinker was listed wholesale at $12.00 a dozen, which put it at $1.50 retail.

Clown Tinker

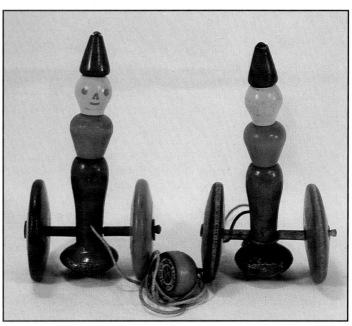

Plate 258

Two Clown Tinker pull toys, $35.00 – $50.00 each. Original box, add $20.00 – 40.00.

This pull toy was first advertised in 1925 and was listed until at least 1929. It consisted of a weighted clown figure on two large wheels and stood about 6" high. It was equipped with the Toy Tinkers pull knob. No matter how jerky the motion of the child, the clown would always regain his upright position because of the weight on his bottom.

The prices found for Clown Tinker are usually in the 50¢ to 60¢ range for the early years, although one store was listing him for $1.25 in 1925. By 1929, the wholesale price for him was $6.00 a dozen, which would put him in the 75¢ range at retail.

Clown Tinker is a fun toy to watch, but you may miss him at a flea market or antique show if you look for his marking as a Toy Tinker item. Very few of the Toy Tinker knobs are found still attached to him, so you will need to recognize him without the knob.

Another thing to keep in mind is that the colors of parts on Clown Tinker are not always the same. The wheels were shown as being one red and one blue, but it is not uncommon to find two of the same color on one Clown Tinker.

Plate 259

Clown Tinker company catalog ad, 1926.

Now Tinker Clown
has come to town,
And a happy clown
is he;
For every time
he tumbles down
He tumbles up
you see.

Plate 260

Clown Tinker brochure plate, mid 1920s.

Dachshund Tinker

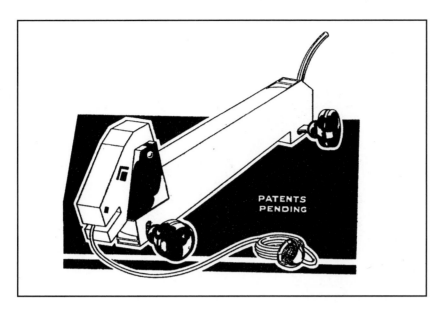

Plate 261

Dachshund Tinker pull toy, $60.00 – 80.00. Original box, add $20.00 – 40.00.

This appears to have been a long wood toy with two sets of knee action wheels, intended to imitate the funny walk of a dachshund. It utilized the Toy Tinker half round hand ball with metal medallion, and retailed for 50¢. 1934 was its first year, but possibly not its last. With luck, more information will turn up about this pooch. It was reported to have been finished with the usual Toy Tinker colors, and may have a leather tail, but that is speculation.

Derby Tinker

Derby Tinker was the second form of a horse racing toy. The first was Jockey Tinker. Derby had two riders racing against each other, and was offered for sale in 1931 and 1932. It may have been offered after those years as well. The addition of a second rider may have increased the sense of action, therefore adding excitement to the toy. The toy measures 11¾" long by 5¼" wide by 6¾" high. It was made of enameled wood and metal rust-proofed parts.

Courtesy of the Evanston Historical Society.

Plate 262

Derby Tinker company catalog ad, 1931. Derby Tinker, $100.00 – 125.00. Original box, add $20.00 – 40.00.

Tinker Dogs

Plate 263

Tinker Dogs pull toy, $80.00 – 100.00. Original box, add $20.00 – 40.00.

Author's collection.

Tinker Dogs are similar to Derby Tinker, with the exception that Tinker Dogs involves three hounds running side by side. Charles H. Pajeau filed a patent for this toy on October 22, 1926. The patent was granted on May 31, 1927. The company catalog lists Tinker Dogs in 1927 through 1930. In 1929, the wholesale price for Tinker Dogs was $15.00 a dozen, which would put the retail price in the $2.00 range.

The dogs were made of wood with felt ears and tails held on by rivets. In the case of the ears, these rivets also served as the dogs' eyes. The wheels are of wood, while the frame and mechanism are of a rust-proof metal. The Tinker Dogs came with a cord and a Toy Tinker pull knob.

The dogs in the author's collection are painted red, yellow, and black. This by no means guarantees that the Tinker Dogs another collector finds would have the same color combination. While the Toy Tinkers endeavored to maintain continuity of the toys, if a certain color of wheel ran out on a given day, it is doubtful that production ceased. Tinker Toys have been seen with the same color wheels when they were normally meant to have contrasting colored wheels; the production supply is the likely explanation.

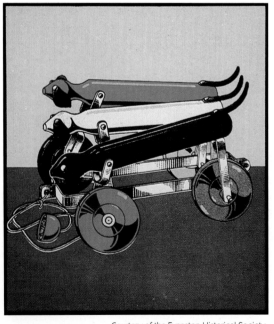

Plate 264

Tinker Dogs company catalog ad, 1927.

Courtesy of the Evanston Historical Society.

Three graceful hounds, Tom, Dick and Harry;
They stand, they point, they fetch and carry;
O'er hill and dale, thru fields and bogs,
They trot all day, these "TINKER DOGS."

Author's collection.

Plate 265

Tinker Dogs brochure plate, late 1920s.

Dragon Tinker

Plate 266

Courtesy of Kathy Trenter.

Dragon Tinker pull toy, $70.00 – 90.00. Original box, add $20.00 – 40.00.

Dragon Tinker was designed by Philip Myers, a resident of Glenview, Illinois. He filed a patent for this toy on September 17, 1923, and it was approved on December 30, 1924. The patent was assigned to the Toy Tinkers of Evanston, Illinois, as was a subsequent design patent.

This toy was designed to be self righting, and to be able to make its way around obstacles without being snagged by something like a table leg. By means of a flexible backbone and the independent movement of the beads that made up this toy, the front wheels could be on the floor while one of the back wheels was riding over something, such as a book.

Dragon Tinker is trumpeted in the 1924 company catalog as "A new principle in pull toys." Dragon Tinker was listed as being 12" long. It had a cord and a handball with the company logo on it. It was enameled in primary colors.

Dragon Tinker must have been a good seller, for it shows up in catalogs from 1924 through at least 1932. In 1924 it was wholesaling for $8.00 a dozen, which translates to about $1.00 each retail. Some local store ads have it at 85¢ in 1925, which might have been as a loss leader; yet Montgomery Wards 1924 – 1925 catalogs listed it at 83¢. In 1929, the wholesale price was $10.20 a dozen, which would have it retailing for about $1.25 to $1.30.

"Drag-on Tinker" looks quite fierce,
But he's kind as kind can be;
He rolls along on any side,
He can't upset you see.

Plate 267

Author's collection.

Dragon Tinker brochure plate, mid to late 1920s.

Follo-Me-Tinker

Plate 268

Courtesy of the Evanston Historical Society.

Two sizes of Follo-Me-Tinker pull toy, $30.00 – 50.00 each. Original box, add $20.00 – 40.00.

Follo-Me-Tinker was an eight-wheeled toy. Attached to a straight length of wood were four wheels, two on each side. The other four wheels were at 90° to the first group, and offset so as not to interfere with them. This was a real success for the Toy Tinkers. It was also a toy with at least two variations. The patent was filled on September 22, 1919, and approved March 9, 1920. The first advertisements for Follo-Me-Tinker show up in 1920. The original version was 14⅛" long. It sold for about $1.00, with Sears listing it for 98¢ in the 1921 catalog. In 1924,

Follo-Me-Tinker was listed as being 10½" long. It was wholesaling at $4.80 a dozen, and a retail price of 60¢, although some stores were still selling it for $1.00.

Follo-Me-Tinker was not listed after 1928 in the company catalogs. Follo-Me-Tinker was designed to be a self-righting toy; no matter how often it tipped over, it always landed on a set of wheels. Charles Pajeau invented this ingenious toy, of which I found a look-a-like being produced by another company in 1961.

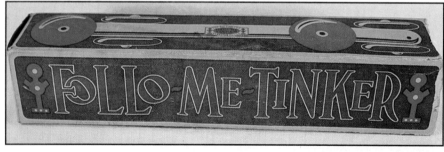

Plate 269

Folo-Me-Tinker box.

Courtesy of the Evanston Historical Society.

Plate 270

Follo-Me-Tinker brochure plate, mid 1920s.

Follo-Me Tinker you can't upset;
I guess that is why he's Billy pet.
Pull him and jump him and turn
Him around— He'll land on his
Wheels all safe and sound!

Author's collection.

Jockey Tinker

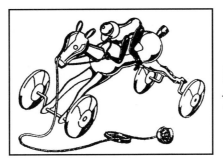

Plate 271
Jockey Tinker pull toy, $110.00 – 135.00.
Original box, add $20.00 – 40.00

Jockey Tinker was offered for sale in 1930 only. This was a racing theme pull toy with one rider on one horse. When pulled, the toy mimicked the action of a horse and rider in a race. It is made of wood and rustproof colors, and is described as being finished in natural colors. For unknown reasons, the Toy Tinkers discontinued this toy after one year, replacing it with Derby Tinker. A guess would be that Jockey Tinker looked too much like a Hustler toy, and retailers were confused by that.

Life Guard Tinker

Plate 272
Courtesy of the Evanston Historical Society.

Life Guard Tinker pull toy, $100.00 – 125.00. Original box, add $20.00 – 40.00.

Life Guard Tinker is a mighty nifty pull toy. He is about 8¼" long. His wheels are painted green, his body red, his hair black, and his face, arms, and legs are painted pale peach. His body is all wood, and his frame and mechanism are rustproof steel.

He was listed from 1928 to 1930 in company catalogs and ads. He wholesaled in 1929 for $12.00 a dozen, or a retail price of $1.50.

Life Guard Tinker seems to have had a short life on the store shelf, which is hard to understand as he is such an interesting character.

Life Guard Tinker is so brave
He does not fear the tallest wave;
Australian crawl or over-hand,
He teaches swimming while on land.

Plate 274
Life Guard Tinker brochure plate, late 1920s.

Author's collection.

Plate 273
Life Guard Tinker pull toy, front view.

Courtesy of the Evanston Historical Society.

Tinker Mule

Plate 275

Author's collection.

Tinker Mule pull toy, $100.00 – 125.00. Original box, add $20.00 – 40.00.

Tinker Mule pull toy features an ornery mule and a poor guy trying to hang onto its tail. It is made of wood, metal, and hard fiber. The body of the mule is wood and painted a pale caramel color, while his ears, legs, and tail are of black fiber. The man has a wood body and head, with the body painted red and his face black. He has on a yellow top hat with the Toy Tinker logo on top. His arms and legs are made of black fiber. The wheels are red and green enameled wood. The frame and mechanism are made of rustproof metal. Since the toy is already marked with the company logo, the pull knob is simply a painted ball.

Tinker Mule is one of the few toys made by the Toy Tinkers with a black character featured. Unfortunately, they all seem to rely on a stereotype of blacks. This can be seen in a company catalog excerpt: "Tinker Mule combines more realistic action than most pull toys, as he goes through all his antics in an endeavor to loosen the darky boy's grip on his tail; at the same time the darky is given a severe shaking up." In a time when offensive ethnic toys were commonly offered in toy departments, this type of catalog wording is not surprising. Other black offerings by Toy Tinkers include Mammy Tinker, Topsy Tinker, and a Tinker Sand set featuring black African natives of which I have heard but not seen.

Tinker Mule was offered from 1928 to at least 1931. In 1929 he was wholesaling for $18.00 a dozen, which would put the retail price at about $2.25 each. Tinker Mule measured 10½" long and was packed in a cardboard box.

Plate 276

Courtesy of the Evanston Historical Society.

Tinker Mule company catalog ad, late 1920s.

Plate 278

Medallion on the top of Tinker Mule man's hat.

Author's collection.

This Tinker Mule can kick so high
You'd think his heels would reach the sky;
He has his master on the run
Although, of course, it's all in fun.

Plate 277

Tinker Mule brochure plate, late 1920s.

Author's collection.

Penguin Tinker

Plate 279

Penguin Tinker pull toy, $60.00 – 80.00. Original box, add $20.00 – 40.00.

Advertised in the 1934 trade journals, Penguin Tinker may have been available for only that year, or perhaps longer. Hopefully, more information will surface to answer this unknown. This toy retailed for 50¢ each. It was identified as being a big toy and a big value. The ads also noted that the finish was the usual long-lasting Tinker Toy finish. From that information and the appearance, it would seem that it was a mostly wood toy.

Three penguins are mounted on a rail, one behind the other, each with a set of wheels. The wheels were utilizing the knee action in automobiles, a new action for pull toys. The penguins appeared to waddle as they were pulled along. The hand ball was still the standard Toy Tinker half ball with the medallion.

Pony Tinker

Author's collection.

Plate 280

Pony Tinker pull toy, $75.00 – 100.00. Original box, $20.00 – 40.00.

The little man posts up and down;
The pony wears no blinker;
The little man will not fall off,
He's riding "Pony Tinker."

Author's collection.

Plate 281

Pony Tinker brochure plate, mid 1920s.

— 139 —

Pony Tinker is an enigma as far as explaining the mechanism that made the rider bob up and down. The patent shows a flat metal bar attached to the rear axle, and inclined up to a bracket near the front wheels. The center portion of the rear axle was bent and attached to the flat bar. When this bend rotated and moved away from the rest of the axle, the flat bar lifted and lowered the rider. In the catalog drawings from 1924 and 1925, the flat lifting bar is also bent and attached further back on the underside of the pony. Later versions show the original patent design for the mechanism. Both of these variations were actually produced. The ones with the highly bent lifting bar were likely first, and the straight bar ones were later. Pony measures 3½" wide by 6" high by 8" long.

As with most of the Tinker Toys, there are variations of color and other features, such as the reins which vary from cord to leather. Pony Tinker was available until 1930. For most of that time it was retailing for $1.25, and by 1929 it sold for $1.50 each. One Christmas ad from 1930 sold him for $1.00, which may have been a response to slow sales during the Depression.

Rattle Box Tinker

Plate 282
Courtesy of Anne Lewis.

Rattlebox Tinker pull toy, $70.00 – 100.00.

Rattle Box Tinker was advertised for sale in 1921 through 1924 store ads. This toy is exactly what the name says: a box that rattles. It is a pull toy with two large wheels on either side of a varnished, dovetailed box. The box has beads inside that make noise when the toy is pulled along. It was manufactured with a decal on the box, but the decals have not always survived the years, so it helps to know what to look for with this toy. Rattle Box Tinker measures about 5" from wheel to wheel by 2⅞" deep.

Plate 283
Courtesy of Anne Lewis.

Rattle Box Tinker box. Original box, $20.00 – 40.00.

Rowly-Boat Tinker

Plate 284

Author's collection.

Rowly-Boat Tinker pull toy, two variations, $100.00 – 150.00 each. Original box, add $20.00 – 40.00.

Rowly-Boat Tinker is a pull toy that simulates a person rowing a boat, including little oars which actually move. Introduced in 1924, he retailed for $1.00 each. The man and wheels are made of wood, while the frame and mechanism are made of steel. The man is painted blue, and his head is light peach. He is wearing a little hat with the Toy Tinkers yellow metal label on it. The wheels and pull ball are painted red. There are two variations of Rowly-Boat

Tinker, involving the legs. In one version, the legs are made of sheet metal, while in the other they are made of wire.

Rowly-Boat Tinker was not listed in the catalog after 1927, yet continued to appear in store ads until 1930. Even if the company had discontinued manufacture in 1927, it is possible that they were able to fill orders from stocks for years afterwards. This toy measured about 11" long.

Plate 285

Author's collection.

Rowly-Boat Tinker brochure plate, mid 1920s.

Seven In One Tinker

Plate 286

Courtesy of Anne Lewis.

Seven In One Tinker pull toy, painted red. With box, $75.00 – 100.00.

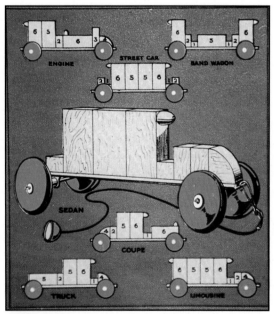

Plate 287

Courtesy of the Evanston Historical Society.

Seven In One Tinker company catalog ad, 1927.

This is a combination pull toy and construction toy. It was invented by Philip Myers of Glenview, Illinois. This toy had a frame with four wheels on it. Several interchangeable wood blocks could be slid into the frame and then locked in place. By varying the order of the blocks, you were able to make seven different vehicles. The suggested models were a train engine, a band wagon, a streetcar, a sedan, a coupe, a truck, and a limousine. Of course, as with any Tinker construction toy, you were free to make up more models.

The toy was 10" long and was packed in its own box. The frame was rustproof metal, the wheels were red enameled wood, and the interchangeable blocks were natural hardwood with no finish. Some collectors have noted red painted wood blocks with some sets. The toy was equipped with a cord and Toy Tinkers pull knob.

It was listed for sale in 1926 and 1927. The patent was filed November 18, 1925, and approved April 6, 1926. The patent was assigned to the Toy Tinkers of Evanston, Illinois.

Steam Roller Tinker

Steam Roller Tinker had two flywheels that turned in opposite directions when the toy was drawn across the floor. The wheels relied on rubber bands to connect the rear wheels to the flywheels. Constructed of wood with some metal parts, it was approximately 7" long and 5" wide. It was enameled in several bright colors and equipped with the Toy Tinkers pull knob. It was first listed in 1927 as selling for $1.00, and made its last appearance in 1928.

> "This little contractor has taken a job
> To pave all the streets in the county;
> His 'Steam Roller Tinker' will
>   Make them smooth.
> They'll probably pay him a bounty."
>
> Charles H. Pajeau

Plate 288   Courtesy of the Evanston Historical Society.
Steam Roller Tinker company catalog ad, 1927. Steam Roller Tinker, $100.00 – 150.00. Original box, add $20.00 – 40.00.

Tumble Tinker

Tumble Tinker was advertised in the Sears catalog in 1920 and 1921. This toy was made mostly of metal, except for the four wheels and three balls that were wood. Tumble Tinker featured an arm that rotated on a central axis. This arm had a large red ball and two smaller balls that were painted like heads. Connected to the wheels of the toy by a rubber band, this arm would rotate when the toy was pulled along a surface. The three balls would slide up and down a rod inside of the arm each time the arm made a rotation.

The wheels were painted red, and the metal frame was painted green. The red ball had a Toy Tinker decal on it and therefore the hand ball at the end of the cord was just a bead painted black. The size was given as 9¼" by 8½" with the wheels measuring 2⅝" in diameter.

Plate 289
Tumble Tinker pull toy, $100.00 – 125.00. Original box, add $20.00 – 40.00.

Plate 290
Side view of Tumble Tinker.

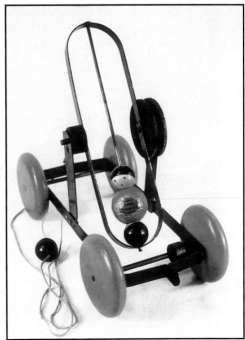

Courtesy of Gale Bailey.

Courtesy of the Evanston Historical Society.

Tumble-Bead Tinker

Plate 291

Courtesy of Kathy Trenter.

Tumble-Bead Tinker pull toy, $80.00 – 100.00. Original box, add $20.00 – 40.00.

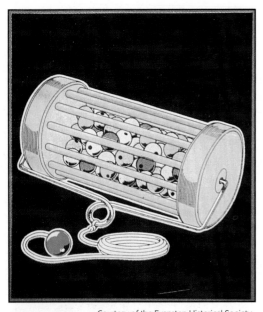

Plate 292

Courtesy of the Evanston Historical Society.

Tumble-Bead Tinker company catalog ad, 1931.

Tumble-Bead Tinker consisted of two round wheels that measured 3⅝" in diameter joined by twelve ¼" dowel rods to create a rolling cage finished in lacquer. The cage held 100 brightly-colored loose wooden balls, each ⅝" in size. The beads came in seven colors. There was a removable plug in one of the side wheels to allow for the beads to be taken out for play or to be strung and then replaced inside the toy. There was a metal handle that fit into holes on either side of the wheels, allowing the whole to rotate when pulled. The result was a rattle of the beads tumbling, and a multicolored show as the beads rolled over each other.

The overall size was 8" by 3⅝", and it weighed about 13 ounces. Tumble-Bead Tinker was shown in the company catalog from 1931 to 1936. It included the Toy Tinker pull knob.

Turtle Tinker

Plate 293

Turtle Tinker pull toy, $70.00 – 90.00. Original box, add $20.00 – 40.00.

Courtesy of Kathy Trenter.

Turtle Tinker shows up for sale in 1921 and is listed until 1924 in the company catalog. It had two wheels at the back, and a large ball in the middle that served as a support wheel. There was a small ball at the front that was the turtle's head, and attached to this is the hand ball and cord.

Turtle Tinker was yet another in the line of noncapsizable pull toys put out by the Toy Tinkers. I first saw the name Turtle Tinker with no drawing or photo to go by, and envisioned something close to Rowly Boat Tinker, like a turtle with feet that moved when the toy was pulled. The actual appearance came as quite a surprise. But with a little imagination, this toy can be seen as a turtle. In some ways, it is more interesting in its design than if it had looked obviously like a turtle.

Turtle Tinker measured about 3" by 4½" by 8", and weighed about 12 ounces. The frame was made of steel. The toy had a decal on its head to identify it as Turtle Tinker.

A 1929 advertisement in the Sheboygan, Wisconsin, newspaper lists Turtle Tinker Toy as a 75¢ toy on sale as an odd lot of shopworn toys for 15¢. The catalog encouraged store buyers to give this unique toy year 'round representation in the toy department.

Catalog copy:

"Right out of the fairy stories comes this Turtle Tinker, his big ball body and bobbing head kindles the imagination of all the little folks. A slight jerk of the string and he turns turtle, coming up smiling the other side up.

From *The Story of the Little Tinker Men*

"'Turtle Tinker' — childhood plaything,
    more fun than a top;
When you turn the corner quickly,
    over he will flop."

The Toy Tinkers, Evanston, Ill., U.S.A.

Whirly Tinker

Plate 294

Courtesy of Lonnie and Joanne Litwiller.

Three examples of Whirly Tinker pull toy. The front two are sailor style, and the back one is bowler hat style. Sailor style, $70.00 – 90.00. Bowler style, $90.00 – 140.00.

Whirly Tinker was most likely the greatest success in a pull toy ever produced by the Toy Tinkers of Evanston, Illinois. It was available from at least 1920 to 1930, in continuous production. Whirly Tinker had two little sailors that would spin around as the toy was pulled. The platforms for the figures sat right on top of the toy's side wheels. That direct contact is what allowed the platforms and figures to move.

A 1920 wholesale advertisement for Whirly Tinker shows two little men wearing bowler hats. This was the original design put into production, yet it was very quickly replaced by the two sailors. The 1920 Sears advertisement shows the sailors in a very angular design which must have been a transitional form. The majority of Whirly Tinkers are more rounded in appearance.

Whirly is marked on the cross frame with a decal. These decals must have been put on before assembly, as many of them are upside down. The frame holds the two front wheels and supports the little men. On the majority of toys, the frame is made of metal, yet some had a wooden cross piece.

As you can see, Whirly is rife with variations. The colors of the toy vary. Sometimes the sailors are painted blue with light colored faces, and other times their suits are greenish, or plain varnish. The front wheels seem to be

From *The Story of the Little Tinker Men*
"Just walk or run and pull the string
To keep the sailors prancing;
These whirly tinkers dance and spin
In ways that are entrancing."
The Toy Tinkers, Evanston, Ill., U.S.A.

mostly bright red with blue for the back wheel. The arms and hands are typically painted red.

Whirly started out priced from 98¢ at Sears to $1.25 at other stores. By 1929 it was selling for about $1.50 each. One early 1920 advertisement noted that the Whirly Tinker required some assembly, yet a photo from 1921 shows it being fully assembled at the factory. It is possible that the company shipped the earliest models partially assembled, and later decided to change that. Whirly measures 8½" by 7½" by 7½".

Plate 295   Courtesy of Lonnie and Joanne Litwiller.
Close-up of bowler style Whirly Tinker.

Plate 296   Author's collection.
Whirly Tinker brochure plate, mid 1920s.

 Mystery Toys

Bottle Tinker

Okay, what is a Bottle Tinker? No one seems to know, but if one should turn up, it is most likely worth more than a two-cent deposit! Advertised in 1919 as one of the Tinker Toys, this little gem plays wildly with one's imagination. Was it a bottle filled with something, one that did tricks, or some other use or function as yet unimagined by Tinker Toy collectors? This one will have to go on the Ten Most Wanted List. As this is unidentified, no value has been given for it.

Snappy Tinker

This one falls under the "your guess is as good as mine" category. Advertisements of 1919 listed this as one of the Tinker Toys, but provided no description or price. Was it a toy that made a snapping sound or a rubber band type toy? Time will tell. Tinker Toys have an astounding way of turning up right when the hope of ever finding them is about gone. As this is unidentified, no value has been given for it.

Target Tinker

As of press time, alas, all that is known about this toy is its name. It is obviously a target type game, but its appearance or how it was played are as yet unknown. Target Tinker was offered as part of the 1919 company product line. As this is unidentified, no value has been given for it.

Non-Toy Products

Tinker Cane

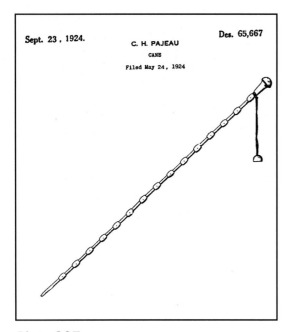

Plate 297

Tinker Cane patent drawing, $10.00 – 20.00.

The design patent was filed by Charles H. Pajeau on May 24, 1924, and it was approved on September 23, 1924. This cane had fifteen beads, spaced on a dowel with a turned handle, and the Toy Tinker knob on a short cord. This was not listed in any of the information that I have seen, and the patent was only for 3½ years. But the Toy Tinkers did seem to put most of Charles Pajeau's ideas into production on some scale, so there may be a few of these canes still floating around out there.

Tinker Collapsible Necktie Holder

The Tinker Collapsible Necktie Holder was filed with the patent office on October 29, 1932, and found approval on December 5, 1933. The first Tinker Tie Tree must have been a reasonable success for Charles Pajeau to patent this second type. This version had tie hooks that would fold out of the way when not in use. They resembled a wheel hub and spokes without the outer rim, and could accommodate sixteen neckties when all hooks were down. The holder was suspended by a leather cord with a knob at the end. The design of this holder seemed much more involved than the earlier one. Maybe someone will find one of these, and we will know the answer to whether it was put into production.

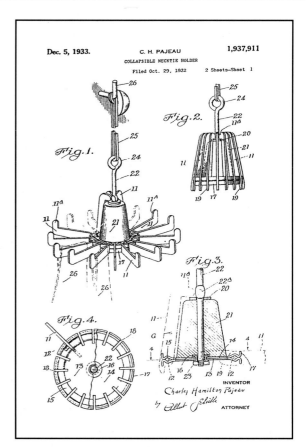

Plate 298

Tinker Collapsible Necktie Holder patent drawing. With box, $30.00 – 40.00.

Tinker Flash Light

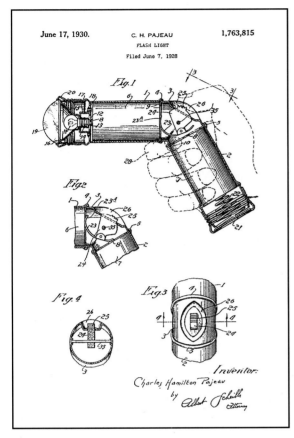

Plate 299
*Tinker Flash Light patent drawing. Tinker Flash Light,
$15.00 – 25.00. Original box, $10.00 – 20.00.*

Patented by Charles H. Pajeau and assigned to the Toy Tinkers of Evanston, Illinois, this flash light was intended to be ergonomic in its design. It had a hand grip angled down from the lamp portion of the light. The control switch was located at the elbow of the device, so that it could easily be switched on with the thumb. The patent was applied for on June 7, 1928, and approved on June 17, 1930. I cannot say whether this item was ever produced. The timing of the Great Depression may have stopped it, or maybe not.

Tinker Rotary Blotter

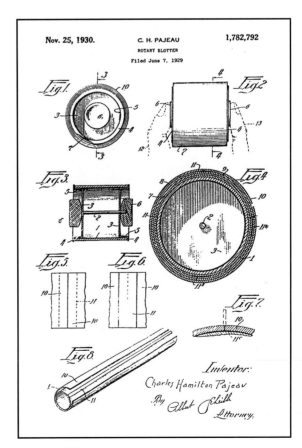

Plate 300
*Tinker Rotary Blotter patent drawing. With box, $10.00
– 20.00.*

On June 7, 1929, Charles H. Pajeau filed for a patent on a rotary blotter. It could be held between thumb and forefinger, thus not requiring the cumbersome handles common to the blotters of the time. The patent was approved on November 25, 1930. This invention was assigned to the Toy Tinkers of Evanston, Illinois. I have never seen one of these, and can only speculate as to whether they were produced in any quantity, unless someone finds one that is marked or in a box.

Tinker Tie Tree

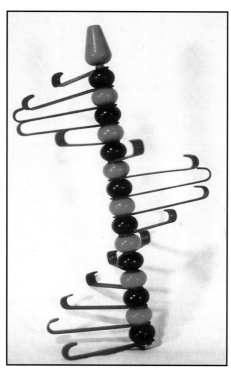

This was a collapsible tie rack that you could hang from a hook or over a hanger. It was constructed of wood beads and metal hooks with the beads acting as spacers for the hooks. The hooks were wide enough to hang a necktie, and could be fanned out to see several ties displayed. The rack was another of Charles H. Pajeau's inventions. The patent application was filed February 7, 1928, and approved on November 13, 1928.

This item was definitely made and sold, as several collectors have found these, including Gale Bailey who bought a boxed Tinker Tie Tree. These were marked with the Toy Tinker knob, but the small yellow metal plates do not always survive.

Plate 301

Tinker Tie Tree. With box, $30.00 – 40.00.

Courtesy of Anne Lewis.

Plate 302

Tinker Tie Tree.

Courtesy of the Evanston Historical Society.

Odds and Ends at Toy Tinkers

Larry J. Basting, a long time employee of the Toy Tinkers, told me about a couple of inventions that he recalled Charles Pajeau trying out. First there was a shave cream. Larry said the whole plant reeked from the perfume that was added to the shave cream. The employees tried it, Larry recalled. Value $5.00 good to $10.00 excellent.

Then there was a wood cone that had sandpaper on the bottom and matches on the sides. You would break off a match and light it on the bottom. This item was in pro-

duction for awhile. Value $5.00 good to $10.00 excellent.

Charles Pajeau was always working on something. He was a clever guy with lots of ideas. Unfortunately, not very many of his ideas ever received the same reception as had the original Tinkertoy. A lot of money was spent on development and production of toys and other inventions that never went very far, were discontinued, and sold at discounts to move them out.

Spalding — Big Boy Tinkertoy

Plate 303

Author's collection.

Right is an early Big Boy Tinkertoy can, left is a later Big Boy Tinkertoy. Complete can and parts, $30.00 – 40.00.

Plate 304

Big Boy Tinkertoy trade ad, late 1950s.

Spalding introduced the Big Boy Tinkertoy as part of its expanding line. This was a set of tremendous proportions with 365 pieces until 1963. It included 62 spools and 224 sticks of various lengths. This set was listed as being for ages 8 to 12 years. This set became available in about 1957, and was in the line through 1967 for certain. From 1964 on, the set contained 318 pieces. The stock number was 155.

Spalding — Curtain Wall Builder

Plate 305

Author's collection.

Curtain Wall Builder.

Curtain Wall Builder is an interesting toy. It was definitely not intended for young children. The set consists of preformed steel wall sections and corners that interlock to form the outline of a modern 1960s office or apartment building. The design allows wall sections to be attached on top of one another to make a structure several floors high. The plastic coping pieces are added to dress the top of the wall and to provide support for the cardboard roof included with the set. The windows were represented by thin yellow plastic sheeting that fit into flanges inside the wall sections. Also included were door sections and pennants as well as a 17" by 11" two-sided instruction sheet.

Curtain Wall Builder is not an easy toy to assemble. The steel wall sections have thin edges that can present a cutting danger. When sliding the wall pieces together, pinching was common. The set owned by the author still has most of the straight coping pieces attached to the original mold-injection bars, probably indicating that prior owners had quickly lost interest in actually using this toy.

In the style of buildings that could be made, Curtain Wall Builder is similar to the Kenner Panel and Girder sets of the same period. However, the Kenner set was all plastic and generally easier and safer to use. Curtain Wall Builder was offered from 1959 to 1964, and possibly longer. Yet, not many are seen at flea markets and antique stores.

These H. O. scale sets came in five sizes:

No. 650 — 417 pieces, $70.00 – 90.00.
No. 640 — 317 pieces, $50.00 – 70.00.
No. 630 — 197 pieces, $40.00 – 50.00.
No. 620 — 123 pieces, $30.00 – 40.00.
No. 610 — 82 pieces, $20.00 – 30.00.

(Prices for complete sets.)

Spalding — Deluxe Tinkertoy

This toy was the same as the Toy Tinkers DeLuxe Tinkertoy. See the listing for DeLuxe Tinkertoy under Toy Tinkers. Value $20.00 good to $30.00 excellent, with original can and lid.

Spalding — Easy Tinkertoy

First listed in 1960 as a new item, Easy Tinkertoy contained 43 pieces and was sold in a canister with a metal top. It was listed as Stock #96 through 1964, when it seems to have been dropped from the company line. In 1964, it was the only canister set to not suffer a reduction in parts. Value $10.00 good to $20.00 excellent, with original can and lid.

Spalding — Executive Tinkertoy

In 1966 Spalding introduced Executive Tinkertoy. The sticks and spools were finished with walnut stain. The canister had what was described as leather-graining. The set contained about 61 parts, an instruction sheet made to look like blue prints, an Executive Tinkertoy Engineer Certificate of Award, and an Executive Development Memo.

The set was touted as being for the executive who had everything. It was listed through 1970.

Plate 306   Author's collection.
Executive Tinkertoy. Complete set, $15.00 – 30.00.

Spalding — Grad Tinkertoy

This was another of the Spalding color-coded sets. It contained 215 pieces, including windblades through 1963. The set was recommended for children from ages 8 to 12. Identified as stock #146. From 1964 on, it contained 183 parts. It was available from 1955 to 1967.

Plate 307   Author's collection.
Grad Tinkertoy, $15.00 – 25.00.

Spalding — Junior Tinkertoy

Junior Tinkertoy was part of the Spalding line. It was stock #106, and up to 1963 contained 53 pieces. From 1964 on, it was listed as having 45 pieces. It was available from 1955 to 1969, at least. Value $10.00 good to $20.00 excellent, with original can and lid.

Spalding — Major Tinkertoy

Major Tinkertoy consisted of 127 parts from 1964 through 1967. It is identified as #136. It contained 149 pieces in 1963 and earlier. It was available from 1955 to 1967, for certain. Value $15.00 good to $25.00 excellent, with original can and lid.

Spalding — Tinkertoy Motorized Sets

Plate 308

Master Tinkertoy set shown in original box, from company advertisement. Complete set, $75.00 – 100.00.

From 1954 through at least 1957, Spalding offered a boxed Tinkertoy set for $9.99. It was called "Master Tinkertoy Electric Motor Drive." This set came with red rods, green windblades, and natural birch spools and parts. The motor in this set was a wall-plug type used to run the models made with the set.

Spalding also offered a motorized Tinkertoy set that used a battery-operated motor. This was set number 177. This motor was mounted on a plastic case that held two size D batteries. The whole arrangement could be attached

to any model. The holes for rods to slide through were located on the bottom of the unit. The motor was designed to run forward or backward, depending on the direction to which the operating switch was moved.

At least four motorized sets were offered: the Master set, the No. 166, No. 177, and No. 178. They were available from about 1960 to 1970. The No. 166 came in a giant can with a Tinkertoy motor model 166M AC 110 – 120 volt 60 cyc. 35 amps.

Plate 309   Author's collection.

#166 Electric Motor Tinkertoy set.
Complete set, $50.00 – 75.00.

Author's collection.

Plate 310

#177 Battery Motorized Tinkertoy
set. Complete set, $40.00 – 60.00.

Spalding — Panel Builder

Spalding introduced Panel Builder in 1958. This was a spools-and-sticks set with the addition of several parts. The new parts were squares, rectangles, and circles made of a material called Duron. These parts have the appearance of pegboard with regularly-spaced holes. There were also small rectangular wood blocks with holes that seem intended to act as the base for vehicles. End caps for the dowel rod sticks were also included.

The first year, set No. 800 was sold, containing 402 pieces and a 16-page instruction booklet. For 1959, set No. 600 was added to the line, containing 250 pieces and a 12-page instruction booklet. Panel Builder was listed as available through at least 1964, and could well have been sold after that.

Plate 311   Author's collection.

Panel Builder set. Set #800, $30.00 –
40.00. Set #600, $20.00 – 30.00. Prices
listed for complete sets.

Plate 312

Panel Builder 1959 company catalog page.

Author's collection.

Plate 313

Late 1950s Panel Builder ad.

Author's collection.

Spalding — Prep Tinkertoy

The Prep Tinkertoy set contained 78 pieces until 1963. It was recommended for ages 2 and up. In 1956 it was selling for 89¢ at Sears. In 1964 the part count dropped to 62 pieces. The stock number was 116. It was for sale from 1955 to at least 1967. Value $10.00 good to $20.00 excellent with original can and lid.

Spalding — Teck Tinkertoy

The Teck Tinkertoy set contained 113 parts until 1963, and was recommended for ages 5 to 9 years. From 1964 on, it was listed as having 98 pieces. The stock number was 126. It is listed from 1955 to 1967 as available for sale. Value $10.00 good to $20.00 excellent with original can and lid.

Spalding — Toy Maker

Toy Maker was desfinitely a young kid's toy. It was a snap-together toy for making vehicles, from cars to tractors to boats. It was made of smooth plastic and available in three sizes. It was sold in a can with a metal push-in lid. It was available from 1963 to 1970, and most likely thereafter. It was recommended for boys and girls ages 2 to 8 years. Values are for Toy Maker with original can and lid. Toy Maker was available in three sizes:

No. 474 — 137 pieces, $15.00 – 20.00.
No. 454 — 105 pieces, $10.00 – 15.00.
No. 434 — 53 pieces, $5.00 – 10.00.

Plate 314   Author's collection.

Back page of Tinkertoy instruction book showing Tinker Zoo and Toy Maker can.

Author's collection.

Spalding — The Wonder Builder

Spalding only offered the Wonder Builder for two years, 1953 and 1954, so do not expect to find many of these. The Spalding version contained 100 pieces in the small-T can.

Plate 315

Spalding Wonder Builder Tinkertoy. Complete set, $15.00 – 25.00.

Spalding — Tinker Zoo

Tinker Zoo was a mix of dowels and flexible-plastic perforated sheets cut into different shapes. This toy came in the familiar can with an outside-screw lit. Children were encouraged to use the set to create imaginative interpretations of animals, or to invent some animals of their own. Four sizes were offered. A 1961 copyrighted instruction sheet offered kids a chance to receive a certificate to be a "Junior Tinker-Zooligist," if their ideas for animals were used in future direction sheets.

The company ads list Tinker Zoo as new for 1962. It was being sold in two sizes, priced at $1.00 and $2.00, as well as a 98¢ rack package. By 1963, two larger sizes had been added. Tinker Zoo was part of the line until at least 1970. Values are for Zoo with original can and lid.

No. 747 — Circus Tinker Zoo, 222 pieces, $20.00 – 30.00.
No. 737 — Carnival Tinker Zoo, 147 pieces, $15.00 – 25.00.
No. 727 — 101 pieces, $10.00 – 20.00.
No. 717 — 51 pieces, $5.00 – 10.00.
No. 707 — 51 pieces, rack package, $5.00 – 10.00.

Plate 316
Tinker Zoo set.

Author's collection.

Spalding — No. 179 Tinkertoy

This was a rack package set consisting of 53 pieces, designed to be hung on a peg board display. It seems to have been introduced in 1959, and stayed in the line until 1964, for sure.

Plate 317
Company ad for #179 Tinkertoy set. In original box, $10.00 – 15.00.

Spalding, Other Toys

Spalding — Block and Roll Pull Toy

Starting in 1957, Block and Roll pull toy began to be listed in company advertisements. It had a suggested retail price of $2.00. The name tells it all. This toy was made up of square and round blocks with the round blocks serving as wheels. A string was attached to one end so that it could be pulled by a young child. This item was available through at least 1959, and possibly later.

BLOCK and ROLL
colorful wood blocks and wheels
Tough, Flexible poly-connectors

retail $2.⁰⁰

Plate 318
Block and Roll pull toy company ad. $15.00 – 25.00. Original box, add $5.00 – 10.00.

Spalding — Tinker Beads

Tinker Beads were brought back to the Toy Tinker line under Spalding. In the late 1950s they were being sold in plastic bags. The bag had a cardboard label across the top with a hole from which the bag could be hung on a peg board. The two sizes, small and large, retailed for 69¢ each.

By 1965 Tinker Beads were being offered in a can with an outside-screw top. The advertisements promised six big, easy-to-handle shapes in six bright, colorsafe colors. Also included were two strong plastic-tipped strings. The plastic tip took the place of the metal bodkin from the original sets.

Plate 319
Author's collection.
Tinker Beads in a bag, $15.00 – 25.00 as pictured.

Plate 320
Author's collection.
Tinker Beads in a bag catalog ad, 1959.

Plate 321
Author's collection.
Tinker Beads in a can. Complete set, $10.00 – 20.00.

Spalding — Count 'N Stack

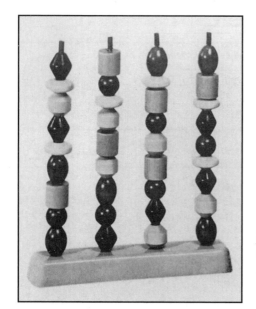

This toy became available in 1967. It consisted of a hardwood base with four sticks inserted into the it, parallel to each other and equally spaced. There were plastic tips on the ends of the sticks. The set appears to have come with six shapes of beads, with a total count of 36. This toy was available through at least 1970, and may have been sold after that date.

Plate 322

Count 'N Stack toy company ad, late 1960s. Complete with box, $15.00 – 25.00.

Spalding — Design Blocks

This was a colored toy made of soft plastic. It consisted of geometrically shaped, colored pieces that could be placed in the tray-like box to make different designs. It was advertised from 1967 through 1970, for certain.

Plate 323

Design Blocks set company ad, late 1960s. Complete set with box, $15.00 – 25.00.

Spalding — Color Coded Dominoes

These turn up in company ads for 1967 with a suggested retail price of $5.00. The dominoes were sold in a canister with a metal lid. The set was listed as containing 28 polyethylene dominoes that were color coded. The ads noted that they could also be used for balancing and counting. It is listed through 1970.

Plate 324

Color Coded Dominoes company ad, late 1960s. Complete set, $15.00 – 25.00.

Spalding — EvenFlo Miniature Baby Bottles

These were miniature baby bottles that came three to a bag with a cardboard printed header. They retailed for 39¢ in 1958, and were made of polyethylene. They were available in 1959 as well, and perhaps after that.

Plate 325

EvenFlo Miniature Baby Bottles, #195, company catalog ad, 1959. Range as shown, $5.00 – 10.00.

Author's collection.

Spalding — Tinker Fun Forms

The Spalding Tinker Fun Forms were added to the line in about 1966 and were available in two sizes. This was a set of interlocking blocks in six colors and four shapes. They could be stacked or connected by means of dowels to make models. The blocks were polyethylene. The $1.00 set was sold in a canister with 10 plastic blocks and 27 hardwood connecting rods. The $3.00 set was sold in a box, and included a large round circular base, 25 plastic blocks, and 42 hardwood connecting rods. It was available through at least 1970.

Plate 326

Tinker Fun Forms company ad, late 1960s. Complete set, $15.00 – 25.00.

Spalding — Tom and Belle Tinker

See the listing under the Toy Tinker section.

Spalding — Pace Setter Line

Plate 327   Author's collection.

Pace Setter line balls company catalog page, 1959. Baseballs, $5.00 – 10.00. Softballs, $5.00 – 10.00. Basketballs, $10.00 – 15.00. Footballs (not shown), $10.00 – 15.00.

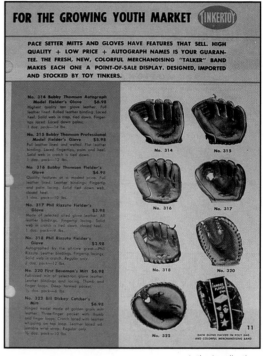

Plate 328   Author's collection.

Pace Setter line gloves company catalog page, 1959. Each, $10.00 – 20.00.

Spalding also decided to add sports equipment to the line of Tinkertoy goods in 1958. This was known as the Pace Setter line of famous players' gloves. Autographs of such names as Bill Diekey, Phil Rizzuto, and Bobby Thomson appeared on the baseball gloves. They retailed from $2.98 to $6.98 each.

In 1960, the line expanded to include names such as Yogi Berra, Bob Shaw, and Don Drysdale, with prices from $3.00 to $8.00. In addition, an assortment of balls were added, some with autographs. Baseballs were priced from $1.00 to $2.25, softballs were priced from $1.00 to $2.00, basketballs sold for $3.49 to $5.00, and footballs were priced at $2.98 each.

The line was designed for sales through toy stores and other non-sports oriented outlets. The expectation was that they would be ideal for impulse purchases due to the price and the celebrity connection.

Spalding — Pound-A-Block

This toy was added to the line of the Toy Tinkers in 1967 and was part of the line through 1970, for certain. It was a bench-type pounding toy consisting of nine color-safe rectangular blocks linked together as one unit, with wooden ends. The blocks were polyethelene, and the set also included a smooth plastic mallet for pounding the blocks. It was recommended for boys and girls ages 1 to 4 years. It came in a four-color chipboard box with a suggested retail of $3.95.

Plate 329

Pound-A-Block company ad, late 1960s. Complete toy, $10.00 – 15.00. Original box, $5.00 – 10.00.

Spalding — Stacking Toys

In the late 1950s and into the 1960s, Spalding offered a large selection of stacking toys. These were reminiscent of the Jack and Jill Tinker set sold in the 1930s. Each toy consisted of a base with a piece of dowel on which the rest of the parts of the set were stacked. The sets offered were Jack Stack, Sally Stack, Cop Stack, Cook Stack, Clown Stack, Tinker Stack, Stack-Me-Sue, and Stack-O the Clown, whose base was curved so that he would roll and bob. These toys came in cardboard and blister-wrap packaging.

Plate 330

Author's collection.

Stack-Me Sue and Jack Stack toys. Complete toy, $15.00 – 25.00.

Plate 331

Author's collection.

Stacking toys from Spalding Tinker Toy catalog, 1959.

Spalding — Tinker Tools

Tinker Tools were available from 1965 until 1970, for sure. They came in three sizes. The sets included a plastic screwdriver, wrench, hammer, nuts, bolts, and nails. They were intended to develop hand-eye coordination in young children. John Wright won awards for the package design for Tinker Tools in 1967.

Plate 332

Tinker Tool company ad, late 1960s. Complete, $15.00 – 25.00. Original package add, $10.00 – 15.00.

Spalding — Toy-O-Ball

Plate 333

Toy-O-Ball company ad, 1955. Toy-O-Ball, $20.00 – 30.00.

Starting in 1955, the Toy Tinkers under Spalding added a line of yo-yos that were made to look like balls. The three styles were a football, a basketball, and a baseball. They do not seem to have lasted long, as no reference is made to them in ads after this year.

Spalding — Treasure Trove for Tiny Tots

Offered in 1957 through at least 1959, the Treasure Trove for Tiny Toys was a boxed assortment of Spalding Tinker Toy items. It retailed for $5 and included a small can of Tinkertoys, a Tom Tinker doll, a Sally Stack toy, and #230 Tinkertown Train coal engine and tender. The box was designed to be set up for display, which was common for the time before toys were routinely stapled and shrink-wrapped shut. Locating this set in the original box would be a nice find.

Plate 334

Treasure Trove for Tiny Tots company ad, late 1950s. Complete as shown, $90.00 – 110.00.

Spalding — Tinkertown Trains

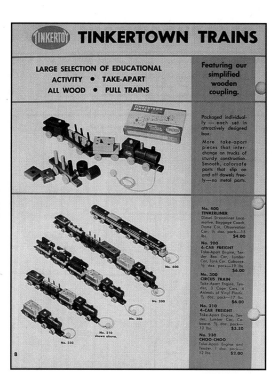

Author's collection.

Tinkertown Trains came in several different sets. Most were variations of a basic coal engine with more or less cars in tow. The one totally different offering was the Tinkerliner. This was intended to look like a streamlined passenger train.

All of the sets were made of wood in brightly enameled colors. The cars could be disassembled, and the parts rearranged. When put together, the train became a pull toy, with the engine having a string and a hand ball. The smallest set, #230, had only the engine and coal tender. Set #210 added a log car and caboose. Set #300 consisted of a coal engine, tender, and three animal cars with small plastic circus animals. #200 consisted of a coal engine, tender, box car, log car, tanker car, and caboose. #400 was the Tinkerliner with an engine, two regular passenger cars, and an observation car. All came packed in cardboard display boxes. Variations on this train were available from 1956 to 1964.

Plate 335

Tinkertown Trains company catalog page, 1959.

Choo Choo, $5.00 – 10.00.
3-car Train, $10.00 – 15.00.
4-car Train, $15.00 – 20.00.
Circus, complete, $25.00 – 30.00.
6-car Train, $30.00 – 35.00.
Tinkerliner, $30.00 – 35.00.

Questor Construction Sets

Questor — Giant Tinkertoy

Plate 336

Author's collection.

Giant Tinkertoy parts. Complate set, $75.00 – 100.00. Original box, add $10.00 – 20.00.

Plate 337

Author's collection.

Comparison between Giant Tinkertoy parts, Original Tinkertoy parts, and Big Tinkertoy parts.

The Giant Tinkertoy was introduced by Questor in 1971. This set should not be confused with Giant Tinker, available 1919 through 1924 from the Toy Tinkers. Giant Tinkertoy was just that: a Tinkertoy that was sixteen times larger than the regular stick-and-spool set. A 1971 set offered by mail, for $29.95 plus postage, contained 90 pieces. There were 52 rods in five different lengths, and 38 spools in five different sizes and styles. As with the regular sets, the possibilities were limitless. With Giant Tinkertoy, what you built was substantially larger than the models made from regular-sized sets. It was available through at least 1977.

Questor — Giant Engineer Tinkertoy

This set was identified as being for ages 3 and up. It was a plastic and wood set, contianing 315 parts. Stock #155. Value $10.00 good to $20.00 excellent, with original can and lid.

Questor — Super Transit

This was set Number 146. It contained 180 parts. As the name suggests, it had a transportation theme showing all manner of vehicles on the canister.

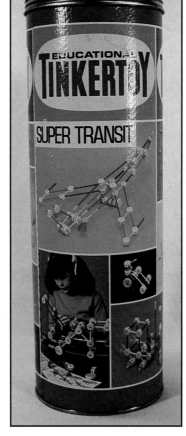

Plate 338

Super Transit Tinkertoy by Questor. Complete, $10.00 – 20.00.

Author's collection.

Questor — Junior Architect

This set consisted of 125 parts, and was basically the same set as Major Tinkertoy under Spalding. It shared the same stock number, #136. Value $10.00 good to $20.00 excellent, with original can and lid.

Questor — Little Designer Tinkertoy

Little Designer Tinkertoy by Questor contained 95 parts. This was a plastic and wood set suggested for ages three and up. Stock #126. $10.00 good to $20.00 excellent, with original can and lid.

Questor — Locomotive and Driver Set

Plate 339

Courtesy of the Evanston Historical Society.

Locomotive and Driver Tinkertoy set. Complete, $5.00 – 10.00.

Stock #193. This was a small set with parts to make a locomotive or other vehicles. It also featured Tinker Tim and Tinker Tina. These were characters that could be constructed out of sticks and spools. Then faces could be applied to one side of a spool to make the head. This set was a mix of plastic and wood. It featured flexible joints for the figure's arms and legs. Several similar small sets were produced with different names and themes.

Questor — Primary Tinkertoy

Stock #5106. This set contained 45 pieces. It was a wood and plastic set. Value $5.00 good to $10.00 excellent, with original can and lid.

Questor — Starter Tinkertoy

Stock #116. Starter Tinkertoy by Questor contained 60 parts. It was recommended for ages 3 and up. Value $5.00 good to $10.00 excellent, with original can and lid.

Questor — Tinkertoy for Little Hands

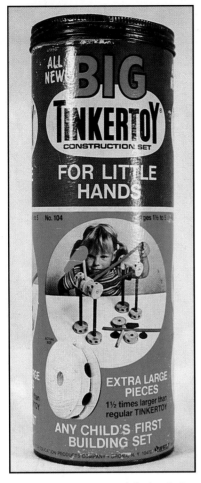

This was available in 1976 as set #104. It was a wood set one and a half times larger than regular Tinkertoys.

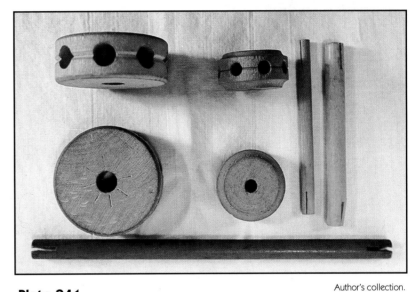

Plate 340   Author's collection.

Big Tinkertoy for Little Hands by Questor. Complete, $15.00 – 25.00.

Plate 341   Author's collection.

Comparing parts for original Tinkeroy and the Big Tinkertoy for Little Hands by Questor.

Questor — Toy Maker

The Questor Toy Maker was essentially the same as the Spalding model. It contained wooden wheels, dowel rods, and plastic pieces for making vehicles. This set also included little figures to fit inside the toys.

Plate 342

Toy Maker by Questor, early version.
Complete set, $15.00 – 20.00.

Plate 343

Toy Maker by Questor, later version.
Complete set, $15.00 – 20.00.

Author's collection.

Author's collection.

Questor — Master Builder

This set was available from 1970 on. It falls between Giant Engineer Tinkertoy and Super Transport Tinkertoy sets in size. Value $10.00 good to $20.00 excellent, with original can and lid.

Questor — Executive Tinkertoy

This toy was the same as the Spalding product. Value $15.00 good to $30.00 excellent, with original can and lid.

Questor — Other Toy Section

The following toys are essentially identical to the Spalding versions:

Questor — Count 'N Stack, $15.00 good to $25.00 excellent.
Questor — Design Blocks, $15.00 good to $25.00 excellent, with box.
Questor — Tinker Fun Forms, $15.00 good to $25.00 excellent, with box.
Questor — Pound-A-Block, $10.00 good to $20.00 excellent.
Questor — Tinker Tools, $15.00 good to $25.00 excellent.

Gabriel Construction Sets

Gabriel/CBS, Inc. — Tinkertoys

Plate 344

Courtesy of the Evanston Historical Society.

Gabriel Tinkertoy sets 1 through 5. Complete sets:
No. 30010, $5.00 – 10.00.
No. 30020, $5.00 – 10.00.
No. 30030, $10.00 – 15.00.
No. 30040, $10.00 – 20.00.
No. 30050, $10.00 – 20.00.
No. 30060 (motorized set), $20.00 – 30.00.

The Gabriel/CBS Inc. sets were made of wood and plastic. All of the sets were recommended for ages 3½ to 7 years, except for the motorized set, recommended for ages 4½ years and up.

#1: Stock #30010 — This was a 50-piece set.
#2: Stock #30020 — This was a 100-piece set.
#3: Stock #30030 — This was a 150-piece set.
#4: Stock #30040 — This was a 200-piece set.

#5: Stock #30050 — This was a 250-piece set.
#6: Stock #30060 — This was a 300-piece set, including a plastic-housed, battery-operated motor.

Hasbro / Playskool — Tinkertoy® Construction Sets

Plate 345
Playskool Tinkertoy® set made through 1991.
Complete sets:
Beginner set, $5.00 – 10.00.
Basic set, $5.00 – 10.00.
Big Builder set, $10.00 – 15.00.
Super set, $10.00 – 20.00.

Author's collection.

<u>1986 to early 1991 (Wood and Plastic)</u>
Values are with original can and lid.
Playskool Beginner Set, 57 pieces (#840), $5.00 good to $10.00 excellent.
Playskool Basic Set (#841), $5.00 good to $10.00 excellent.
Playskool Big Builder Set (#842), $10.00 good to $15.00 excellent.
Playskool Super Set (#843), $10.00 good to $20.00 excellent.

<u>1992 to Present (All Plastic)</u>
Values are not given, as these products are still made.

Playskool Big Builder Tinkertoy®
Playskool Dynamic Designs Tinkertoy®
Playskool King-Size Creations Tinkertoy®
Playskool Colossal Construction Tinkertoy®

<u>1995</u>
Value not given, as this product is still made.
Playskool Crazy Constructions Tinkertoy®

Plate 346

Playskool Big Builder Tinkertoy,® still available.
Playskool Dynamic Designs Tinkertoy,® still available.
Playskool King Size Creations Tinkertoy,® still available.
Playskool Colossal Construction Tinkertoy,® still available.
Crazy Construction Tinkertoy,® new 1995.

Plate 347

An employee at the Hasbro production facilities in Central Falls, Rhode Island, checks quality on Tinkertoy® parts.

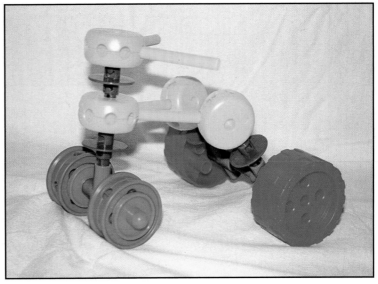

Plate 348

A Tinkertoy® model made using the all-plastic sets made by Playskool.®

☖ Go-Along Items ☖

This term covers items made based on the Tinker Toy theme but not manufactured by the Toy Tinkers or any of their successors.

Tinker Town Tom

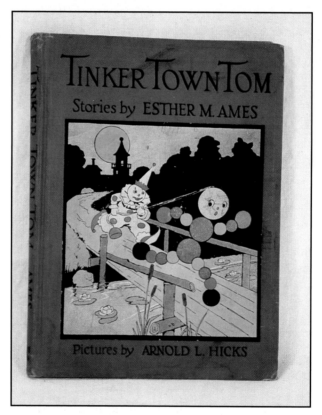

Plate 349

Author's collection.

Tinker Town Tom story book, 1924, by Rand McNally, Chicago, $40.00 – 50.00.

This children's book was published in 1924 by Rand McNally of Chicago, written by Esther Merrian Ames, and illustrated by Arnold Lorne Hicks. Hard covered, this 96-page volume had 43 color illustrations. It measures 9" x 6½".

Tinker Town Tom Brochure

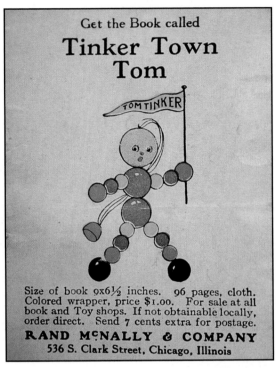

Plate 350

Author's collection.

Tinker Town Tom brochure, $20.00 – 30.00. Front cover shown.

Plate 351

Author's collection.

Front center panel of Tinker Town Tom brochure.

This small brochure promoted the *Tinker Town Tom* book and was included in jars of Tinker Beads. It may have been found also packed in other Tinker Toys. It measures 7" x 3" when open, and folds down to 2⁵/₁₆" x 3".

One side has three panels, two with drawings of Tom Tinker himself and the center panel showing one of the book's illustrations. This side also tells the publisher, author, illustrator, and price. In 1924 the book price was $1.00. The reverse side shows Tom and Belle Tinker, and provides a brief outline of the book's story line.

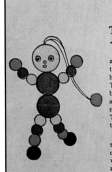

Plate 352

Author's collection.

Three inside panels of Tinker Town Tom brochure.

Tinker Toy Paint Book

This coloring book was published by Whitman Publishing of Racine, Wisconsin. It has a copyright of 1939. Illustrations were by Bernyce Polifka. The book measures 15¾" x 10¾" with 32 pages and a cardboard cover printed in color. The front and back covers are the same.

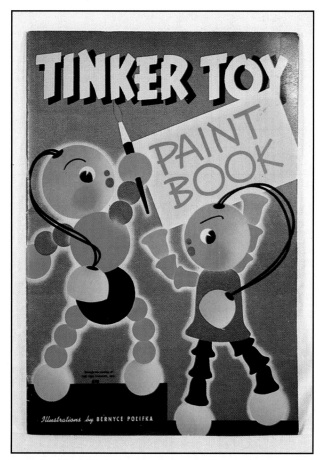

Plate 353

Author's collection.

Tinker Toy Paint Book, 1939, Whitman Publishing, Racine, $20.00 – 40.00.

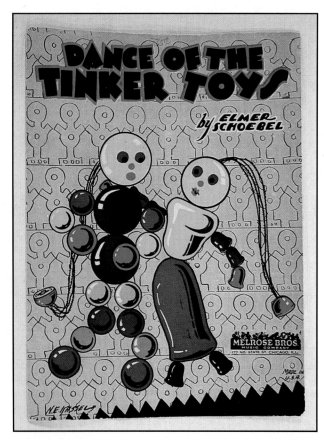

Plate 354

Author's collection.

Dance of the Tinker Toys, 1927, Melrose Bros., Chicago, $15.00 – 25.00.

Dance of the Tinker Toys

This was sheet music published by Melrose Bros. Music Company of Chicago, Illinois. The copyright date is 1927. The writer was Elmer Schoebel. It contains four pages of sheet music with a colored cover featuring Tom and Belle Tinker and a background of line-drawn Tinker Men symbols. The back cover is an advertisement for other items available in the Melrose Bros. line. It measures 12" x 9".

Parade of the Tinkertoys

Parade of the Tinkertoys

This sheet music was written for the piano by Stanford King. It was published by Theodore Presser Company of Philadelphia, Pennsylvania. The cover is blue, red, and white, showing Tinkertoy construction pieces made up as animals and a wagon. The price printed on the cover is 35¢. The copyright date is 1944. It contains three sheets of music and the back cover lists several Presser Company items for sale. The size is 9¼" x 12".

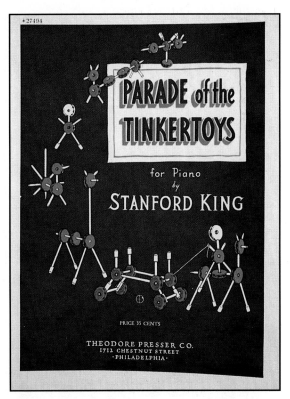

Author's collection

Plate 355
Parade of the Tinkertoys, 1944, Theodore Presser Co., Philadelphia, $15.00 – 25.00.

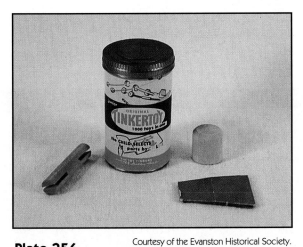

Plate 356
Courtesy of the Evanston Historical Society.

Miniature Tinkertoy can, $3.00 – 5.00. Complete as shown.

Miniature Tinkertoy Can

This was originally sold as part of a store play set.

Paper Items

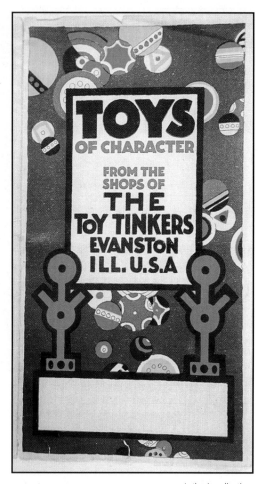

Plate 357

Author's collection.

Toys of Character brochure, four panels each side. Circa 1918, $15.00 – 25.00.

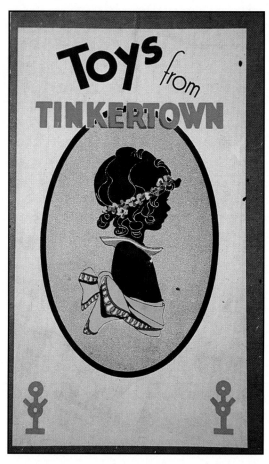

Plate 358

Courtesy of the Evanston Historical Society.

Toys from Tinkertown brochure, three panels front side and one large panel reverse, $15.00 – 25.00.

Plate 359

Reverse side of Toys from Tinkertown brochure, about 1926.

Courtesy of the Evanston Historical Society.

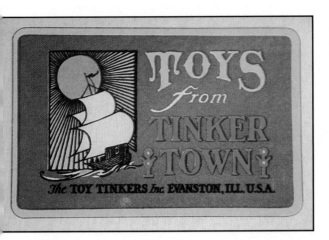

Plate 360 *Author's collection.*

Toys from Tinkertown accordion-style brochure, mid 1920s, $15.00 – 20.00.

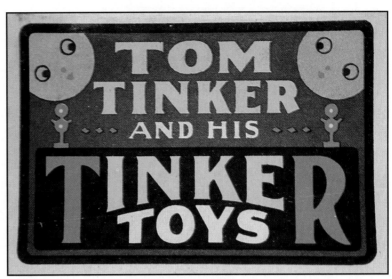

Plate 361 *Author's collection.*

Tom Tinker and His Tinker Toys accordion-style brochure, mid 1920s, $15.00 – 20.00.

Plate 362 *Author's collection.*

Toys from Tinker Town accordion-style brochure, mid 1920s, $15.00 – 20.00.

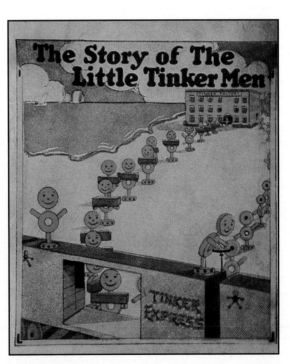

Plate 363 *Author's collection.*

The Story of the Little Tinker Men brochure, early 1920s, $15.00 – 20.00.

Plate 364   Courtesy of the Evanston Historical Society.
Tinker Toys 1924 catalog, $25.00 – 50.00.

Plate 365   Author's collection.
Front of black and white mid-1930s full-page brochure, $5.00 – 10.00.

Plate 366   Author's collection.
Back of black and white mid-1930s full-page brochure.

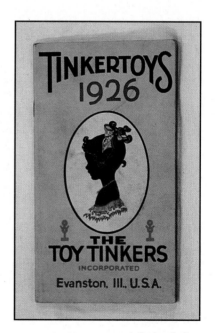

Plate 367   Author's collection.
Tinkertoys 1926 catalog, $25.00 – 50.00.

Courtesy of the Evanston Historical Society.

Plate 368

1927 Tinker Toys catalog, $25.00 – 50.00.

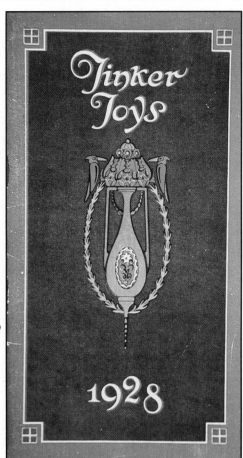

Courtesy of the Evanston Historical Society.

Plate 369

1928 Tinker Toys catalog, $25.00 – 50.00.

Courtesy of the Evanston Historical Society.

Plate 370

1931 Tinker Toys catalog, $25.00 – 50.00.

Plate 371

1932 Tinker Toys catalog, $25.00 – 50.00.

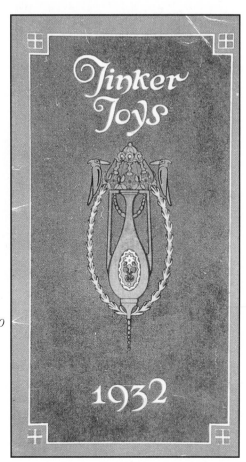

Courtesy of the Evanston Historical Society.

Plate 372   Courtesy of the Evanston Historical Society.

1935 Tinker Toys catalog, $25.00 – 50.00.

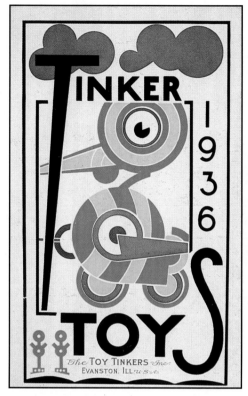

Plate 373   Courtesy of the Evanston Historical Society.

1936 Tinker Toys catalog, $25.00 – 50.00.

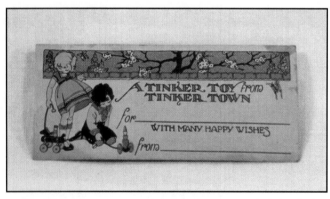

Plate 374   Author's collection.

A Tinker Toy from Tinker Town gift card, $5.00 – 10.00.

Plate 375

The Tinkertoy Wonder Builder instruction book, example in poor condition. Good to excellent, $5.00 – 10.00.

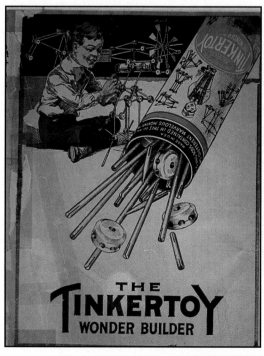

Author's collection.

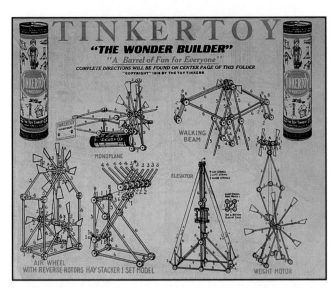

Plate 376
Author's collection.
Tinkertoy The Wonder Builder instruction book, $5.00 – 10.00.

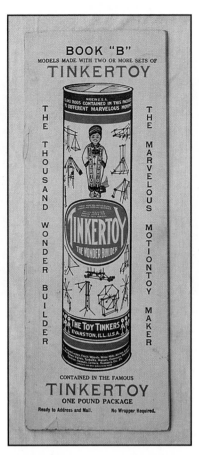

Plate 377
Author's collection.
Book "B" for Tinkertoy, $15.00 – 30.00.

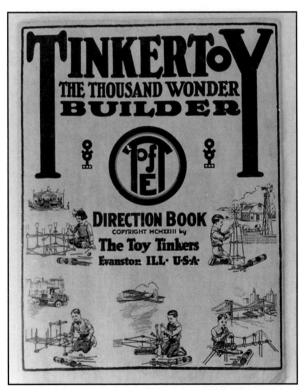

Plate 378
Author's collection.
Tinkertoy the Thousand Wonder Builder instruction book, $5.00 – 10.00.

Plate 379
Author's collection.
Senior Tinkertoy instruction book, $5.00 – 10.00.

Plate 380   Author's collection.

Tinker Tales for Tiny Tots instruction booklet for Tinker Blox Toy, $10.00 – 15.00.

Plate 381   Author's collection.

Tinker Toys advertisement from Child Life magazine, 1927. Black and white full page ads, $5.00 – 10.00.

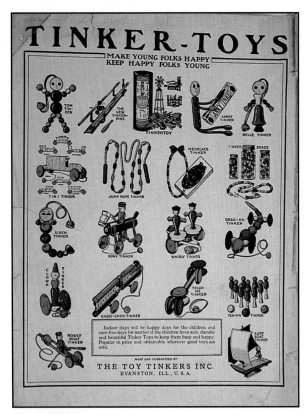

Plate 382   Author's collection.

Tinker Toys full page color magazine ad, 1927. Full page color ads, $7.50 – 15.00.

Plate 383   Courtesy of the Evanston Historical Society.

Tinker Toys and Chistmas full page ad, $7.50 – 15.00.

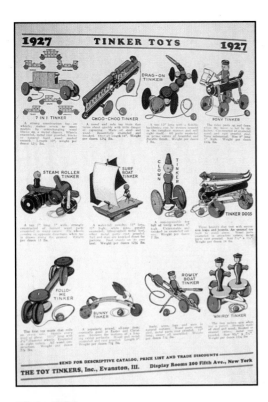

Plate 384

1927 Tinker Toys wholesale catalog page, color,
$7.50 – 15.00.

Plate 385

1930 Tinker Toys wholesale catalog page, color,
$7.50 – 15.00.

Plate 386

Tinker Toys 1931 wholesale catalog page, color,
$7.50 – 15.00.

Author's collection.

Plate 387

Bunny Tinker for Easter company flyer, 8" x 10", color, $20.00 – 40.00.

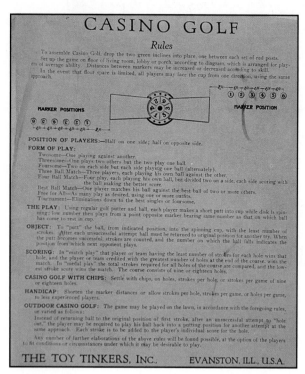

Plate 388

Author's collection.

Casino Golf instruction sheet. Non-Tinkertoy construction set instruction sheets, $5.00 – 15.00.

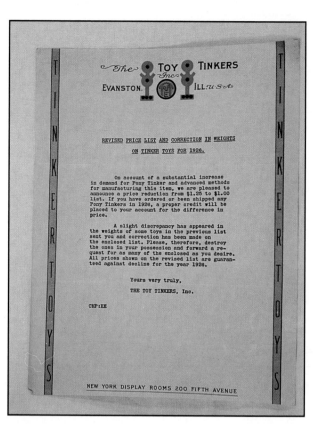

Plate 389

Author's collection.

Toy Tinker letter to dealers, 1926. Letters on company stationary, $10.00 – 15.00.

Plate 390

Author's collection.

Tinker Wind Blades uncut. Red with Toy Tinker graphics, $10.00 – 15.00.

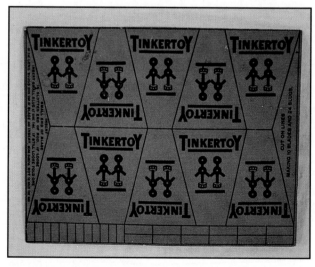

Plate 391

Author's collection.

Tinker Wind Blades uncut. Blue with Toy Tinker graphics, $10.00 – 20.00.

Plate 392

Spalding 1959 Tinkertoy catalog, $20.00 – 30.00.

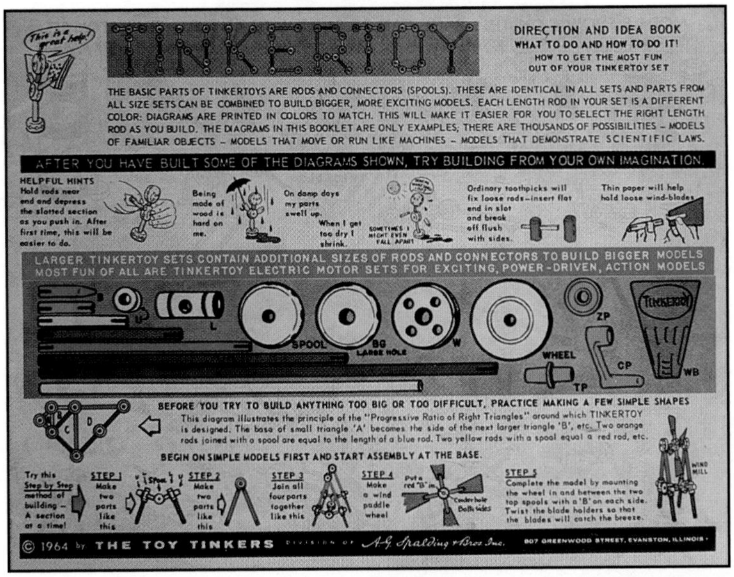

Author's collection.

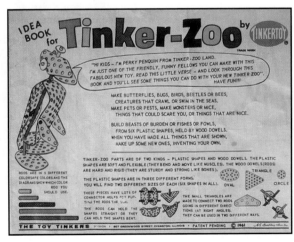

Author's collection.

Plate 393

Spalding Tinkertoy instruction book,
$3.00 – 6.00.

Plate 394

Spalding Tinker Zoo instruction book, $3.00 – 6.00.

Author's collection.

Plate 395   Author's collection.

Spalding Toy Maker ad, mid-1960s.
Full page ads, $3.00 – 5.00.

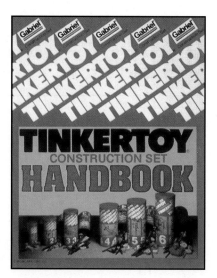

Plate 396   Author's collection.

Gabriel Tinkertoy handbook, $3.00 –
5.00.

Miscellaneous Promotional Items

Plate 397   Courtesy of the Evanston Historical Society.

Glass printer's plate for Tinker Toys from about 1927,
$15.00 – 30.00.

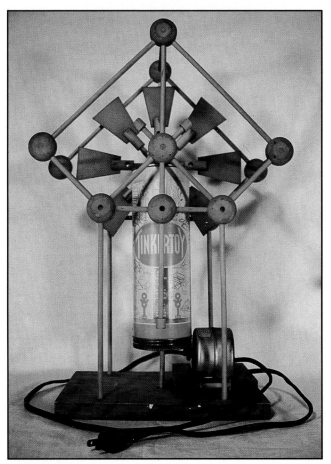

Plate 398

Tinkertoy Motorized Windmill company display piece, $150.00 – 200.00.

Plate 399

Tinkertoy Motorized Oil Well company display piece, $250.00 – 400.00.

Plate 400

Junior Tinkertoy Motorized display piece from 1935 company catalog. Display piece, $75.00 – 125.00.

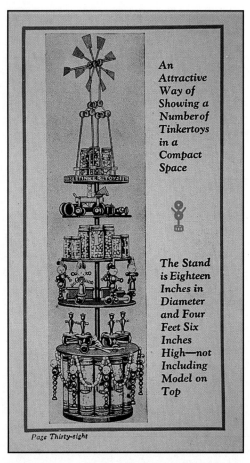

An Attractive Way of Showing a Number of Tinkertoys in a Compact Space

The Stand is Eighteen Inches in Diameter and Four Feet Six Inches High—not Including Model on Top

Plate 401   Courtesy of the Evanston Historical Society.

Four foot, six inch tall Toy Tinker display stand as shown in company catalog. Stand, $100.00 – 150.00.

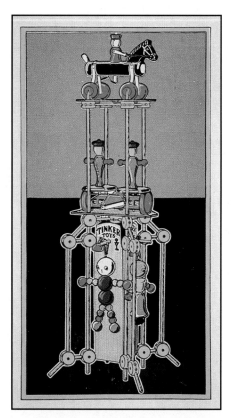

Courtesy of the Evanston Historical Society.

Plate 402

Small company display stand as shown in company catalog, 1924. Stand, $50.00 – 75.00.

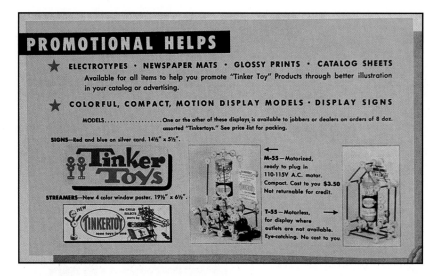

Plate 403

Spalding Tinker Toys promotional helps.
Electrotypes, $5.00 – 10.00.
Newspaper mats, $5.00 – 10.00.
Glossy prints, $10.00 – 15.00.
Catalogs, $20.00 – 30.00.

Signs, $15.00 – 25.00.
Streamers, $20.00 – 30.00.
M-55 motor/display, $90.00 – 120.00.
T-55 display, $40.00 – 60.00.

 Glossary

Blunt Needle: A large blunt-ended needle intended for use by small children for stringing wood beads.

Bodkin: See Blunt Needle.

Fiber: A heavy sturdy pressed board used to make components of some of the Tinker Toys.

Government Return Post Card: These are post cards that indicate that the recipient will pay the cost of the postage when the card is mailed.

Gyroscopic: Acting like a Gyroscope.

Gyrospinner: A part of the Tinkerpins Bowling Game. It operates on the principle of a gyroscope. The skill of the player is required to direct the gyrospinner to knock down as many pins as possible.

Gyrogovernor: Principle behind Spinning Jack Tinker that allows the toy to maintain a continuous rotation once set in motion, with occasional movement of the wrist.

Jobber: Wholesaler or middleman. Someone who buys from the manufacturer and sells to a third party that intends to resell the goods.

Knee Action: When each wheel is allowed independent vertical movement as in the case of a toy creating a motion that mimics some animal movements.

Knockabout Doll: A sturdy wooden doll usually made of beads and held together with string.

Letter Men: The individual blocks of wood from the Tinker Blox spelling game. Each block has a letter of the alphabet impressed upon it. They are drilled to accept a dowel rod in the bottom, and can then be placed in an individual stand or group stand, depending on the age of the set.

Medallions: These are the metal disks impressed into the handballs attached to Tinker Toys. They typically identify the Toy Tinkers of Evanston, Illinois, as the manufacturer. Occasionally they also list the name of the toy.

Monument Business: The design and sale of tombstones and burial monuments.

Pajeau: Pronounced "pash-oh."

Pandora's Box: This is the rumored chest filled with one of each of the Tinker Toys manufactured under the control of Charles H. Pajeau.

Pierrot Suit: The usual costume of a traditional French pantomime character, white face and loose white clothing.

Retail: The practice of adding a mark up or profit to the price charged by a wholesaler when goods are resold to the general public.

Siren: Creatures from Greek mythology that were reputed to lure sailors to destruction with their seductive songs.

Sulky: A two-wheeled cart like those used in horse racing.

Terpsichorean: Relating to dancing.

Tinker Toy: Any toy or novelty manufactured by the Toy Tinkers of Evanston, Illinois.

Tinkertoy: A construction set made up of sticks (dowel rods) and spools with a hole through the center and eight holes drilled around the edge. The sets can be made of all wood, all plastic, or some combination of the two. They also include windblades of either cardboard or plastic.

Whirly Gig: A child's toy that has a whirling motion, such as a pinwheel.

Wholesale: The price charged to a merchant or middleman before the goods are sold to the general public.

Yankee Doodle Sulky: A sulky designed and manufactured by Charles Hamilton Pajeau. It was intended to be used to transport small children, and featured a safety catch that prevented it from falling forward when the handle was lowered to the ground.

1. "A New American Industry," *Scientific American*, Dec. 25, 1920, Vol. 123; p. 634, by H.A. Mount.

2. "Toy Importers Hit Hard," *New York Times*, August 10, 1914.

3. "Germany Losing the Toy Market," *New York Times*, July 16, 1916.

4. "Toy Makers Organize," *New York Times*, June 10, 1916.

5. "Difficulties of the Toy Maker," *New York Times*, Dec. 3, 1916.

6. "Toy Show," *Business Week*, March 30, 1935, p. 15.

7. "Toy Rush," *Business Week*, Nov. 9, 1935, p. 16.

8. "Associations and Industries That Have Brought Fame to Evanston," *Evanston Review*, January 15, 1953, by Olive Carruthers.

9. "A Visit to Santa's Tinkertoy Factory," *Wilmette Life*, Dec. 16, 1971, by Betty Crookes.

10. Evanston Historical Society Archives, interview with Mr. Martin, son-in-law of Robert Pettit.

11. Interview with Annie Pashow, Pasho family genealogical research.

12. 1900 U.S. Census for Hyde Park, Illinois; Joseph Pajeau family.

13. Chicago Lakeside City Directory, 1883 – 1916.

14. Evanston City Directory, 1879 – 1948.

15. Harvard School for Boys Year Books from 1876 – 1889 and 1890 – 1891.

16. Harvard School for Boys Alumni Book for 1940, pp. 27 & 28.

17. "The History of Harvard-Saint George School," 1965 newspaper article from the archives of the Chicago Historical Society, no paper identified, no exact date given. By students of the school: Jim Ryan and Kyle Fowler.

18. "Charles Hamilton Pajeau," *The National Cyclopedia of American Biography*, p. 149.

19. "Evanston Named as Leader Among Toy Makers in State," *Evanston Review*, Dec. 25, 1947.

20. Marriage license for Charles H. Pajeau and Grace C. Fuller, Cook County, Illinois, City of Chicago, Oct. 11, 1899.

21. 1880 U.S. Census for the City of Chicago, Illinois; Alanzo Fuller family.

22. "Charles H. Pajeau Built a Successful Business with an Idea 2,500 Years Old," *Systems* magazine, Dec. 1918, Vol. 34; pp. 834 – 836, by A. Van Vlissinger Jr.

23. *Toys and Novelties* magazine, July 1924, pp. 49 – 50.

24. Patent #833, 541, Serial #290, 087, Charles H. Pajeau, Chicago, Illinois, filed Dec. 4, 1905, approved Oct. 16, 1906.

25. *Biographical Sketches of Loyalists of the American Revolution with an Historical Essay*, by Lorenzo Sabine, Vol. II, Baltimore Genealogical Publishing Co., Inc., 1979.

26. *Lineage Book — National Association of the Daughters of the American Revolution*; Vol. III (CXI), 1914; Flora Myers Gillentine, Historical General, Washington, District of Columbia.

27. The Haverford School Archives.

28. Princeton University Archives, Class of 1905.

29. "Forty Oldest Admitted Members to the Evanston Club," Evanston Club Archives. No date.

30. "Roster of Member, July 1931," *Chronological History of the Evanston Club 1931*.

31. "Evanston Club Haven for Men for More Than Half a Century," *Evanston Review*, July 4, 1963.

32. "M. M. Kirkman was First President of Evanston Club, Sketch Indicates," *Evanston News-Index*, June 6, 1919, by Seymour Currey.

33. "Historic Evanston Club," *Evanston Review*, April 1, 1948, by Dwight F. Clark, President of Evanston Club.

34. "Razing of Evanston Club Marks End of Era: $2,500,000 Apartment Will Be Built On Site," *Evanston Review*, June 26, 1958, by Peg Schafer.

35. "Popularity of Tinkertoys Survives 50 Years," *Evanston Review*, Feb. 13, 1964, by Carol Allen.

36. *Toys and Novelties* magazine, Feb. 1915, p. 24.

37. *Toys and Novelties* magazine, Jan. 1915, p. 29.

38. "M. Pajeau of the Toy Tinkers," *Evanston News-Index*, Feb. 28, 1929, by Lucy Rogers Hawkins.

39. *Toys and Novelties* magazine, April 1915, p. 22.

40. *Toys and Novelties* magazine, June 1915, p. 22.

41. "How We Build More Sales for Jobbers' Salesmen," *Printers Ink Monthly*, April 1922, pp. 40 – 42, by Lawrence D. Ely, General Sales Manager of the Toy Tinkers of Evanston, Illinois.

42. *Toys and Novelties* magazine, Feb. 1917, p. 83.

43. *Playthings* magazine, Dec. 1916, p. 26.

44. *Toys and Novelties* magazine, Jan. 1917, p. 45; Cited 1,750,000 Tinkertoys sold in 1915 and 1916 total.

45. *Toys and Novelties* magazine, June 1917, p. 30.

46. *Toys and Novelties* magazine, Aug. 1917, p. 54.

47. Instruction Booklet for Tinker Blox.

48. *Toys and Novelties* magazine, Feb. 1918, p. 190.

49. Company Brochures.

50. U.S. Patent #1,319,432, Screw Cap Container, Oct. 21, 1919.

51. *Toys and Novelties* magazine, Jan. 1919, p. 20.

52. *Toys and Novelties* magazine, Feb. 1919, p. 149.

53. Trade Mark Filing; Toy Tinkers of Evanston, Illinois, 1919.

54. *Toys and Novelties* magazine, Jan. 1921, p. 143.

55. Trade Mark Filing; Toy Tinkers of Evanston, Illinois, 1920.

56. Interviews with Larry J. Basting.

57. *Toys and Novelties* magazine, April 1921, p. 34.

58. *Toys and Novelties* magazine, Feb. 1921, p. 148.

59. *Toys and Novelties* magazine, May 1921, p. 22.

60. *Sheridan Shore Yacht Club — A Sixty Year History*, prepared by the Sheridan Shore Yacht Club, copyright 1982.

61. *Toys and Novelties* magazine, Jan. 1921, p. 329.

62. *Toys and Novelties* magazine, Feb. 1921, p. 147.

63. *Playthings* magazine, April 1936, p. 136.

64. *Toys and Novelties* magazine, Feb. 1922, p. 122.

65. *Toys and Novelties* magazine, Dec. 1921, p. 100.

66. *Toys and Novelties* magazine, March 1923, p. 109.

67. Corporate papers for the Siren Mills Corporation, County of Cook, State of Illinois.

68. Corporate papers for the Toy Tinkers of Evanston, Illinois, Inc., County of Cook, State of Illinois.

69. "Sheridan Shore Yacht Club Log — 25th Anniversary," prepared by Charles Hamilton Pajeau, 1948.

70. "Star-Class Yachts Ready for Friday Races," *Evanston Review*, May 29, 1930.

71. "Mystery Yacht Wins," *Evanston Review*, June 26, 1930.

72. "Parade of the Tinkertoys" for piano by Stanford King, Theodore Presser Co., 1712 Chestnut Street, Philadelphia; copyright 1944.

73. "Dance of the Tinkertoys," by Elmer Schoebel, Melrose Brothers Music Company; copyright 1924.

74. "Tinker Toy Paint Book," Whitman Publishing Co., Racine, Wisconsin; copyright 1939. Illustrated by Bernyce Polifka.

75. "Toy Tinkers Honor Hiertz," *Evanston Review*, Sept. 1, 1966.

76. McDonald Bros. Co., Minneapolis, Minnesota Wholesale Catalog; 1925 advertisement for the Toy Tinkers of Evanston, Illinois, 3 pages.

77. *Toys and Novelties* magazine, Jan. 1925, pp. 115 – 116.

78. "Toy Tinkers will Erect New Factory," *Evanston News-Index*, Jan. 22, 1926.

79. *Toys and Novelties* magazine, May 1926, p. 62.

80. *Toys and Novelties* magazine, June 1927, p. 38.

81. *Toys and Novelties* magazine, May 1927, p. 8.

82. "Hustler Toy Company Advertisement," Hibbard, Spencer, Bartlett & Co., from wholesale catalog for 1929/1930.

83. Interviews with Muriel Biemolt.

84. Interviews with Margaret Bryant Witt.

85. Interviews with Arlene R. Grewe.

86. Interviews with Julius Gardner.

87. Interviews with Paul Gardner.

88. Interviews with Ken Hoos.

89. Interviews with Bill Powell (correspondence)

90. Interviews with John Wright.

91. *Toys and Novelties* magazine, Feb. 1929, p. 132.

92. *Toys and Novelties* magazine, April 1930, p. 184.

93. *Toys and Novelties* magazine, March 1931, p. 103.

94. Review of toy advertisements from 1927 to 1931.

95. *Toys and Novelties* magazine, Feb. 1932, p. 32.

96. "Plant to Occupy Toy Tinkers' Factory," *Evanston Review*, Dec. 30, 1943.

97. *Playthings* magazine, April 1934, p. 68.

98. *Playthings* magazine, July 1934, p. 25.

99. *Toys and Novelties* magazine, June 1940, p. 66.

100. *Playthings* magazine, April 1939, p. 149.

101. *Playthings* magazine, April 1939, p. 171.

102. "Obituary — Henry Martin Svebilius," *Evanston News-Index*, Feb. 22, 1936.

103. "Charles Pajeau Hurt as Plane Crashes," *Evanston Review*, June 23, 1938.

104. "Flyer is Killed in North Shore Crash: One Hurt," *Chicago Tribune*, June 22, 1938.

105. "One Dead, One Hurt in Plane Crash," *Evanston Daily News Index*, June 22, 1938.

106. "Evanston Aviator Has 'Fair' Chance to Recover," *Evanston Daily News Index*, June 22, 1938.

107. "Condition of Pajeau, Plane Crash Victim, Is Reported 'Critical,'" *Evanston Daily News Index*, June 23, 1938.

108. "Injured Aviator Conscious Again," *Evanston Daily News Index*, June 27, 1938.

109. "Pajeau Reported On Recovery Road," *Evanston Daily News Index*, July 14, 1938.

110. "228-Acre Tract Sold in Big Glenview Deal," *Chicago Daily News*, Feb. 16, 1929.

111. Archives of the Glenview Historical Society.

112. "Tinkertoy Firm Sold to Spalding," *Evanston Review*, Dec. 1, 1952.

113. "Obituary — Robert Pettit," *Evanston Review*, July 15, 1943.

114. *Toys and Novelties* magazine, July 1944, p. 43.

115. *Toys and Novelties* magazine, March 1944, p. 229.

116. *Toys and Novelties* magazine, March 1945, p. 287.

117. *Toys and Novelties* magazine, March 1946, p. 83.

118. *Toys and Novelties* magazine, March 1947, p. 26.

119. *Toys and Novelties* magazine, March 1950, p. 61.

120. *Playthings* magazine, Jan. 1953, p. 151.

121. "The Toy That Won't Die," *Business Week*, 1964.

122. "Obituary — Charles H. Pajeau," *Chicago Tribune*, Dec. 19, 1952.

123. "Obituary — Charles H. Pajeau," *Evanston Review*, Dec. 25, 1952.

124. "Obituary — Charles H. Pajeau," *New York Times*, Dec. 19, 1952, p. 31, col. 5.

125. "Obituary — Joseph Pajeau," *Evanston News-Index*, July 13, 1920.

126. "Pajeau Sets Up Foundation For Children In Will," *Evanston Review*, March 5, 1953.

127. Coroner's Certificate of Death, State of Illinois, County of Cook for Charles Hamilton Pajeau, Died Dec. 17, 1952.

128. "Old Time Evanstonians Aid Toy Tinker Sale to Spalding," *Evanston Review*, Dec. 4, 1953.

129. "Spalding Men Take Over Toy Tinker," *Evanston Review*, Dec. 4, 1953.

130. "Toy Tinkers Will Remain in Evanston," *Evanston Review*, Feb. 2, 1953.

131. *Playthings* magazine, April 1967, p. 104.

132. Spalding Brothers 1959 Tinker Toy Products catalog.

133. *Playthings* magazine, Dec. 1967, p. 10.

134. *Playthings* magazine, June 1968, p. 65.

135. *Playthings* magazine, May 1967, p. 65.

136. *Playthings* magazine, July 1967, p. 53.

137. *Playthings* magazine, Sept. 1961, p. 14.

138. *Playthings* magazine, Aug. 1960, p. 37.

139. *Playthings* magazine, Aug. 1963, p. 85.

140. *Playthings* magazine, Sept. 1953, p. 26.

141. *Playthings* magazine, May 1964, p. 81.

142. *Playthings* magazine, Oct. 1966, p. 77.

143. *Playthings* magazine, Dec. 1960, p. 58.

144. *Toys and Novelties* magazine, Jan. 1959, p. 56.

145. *Playthings* magazine, Nov. 1960, p. 29.

146. *Playthings* magazine, Feb. 10, 1961, p. 26.

147. "Obituary — Grace Fuller Pajeau," *Evanston Review*, May 23, 1957.

148. "Obituary — Grace Pajeau Ross," *Chicago Tribune*, March 20, 1958.

149. "R. A. Smallwood is Promoted by Toy Tinkers Co.," *Evanston Review*, July 21, 1966.

150. "Collapse of 1310 Sherman Warehouse," with photo, *Evanston Review*, March 2, 1967.

151. "Evanston Toy Company Tinker Tools, Wins Two Awards for Packaging," *Evanston Review*, Sept. 7, 1967.

152. *Playthings* magazine, March 1962, p. 482.

153. *Toy Tinker Review* (company newsletter), Vol. 4, No. 2, June 1970.

154. *Playthings* magazine, Nov. 1971, p. 34.

155. *Playthings* magazine, Sept. 1974, p. 46.

156. *Playthings* magazine, March 1977, p. 37.

157. "Tinkertoy — Yes, Rust-Oleum — No," *Evanston Review*, Oct. 26, 1972.

158. Hasbro Inc., corporate history, including the history of Playskool Division of Hasbro Inc.

159. "Chicago as a Maker of Christmas Toys," *Fort Dearborn* magazine, Dec. 1920, p. 4 – 8.

160. "Tinker Toys for 1924," Toy Tinker Company Catalog for 1924, 42 pages.

161. Catalogs for the Toy Tinkers of Evanston, Illinois:
    Tinkertoys for 1924, 42 pages.
    Tinkertoys for 1926, 48 pages.
    1927 Tinker Toys, 50 pages.
    Tinker Toys 1928, 34 pages.
    Tinker Toys 1931, 30 pages
    Tinker Toys 1932, 26 pages.
    Tinker Toys 1935, 22 pages.
    Tinker Toys 1936, 20 pages.

Assorted undated flyers, brochures, advertisements, catalogs, and posters from Toy Tinkers.

162. Newspaper Advertisements:

Aurora Daily Beacon News, Aurora, Illinois
Nov. 26, 1915, Schickler & Miller
Dec. 1, 1916, Economy Store
Dec. 17, 1916, Schickler & Miller
Dec. 6, 1917, Cooper Bros.
Dec. 17, 1919, Economy Story
Dec. 9, 1920, Fagerholm's
Dec. 16, 1921, Leath's
Dec. 9, 1923, Fagerholm's
Dec. 3, 1924, Cooper Bros.

Chicago Tribune, Chicago, Illinois
Dec. 5, 1915, Mandel Bros.
Dec. 12, 1915, Erector Set
Dec. 3, 1916, Mandel Bros.
Dec. 1, 1918, Joy-Toy
Dec. 1, 1918, Boston Store
Dec. 14, 1919, Rothschild's Store

Evanston News-Index, Evanston, Illinois
Dec. 8, 1914, William S. Lord (*Daily News-Index*)
Dec. 8, 1914, Rosenberg's (*Daily News-Index*)
Dec. 21, 1914, Rosenberg's
Dec. 10, 1915, Rosenberg's
Dec. 14, 1915, Rosenberg's
Dec. 14, 1915, Lord's
Dec. 17, 1915, Rosenberg's
Dec. 20, 1915, Rosenberg's
Dec. 1, 1916, Lord's
Dec. 15, 1916, Rosenberg's
Dec. 18, 1916, Chandler's
Dec. 18, 1916, Rosenberg's
Dec. 20, 1916, Rosenberg's
Dec. 22, 1919, Thos. E. Connor Hardware
Dec. 8, 1920, Chandler's
Dec. 10, 1921, Rosenberg's
Dec. 20, 1921, Thos. E. Connor
Dec. 4, 1922, Lord's
Dec. 18, 1922, Rosenberg's
Dec. 7, 1923, Lord's
Dec. 7, 1923, Rosenberg's
Dec. 14, 1923, Rosenberg's
Dec. 17, 1923, Lord's
Dec. 12, 1924, Lord's
Dec. 4, 1925, Chandler's
Dec. 4, 1925, Rosenberg's
Dec. 11, 1925, Lord's
Dec. 15, 1925, Lord's
Dec. 16, 1925, Roseberg's
Dec. 18, 1925, Rosenberg's

Dec. 18, 1925, Chandler's
Dec. 21, 1925, Lord's
Nov. 27, 1926, Lord's
Dec. 3, 1926, Rosenberg's
Dec. 10, 1926, Rosenberg's
Dec. 5, 1927, Lord's
Dec. 12, 1927, Rosenberg's
Dec. 6, 1928, Lord's
Dec. 7, 1928, Loren Miller & Co.
Dec. 18, 1929, Lord's
Dec. 20, 1929, Royal Dry Goods Co.
Dec. 23, 1929, Rosenberg's-Wiebolts
Dec. 1, 1930, Marshall Fields & Co.
Dec. 9, 1930, Lord's
Dec. 22, 1930, Marshall Fields & Co.
Dec. 15, 1931, Lord's
Dec. 22, 1931, Lord's
Dec. 23, 1931, Lord's
Dec. 7, 1932, Lord's
Dec. 14, 1932, Lord's
Dec. 6, 1933, Lord's
Dec. 8, 1933, Lord's
Nov. 30, 1934, Chandler's
Dec. 5, 1934, Article: "Christmas Toys Are More Educational Tour Shows," by Mary Kay Reif.
Dec. 7, 1934, Lord's
Dec. 14, 1934, Marshall Fields & Co.
Nov. 29, 1935, Chandler's
Nov. 29, 1935, Lord's

The Evanston Review, Evanston, Illinois
Dec. 17, 1925, Chandler's
Dec. 16, 1926, Chandler's
Dec. 13, 1928, Chandler's
Dec. 29, 1928, Lord's
Nov. 13, 1930, Chandler's

Highland Park Press, Highland Park, Illinois
Dec. 2, 1915, Chas. H. Waren & Co.
Dec. 9, 1915, Chas. H. Warren & Co.

Racine Journal News, Racine, Wisconsin
Dec. 12, 1921, Mohr-Jones
Dec. 12, 1922, Folwell's
Dec. 1, 1922, Mohr-Jones
Dec. 5, 1922, Mohr-Jones
Dec. 13, 1923, Mohr-Jones
Dec. 18, 1923, Mohr-Jones
Dec. 12, 1924, Mohr-Jones
Dec. 17, 1924, Mohr-Jones
Dec. 22, 1924, Mohr-Jones
Dec. 8, 1925, Mohr-Jones
Dec. 11, 1925, Mohr-Jones
Dec. 17, 1926, Folwell's

Dec. 3, 1926, Boston Store
Dec. 10, 1926, Mohr-Jones
Nov. 25, 1927, J.C. Penney Co.
Dec. 16, 1927, Zahn's Downstairs Store
Nov. 29, 1929, Folwell's
Dec. 11, 1929, Zahn's
Dec. 5, 1930, Sears
Dec. 10, 1930, Racine Dry Goods
Dec. 19, 1930, Racine Dry Goods

Racine Journal-Times, Racine, Wisconsin
Dec. 4, 1932, Folwell's
Dec. 1, 1933, Racine Dry Goods Co.
Dec. 3, 1933, Folwell's
Dec. 6, 1933, Racine Dry Goods Co.
Dec. 8, 1933, Racine Dry Goods Co.
Dec. 10, 1933, Racine Dry Goods Co.
Dec 13, 1933, Racine Dry Goods Co.
Dec. 14, 1933, Mohr-Jones
Dec. 18, 1933, Mohr-Jones
Dec. 5, 1934, Mohr-Jones
Dec. 13, 1934, Mohr-Jones
Dec. 12, 1935, Mohr-Jones
Nov. 27, 1936, Racine Dry Goods
Dec. 15, 1937, Zahn's
Dec. 11, 1938, Racine Dry Goods Co.
Dec. 11, 1938, Badger Paint & Hardware Co.
Dec. 17, 1938, Badger Paint & Hardware Co.

Rockford Morning Star, Rockford, Illinois
Dec. 3, 1915, Gust. E. Ekeberg Dry Goods
Dec. 12, 1915, Allen's
Dec. 19, 1915, A. W. Wheelock
Dec. 3, 1916, Hess Bros. & Co.
Dec. 10, 1916, Allen's
Dec. 10, 1916, Ashton's
Dec. 9, 1917, Allen's
Dec. 9, 1917, Ashton Dry Goods
Dec. 15, 1917, Ashton Dry Goods
Dec. 15, 1918, Allen's
Nov. 27, 1919, Hess Bros.
Nov. 30, 1919, Allen's
Dec. 12, 1920, Allen's Crockery Store
Dec. 11, 1921, Allen's Crockery Store
Dec. 18, 1921, Allen's
Dec. 3, 1922, Allen's Crockery Store
Dec. 10, 1922, Gust. E. Ekeberg
Dec. 2, 1923, William's Sport Shop
Dec. 8, 1923, Allen's Crockery
Dec. 9, 1923, William's Sport Shop
Dec. 14, 1923, Hess Bros.
Dec. 21, 1924, Allen's Crockery Store
Dec. 3, 1925, Ekeberg's
Nov. 29, 1925, Allen's Crockery

Dec. 4, 1925, Hess Bros.
Dec. 20, 1925, Allen's Crockery
Nov. 28, 1926, Allen's Crockery
Dec. 19, 1926, Allen's Crockery

Sheboygan Press, Sheboygan, Wisconsin
Dec. 7, 1920, Prange-Geussenhainer Co.
Dec. 7, 1923, Jung Co.
Dec. 5, 1923, Prange Co.
Dec. 2, 1924, Prange Co.
Dec. 4, 1924, Sell Bros.
Dec. 15, 1924, Sell Bros.
Dec. 3, 1925, Prange Co.
Dec. 12, 1925, Jung Co.
Nov. 25, 1925, Sell Bros.
Dec. 27, 1925, J.C. Penney
Dec. 8, 1928, Prange Co.
Dec. 11, 1928, Sheboygan Dry Goods
Dec. 18, 1928, Sell Bros.
Nov. 19, 1929, Prange Co.
Nov. 19, 1929, Sell Bros.
Nov. 19, 1929, Ward's
Nov. 26, 1929, Sheboygan Dry Goods Co.
Nov. 30, 1929, Sheboygan Dry Goods Co.
Dec. 4, 1929, Sheboygan Dry Goods Co.
Dec. 6, 1929, Sheboygan Dry Goods Co.
Dec. 7, 1929, F. Gelle Hardware Co.
Dec. 7, 1929, Prange Co.
Dec. 12, 1929, Sell Bros.
Dec. 19, 1929, Sheboygan Dry Goods Co.
Dec. 4, 1930, Trilling Hardware Co.
Dec. 9, 1930, Sheboygan Dry Goods Co.
Dec. 13, 1930, Sheboygan Dry Goods Co.
Dec. 18, 1930, Trilling Hardware
Dec. 21, 1931, Sheboygan Dry Goods Co.

Waukegan Daily Gazette, Waukegan, Illinois
Dec. 15, 1916, Rubin's
Dec. 21, 1916, The Globe Department Store
Dec. 11, 1917, The Globe Department Store
Dec. 14, 1917, Rubin's
Dec. 21, 1917, Rubin's
Dec. 21, 1917, The Globe Department Store
Dec. 13, 1918, The Globe Department Store
Dec. 16, 1918, The Globe Department Store

Waukegan Daily News, Waukegan, Illinois
Dec. 6, 1922, The Globe Department Store
Dec. 8, 1922, The Globe Department Store
Dec. 5, 1923, The Globe Department Store
Dec. 4, 1925, The Globe Department Store
Nov. 25, 1927, The Globe Department Store
Nov. 30, 1928, Rubin's
Nov. 30, 1928, The Globe Department Store

Dec. 12, 1928, The Globe Department Store
Nov. 29, 1929, Waukegan Dry Goods Co.
Dec. 18, 1929, Waukegan Dry Goods Co.

The Daily Sun, Waukegan, Illinois
Dec. 8, 1916, The Globe Department Store
Dec. 15, 1916, Rubin's
Dec. 7, 1917, The Globe Department Store
Dec. 13, 1918, The Globe Department Store
Dec. 16, 1918, The Globe Department Store
Dec. 12, 1919, Bon Ton Department Store
Dec. 3, 1920, Bon Ton Department Store
Dec. 2, 1921, The Globe Department Store
Dec. 14, 1923, Rubin's
Nov. 28, 1924, The Globe Department Store
Nov. 26, 1926, Rubin's
Nov. 26, 1926, The Globe Department Store
Dec. 10, 1926, Landover Stores
Nov. 29, 1929, Waukegan Dry Goods Co.
Dec. 6, 1929, The Globe Department Store

The Waukegan News Sun, Waukegan, Illinois
Dec. 9, 1930, Mother Goose Shop
Dec. 12, 1930, The Globe Department Store
Dec. 17, 1930, Rubin's
Dec. 19, 1930, The Globe Department Store
Dec. 4, 1931, The Globe Department Store
Dec. 9, 1932, The Globe Department Store
Nov. 29, 1935, Rubin's

Dec. 6, 1935, The Globe Department Store
Dec. 4, 1936, Rubin's
Dec. 4, 1936, The Globe Department Store
Dec. 22, 1936, Rubin's
Nov. 26, 1937, The Globe Department Store
Dec. 2, 1937, Photo Ward's Toy Town
Dec. 3, 1937, Grank Burke Hardware
Dec. 2, 1938, Rubin's
Dec. 5, 1939, The Globe Department Store

Wilmette Life Newspaper, Wilmette, Illinois
Nov. 29, 1934, Chandler's

163. Magazine Advertisements:
Boys Life, 1929, p. 78.
Childhood Education, Dec. 1931, pp. 184 – 185.
Child Life, Dec. 1923, p. 177.
Child Life, Oct. 1926, p. 648.
Junior Home Magazine, Dec. 1926.
Junior Home Magazine, Dec. 1928, inside front cover.
Parents, Nov. 1929.
Parents, Dec. 1929, p. 86.
Parents, Nov. 1931, p. 24.
Saturday Evening Post, Winter 1971.
Woman's World, April 1916.

164. *Playthings* magazine, July 1937, p. 19.

165. *Toys and Novelties* magazine, March 1947, p. 26.

Other Sources of Information

Magazine and Newspaper Articles

Atlanta Journal-Constitution, Atlanta, Georgia; Fall 1992, "Companies Are Continuing to Tinker with Classic Toys."

Current Opinion, June 1919, Vol. 66; "Uncle Sam is Now the Second Biggest Toy Maker in the World," pp. 401 – 402.

Evanston News-Index, Evanston, Illinois; June 23, 1927, "Night High School Winning Favor Among Young People Here."

Evanston Review, Evanston, Illinois; April 16, 1953, "Toys Win Award."

Evanston Review, Evanston, Illinois; July 4, 1963, "Evanston Made Wares Spread Name of City."

Evanston Review, Evanston, Illinois; Oct. 20, 1966, "Article Features Tinkertoy Contest Award Program."

Evanston Review, Evanston, Illinois; Aug. 28, 1969, Photo: Robert A. Christofferson, Vice President Spiro Agnew, and Becky Wright.

Evanston Review, Evanston, Illinois; July 16, 1970, "A Tinkertoy Bird Wins Her An Award."

Evanston Review, Evanston, Illinois; Dec. 23, 1971, "Santa Makes Visit to Tinkertoy Factory."

Evanston Review, Evanston, Illinois; Dec. 16, 1982, "Tinkertoy."

The House Beautiful, Dec. 1915, Vol. 39; "Unusual American Toys," by R. Bergengren, pp. 17 – 19+.

Illustrated World, Dec. 2, 1921, Vol. 36; "Uncle Sam — The World's Greatest Toy Maker," by Frederick Grinde, pp. 520 – 522.

Industrial Management, April 1922, Vol. 63; "The Application of Production Methods to Toy Manufacture," by Nicholas Heyman, pp. 246 – 250.

Industrial Management, October 1923, Vol. 66; "Charges & Costs in Toy Manufacture," by Arthur Lazarus, pp. 243 – 246.

Literary Digest, May 2, 1936, Vol. 121; "Toy Wonderland," p. 42.

Literary Digest, April 17, 1937, Vol. 123; "Seven Acres of Toys," p. 38.

New York Times, New York, New York; Nov. 16, 1914, "Toy Factories Rushed."

New York Times, New York, New York; Dec. 22, 1914, "Toy Makers Hurt By War."

Pictorial Review, Dec. 1929, Vol. 31; "The Best of Toys," by Dr. Emelyn L. Coolidge, p. 48.

Scientific American, October 1989; "Computer Recreations — A Tinkertoy Computer that Plays Tic-Tac-Toe," by A.K. Dewdney.

The Chicago Tribune Magazine, Chicago, Illinois; Dec. 8, 1963, "A Successful Idea Grinds On And . . ."

The Chicago Tribune Magazine (suburban north), Chicago, Illinois; Jan. 12, 1983, "Exhibit Puts Together Pieces of Tinkertoy Past."

The Chicago Sun-Times, Chicago, Illinois; Jan. 20, 1983, "Tinkering with Toy Idea Paid Off."

Special Toy Show Reprint of These Articles

Industrial Woodworking, 1964, "Birchwood Bits are Big Business."

Kodakery (company newsletter), 1964, Eastman Kodak Co., Rochester, New York; "Tinkertoy of Tenite, Too."

Playthings, March 1964, "Tinkertoy Celebrating Its 50th Anniversary."

Toys and Hobby World, Feb. 17, 1964, "New Faces For 50-Year-Old Tinkertoys."

Toys and Novelties, April 1964, "Tinkertoy Is 50, But It Won't Grow Old."

Toys and Novelties, June 15, 1964, "Tinkertoy."

Obituaries

Evanston Review, Evanston, Illinois; Sept. 7, 1978, Arnold Svebilius.

The Chicago Tribune, Chicago, Illinois; July 13, 1920, Joseph Pajeau.

Index of Patents

April 7, 1914; 1,092,591 — Mechanical Construction Blocks
Oct. 13, 1914; 1,113,371 — Construction Blocks
June 20, 1916; 1,187,923 — Tinker Pins (old)
Sept. 12, 1916; 1,198,263 — Construction Blocks
July 31, 1917; 1,235,050 — Tilly Tinker
Sept. 25, 1917; 1,241,009 — Tinker Blox
Oct. 21, 1919; 1,319,432 — Screw Top Container
Dec. 23, 1919; 1,325,651 — Tom Tinker
March 9, 1920; 1,333,216 — Follo-Me-Tinker
Feb. 21, 1922; 1,407,165 — Bag Doll Tinker
May 22, 1923; Des62,409 — Tom Tinker
Sept. 23, 1924; Des65,667 — Tinker Cane
Oct. 21, 1924; Des65,826 — Choo-Choo Tinker
Nov. 11, 1924; Des65,974 — Dragon Tinker
Dec. 30, 1924; 1,521,573 — Dragon Tinker
Jan. 13, 1925; Des66,433 — Surf Boat Tinker
March 17, 1925; Des66,808 — Pony Tinker

July 14, 1925; 1,545,971 — Marathon Tinker
April 6, 1926; 1,579,884 — Seven-In-One-Tinker
March 1, 1927; 1,619,630 — Spinning Jack Tinker
April 19, 1927; 1,625,676 — Tinker Pins (new)
April 19, 1927; Des72,497 — Bunny Tinker
May 31, 1927; Des72,778 — Dogs Tinker
June 28, 1927; Des72,964 — Spinning Jack Tinker
Nov. 13, 1928; 1,691,123 — Necktie Rack
June 17, 1930; 1,763,815 — Flashlight
Nov. 25, 1930; 1,782,792 — Rotary Blotter
June 27, 1933; 1,915,835 — Construction Blocks
June 27, 1933; 1,915,840 — Toy Motor Support
July 4, 1933; 1,916,634 — Construction Blocks
July 25, 1933; 1,920,021 — End Expander for Toy Rods
Dec. 5, 1933; 1,937,911 — Collapsible Necktie Holder
July 16, 1940; 2,208,049 — Construction Blocks
March 9, 1943; 2,313,357 — Construction Blocks

Permits and Inspection Reports

Feb. 3, 1926: Building permit, Toy Tinkers, for construction at 2012 Ridge, Evanston, Illinois.

Feb. 24, 1926: Building Permit, Toy Tinkers, for construction at 2012 Ridge, Evanston, Illinois.

March 1, 1933: Inspection Report for 1948 Ridge, Evanston, Illinois.

March 2, 1933: Letter from building commissioner regarding 1948 Ridge, Evanston, Illinois

Will

Last will and testament of Charles H. Pajeau, dated Dec. 16, 1952. Prepared by Eckert, Peterson & Leeming.

Brochure

"Tinker Town Tom" promotional brochure for the book, printed by Rand McNally & Co., Oct. 1924; 536 Clark, Chicago, Illinois.

Catalogs

Butler Bros. Co., Chicago, Minneapolis, New York.
Holiday 1915, p. 237
Holiday 1920, p. 203
March 1920, p. 269
Winter 1920, p. 66
Early 1920s, p. 44
1942, p. 328

Carson Pirie Scott Co., Chicago
1952, p. 24H, p. 34
1953, p. 8, p. 26K
1957, p. 15, p. 20
1958, p. 13, p. 16
1959, p. 15

Sears, Roebuck & Co., Chicago
1920, Fall
1920
1921
1922, Spring
1923, Spring
1923, Fall

1924, Spring
1924 – 1925, Fall/Winter
1926 – 1927, Fall/Winter
1927, Spring
1927 – 1928, Fall/Winter
1928 – 1929, Fall/Winter
1930 – 1931, Fall/Winter
1931 – 1932, Fall/Winter
1932 – 1933, Fall/Winter
1933 – 1934, Fall/Winter
1935 – 1936, Fall/Winter
1936 – 1937, Fall/Winter
1937
1937 – 1938, Fall/Winter
1939
1939 – 1940, Fall/Winter

Shure Winner Catalog, N. Shure Co., Chicago
1933, p. 792
1937, p. 987
1942 – 1943, p. 631

Directories

Elite Blue Book, Chicago
1884 – 1885
1885 – 1886
1886 – 1887
1887 – 1888

Evanston, Illinois Telephone Directory

1928	1936	1944	1953	1962 – 1963	1971
1929	1937	1945	1954	1963 – 1964	1972
1930	1938	1946	1955	1964 – 1965	1973
1931	1939	1947	1956	1965 – 1966	1974
1932	1940	1948	1957	1967	1975
1933	1941	1949	1958	1968	1976
1934	1942	1950	1959	1969	1977
1935	1943	1952	1961 – 1962	1970	1978

Government Agencies

Federal Aviation Administration • The National Transportation Safety Board • Smithsonian Institution, Washington, D.C.

About the Author

Craig Strange was born in Chicago, Illinois, in 1955, and received two degrees from the University of Illinois in 1978. He has run his own business involving property development since graduation. Mr. Strange's past includes a stint as a stand-up comedian and co-founder of the Chicago Comedy College in the mid-1970s at the Kingston Mines Club in Chicago. In 1987 he opened the Chicago Hysterical Society with a partner, offering improvisational comedy.

Mr. Strange has been an avid collector for many years. He served as a board member for the 20-30-40 Society, a club dedicated to the preservation of information about glassware made in the early part of this century. He collects several categories of items ranging from decorated tumblers made from the 1920s to 1960s to hundreds of Tinker Toy Items.

Mr. Strange is recognized by the Evanston Historical Society and by collectors of Tinker Toys as an expert on the subject. Mr. Strange's articles about Tinker Toys have been printed in national collector publications.

Mr. Strange can be contacted at P.O. Box 306, Northbrook, IL 60065-0306. Please enclose a self-addressed stamped envelope if you wish a reply.

COLLECTOR BOOKS
Informing Today's Collector

BOOKS ON COLLECTIBLES

This is only a partial listing of the books on antiques that are available from Collector Books. All books are well illustrated and contain current values. Most of the following books are available from your local bookseller, antique dealer, or public library. If you are unable to locate certain titles in your area, you may order by mail from COLLECTOR BOOKS, P.O. Box 3009, Paducah, KY 42002-3009. Customers with Visa or MasterCard may phone in orders from 7:00–4:00 CST, Monday–Friday, Toll Free 1-800-626-5420. Add $2.00 for postage for the first book ordered and $0.30 for each additional book. Include item number, title, and price when ordering. Allow 14 to 21 days for delivery.

DOLLS, FIGURES & TEDDY BEARS

2382	**Advertising Dolls**, Identification & Values, Robison & Sellers	$9.95
2079	**Barbie** Doll Fashions, Volume I, Eames	$24.95
3957	**Barbie** Exclusives, Rana	$18.95
4557	**Barbie**, The First 30 Years, Deutsch	$24.95
3310	**Black Dolls**, 1820–1991, Perkins	$17.95
3873	**Black Dolls**, Book II, Perkins	$17.95
3810	**Chatty Cathy** Dolls, Lewis	$15.95
2021	Collectible **Action Figures**, 2nd Ed., Manos	$14.95
1529	Collector's Encyclopedia of **Barbie** Dolls, DeWein	$19.95
4506	Collector's Guide to **Dolls in Uniform**, Bourgeois	$18.95
3727	Collector's Guide to **Ideal Dolls**, Izen	$18.95
3728	Collector's Guide to Miniature **Teddy Bears**, Powell	$17.95
3967	Collector's Guide to **Trolls**, Peterson	$19.95
4569	**Howdy Doody**, Collector's Reference and Trivia Guide, Koch	$16.95
1067	**Madame Alexander** Dolls, Smith	$19.95
3971	**Madame Alexander** Dolls Price Guide #20, Smith	$9.95
3733	**Modern Collector's** Dolls, Sixth Series, Smith	$24.95
3991	**Modern Collector's** Dolls, Seventh Series, Smith	$24.95
4571	**Liddle Kiddles**, Identification & Value Guide, Langford	$18.95
3972	Patricia Smith's **Doll Values**, Antique to Modern, 11th Edition	$12.95
3826	Story of **Barbie**, Westenhouser	$19.95
1513	**Teddy Bears & Steiff** Animals, Mandel	$9.95
1817	**Teddy Bears & Steiff** Animals, 2nd Series, Mandel	$19.95
2084	**Teddy Bears, Annalee's & Steiff** Animals, 3rd Series, Mandel	$19.95
1808	Wonder of **Barbie**, Manos	$9.95
1430	World of **Barbie** Dolls, Manos	$9.95

FURNITURE

1457	American **Oak** Furniture, McNerney	$9.95
3716	American **Oak** Furniture, Book II, McNerney	$12.95
1118	Antique **Oak** Furniture, Hill	$7.95
2132	Collector's Encyclopedia of **American** Furniture, Vol. I, Swedberg	$24.95
2271	Collector's Encyclopedia of **American** Furniture, Vol. II, Swedberg	$24.95
3720	Collector's Encyclopedia of **American** Furniture, Vol. III, Swedberg	$24.95
1437	Collector's Guide to **Country** Furniture, Raycraft	$9.95
3878	Collector's Guide to **Oak** Furniture, George	$12.95
1755	Furniture of the **Depression Era**, Swedberg	$19.95
3906	**Heywood-Wakefield** Modern Furniture, Rouland	$18.95
1965	**Pine** Furniture, Our American Heritage, McNerney	$14.95
1885	**Victorian** Furniture, Our American Heritage, McNerney	$9.95
3829	**Victorian** Furniture, Our American Heritage, Book II, McNerney	$9.95
3869	**Victorian** Furniture books, 2 volume set, McNerney	$19.90

JEWELRY, HATPINS, WATCHES & PURSES

1712	Antique & Collector's **Thimbles** & Accessories, Mathis	$19.95
1748	Antique **Purses**, Revised Second Ed., Holiner	$19.95
1278	Art Nouveau & Art Deco **Jewelry**, Baker	$9.95
4558	Christmas Pins, Past and Present, Gallina	$18.95
3875	Collecting Antique **Stickpins**, Kerins	$16.95
3722	Collector's Ency. of **Compacts, Carryalls & Face Powder Boxes**, Mueller	$24.95
3992	Complete Price Guide to **Watches**, #15, Shugart	$21.95
1716	Fifty Years of Collectible **Fashion Jewelry**, 1925-1975, Baker	$19.95
1424	**Hatpins** & Hatpin Holders, Baker	$9.95
4570	Ladies' **Compacts**, Gerson	$24.95
1181	100 Years of Collectible **Jewelry**, 1850-1950, Baker	$9.95
2348	20th Century Fashionable Plastic **Jewelry**, Baker	$19.95
3830	Vintage **Vanity Bags & Purses**, Gerson	$24.95

TOYS, MARBLES & CHRISTMAS COLLECTIBLES

3427	**Advertising Character** Collectibles, Dotz	$17.95
2333	Antique & Collector's **Marbles**, 3rd Ed., Grist	$9.95
3827	Antique & Collector's **Toys**, 1870–1950, Longest	$24.95
3956	Baby Boomer **Games**, Identification & Value Guide, Polizzi	$24.95

3717	**Christmas** Collectibles, 2nd Edition, Whitmyer	$24.95
1752	**Christmas** Ornaments, Lights & Decorations, Johnson	$19.95
3874	Collectible Coca-Cola Toy **Trucks**, deCourtivron	$24.95
2338	Collector's Encyclopedia of **Disneyana**, Longest, Stern	$24.95
2151	Collector's Guide to **Tootsietoys**, 2nd Ed., Richter	$16.95
3436	Grist's Big Book of **Marbles**	$19.95
3970	Grist's Machine-Made & Contemporary **Marbles**, 2nd Ed.	$9.95
3732	**Matchbox®** Toys, 1948 to 1993, Johnson	$18.95
3823	**Mego** Toys, An Illustrated Value Guide, Chrouch	15.95
1540	**Modern Toys** 1930–1980, Baker	$19.95
3888	**Motorcycle** Toys, Antique & Contemporary, Gentry/Downs	$18.95
3891	Schroeder's Collectible **Toys**, Antique to Modern Price Guide, 2nd Ed.	$17.95
1886	Stern's Guide to **Disney** Collectibles	$14.95
2139	Stern's Guide to **Disney** Collectibles, 2nd Series	$14.95
3975	Stern's Guide to **Disney** Collectibles, 3rd Series	$18.95
2028	**Toys**, Antique & Collectible, Longest	$14.95
3975	**Zany Characters** of the Ad World, Lamphier	$16.95

INDIANS, GUNS, KNIVES, TOOLS, PRIMITIVES

1868	Antique **Tools**, Our American Heritage, McNerney	$9.95
2015	Archaic **Indian** Points & Knives, Edler	$14.95
1426	**Arrowheads** & Projectile Points, Hothem	$7.95
2279	**Indian** Artifacts of the Midwest, Hothem	$14.95
3885	**Indian** Artifacts of the Midwest, Book II, Hothem	$16.95
1964	**Indian** Axes & Related Stone Artifacts, Hothem	$14.95
2023	**Keen Kutter** Collectibles, Heuring	$14.95
3887	Modern **Guns**, Identification & Values, 10th Ed., Quertermous	$12.95
4505	Standard Guide to **Razors**, Ritchie & Stewart	$9.95
3325	Standard **Knife** Collector's Guide, 2nd Ed., Ritchie & Stewart	$12.95

PAPER COLLECTIBLES & BOOKS

1441	Collector's Guide to **Post Cards**, Wood	$9.95
2081	Guide to Collecting **Cookbooks**, Allen	$14.95
3969	Huxford's **Old Book** Value Guide, 7th Ed.	$19.95
3821	Huxford's **Paperback** Value Guide	$19.95
2080	Price Guide to **Cookbooks & Recipe Leaflets**, Dickinson	$9.95
2346	**Sheet Music** Reference & Price Guide, 2nd Ed., Pafik & Guiheen	$18.95

GLASSWARE

1006	**Cambridge Glass** Reprint 1930–1934	$14.95
1007	**Cambridge Glass** Reprint 1949–1953	$14.95
2310	**Children's Glass Dishes, China & Furniture**, Vol. I, Lechler	$19.95
1627	**Children's Glass Dishes, China & Furniture**, Vol. II, Lechler	$19.95
4561	Collectible **Drinking Glasses**, Chase & Kelly	$17.95
3719	Coll. **Glassware** from the 40's, 50's & 60's, 3rd Ed., Florence	$19.95
2352	Collector's Encyclopedia of **Akro Agate Glassware**, Florence	$14.95
1810	Collector's Encyclopedia of **American Art Glass**, Shuman	$29.95
3312	Collector's Encyclopedia of **Children's Dishes**, Whitmyer	$19.95
3724	Collector's Encyclopedia of **Depression Glass**, 12th Ed., Florence	$19.95
1664	Collector's Encyclopedia of **Heisey Glass**, 1925–1938, Bredehoft	$24.95
3905	Collector's Encyclopedia of **Milk Glass**, Newbound	$24.95
1523	Colors In **Cambridge Glass**, National Cambridge Soceity	$19.95
4564	**Crackle Glass**, Weitman	$18.95
2275	**Czechoslovakian Glass** and Collectibles, Barta	$16.95
3882	**Elegant Glassware** of the Depression Era, 6th Ed., Florence	$19.95
1380	Encyclopedia of **Pattern Glass**, McClain	$12.95
3981	Ever's Standard **Cut Glass** Value Guide	$12.95
3725	**Fostoria**, Pressed, Blown & Hand Molded Shapes, Kerr	$24.95
3883	**Fostoria Stemware**, The Crystal for America, Long & Seate	$24.95
3318	**Glass Animals** of the Depression Era, Garmon & Spencer	$19.95
3886	**Kitchen Glassware** of the Depression Years, 5th Ed., Florence	$19.95
2394	**Oil Lamps II**, Glass Kerosene Lamps, Thuro	$24.95
3889	Pocket Guide to **Depression Glass**, 9th Ed., Florence	$9.95
3739	Standard Encyclopedia of **Carnival Glass**, 4th Ed., Edwards	$24.95

3740	Standard **Carnival Glass** Price Guide, 9th Ed.	$9.95
3974	Standard Encyclopedia of **Opalescent Glass**, Edwards	$19.95
1848	**Very Rare Glassware** of the Depression Years, Florence	$24.95
2140	**Very Rare Glassware** of the Depression Years, 2nd Series, Florence	$24.95
3326	**Very Rare Glassware** of the Depression Years, 3rd Series, Florence	$24.95
3909	**Very Rare Glassware** of the Depression Years, 4th Series, Florence	$24.95
2224	World of **Salt Shakers**, 2nd Ed., Lechner	$24.95

POTTERY

1312	**Blue & White Stoneware**, McNerney	$9.95
1958	So. Potteries **Blue Ridge Dinnerware**, 3rd Ed., Newbound	$14.95
1959	**Blue Willow**, 2nd Ed., Gaston	$14.95
3816	Collectible **Vernon Kilns**, Nelson	$24.95
3311	Collecting **Yellow Ware** – Id. & Value Guide, McAllister	$16.95
1373	Collector's Encyclopedia of **American Dinnerware**, Cunningham	$24.95
3815	Collector's Encyclopedia of **Blue Ridge Dinnerware**, Newbound	$19.95
2272	Collector's Encyclopedia of **California Pottery**, Chipman	$24.95
3811	Collector's Encyclopedia of **Colorado Pottery**, Carlton	$24.95
2133	Collector's Encyclopedia of **Cookie Jars**, Roerig	$24.95
3723	Collector's Encyclopedia of **Cookie Jars**, Volume II, Roerig	$24.95
3429	Collector's Encyclopedia of **Cowan Pottery**, Saloff	$24.95
2209	Collector's Encyclopedia of **Fiesta**, 7th Ed., Huxford	$19.95
3961	Collector's Encyclopedia of **Early Noritake**, Alden	$24.95
1439	Collector's Encyclopedia of **Flow Blue China**, Gaston	$19.95
3812	Collector's Encyclopedia of **Flow Blue China**, 2nd Ed., Gaston	$24.95
3813	Collector's Encyclopedia of **Hall China**, 2nd Ed., Whitmyer	$24.95
3431	Collector's Encyclopedia of **Homer Laughlin China**, Jasper	$24.95
1276	Collector's Encyclopedia of **Hull Pottery**, Roberts	$19.95
4573	Collector's Encyclopedia of **Knowles, Taylor & Knowles**, Gaston	$24.95
3962	Collector's Encyclopedia of **Lefton China**, DeLozier	$19.95
2210	Collector's Encyclopedia of **Limoges Porcelain**, 2nd Ed., Gaston	$24.95
2334	Collector's Encyclopedia of **Majolica Pottery**, Katz-Marks	$19.95
1358	Collector's Encyclopedia of **McCoy Pottery**, Huxford	$19.95
3963	Collector's Encyclopedia of **Metlox Potteries**, Gibbs Jr.	$24.95
3313	Collector's Encyclopedia of **Niloak**, Gifford	$19.95
3837	Collector's Encyclopedia of **Nippon Porcelain I**, Van Patten	$24.95
2089	Collector's Ency. of **Nippon Porcelain**, 2nd Series, Van Patten	$24.95
1665	Collector's Ency. of **Nippon Porcelain**, 3rd Series, Van Patten	$24.95
3836	**Nippon Porcelain** Price Guide, Van Patten	$9.95
1447	Collector's Encyclopedia of **Noritake**, Van Patten	$19.95
3432	Collector's Encyclopedia of **Noritake**, 2nd Series, Van Patten	$24.95
1037	Collector's Encyclopedia of **Occupied Japan**, Vol. I, Florence	$14.95
1038	Collector's Encyclopedia of **Occupied Japan**, Vol. II, Florence	$14.95
2088	Collector's Encyclopedia of **Occupied Japan**, Vol. III, Florence	$14.95
2019	Collector's Encyclopedia of **Occupied Japan**, Vol. IV, Florence	$14.95
2335	Collector's Encyclopedia of **Occupied Japan**, Vol. V, Florence	$14.95
3964	Collector's Encyclopedia of **Pickard China**, Reed	$24.95
1311	Collector's Encyclopedia of **R.S. Prussia**, 1st Series, Gaston	$24.95
1715	Collector's Encyclopedia of **R.S. Prussia**, 2nd Series, Gaston	$24.95
3726	Collector's Encyclopedia of **R.S. Prussia**, 3rd Series, Gaston	$24.95
3877	Collector's Encyclopedia of **R.S. Prussia**, 4th Series, Gaston	$24.95
1034	Collector's Encyclopedia of **Roseville Pottery**, Huxford	$19.95
1035	Collector's Encyclopedia of **Roseville Pottery**, 2nd Ed., Huxford	$19.95
3357	**Roseville** Price Guide No. 10	$9.95
2083	Collector's Encyclopedia of **Russel Wright** Designs, Kerr	$19.95
3965	Collector's Encyclopedia of **Sascha Brastoff**, Conti, Bethany & Seay	$24.95
3314	Collector's Encyclopedia of **Van Briggle** Art Pottery, Sasicki	$24.95
2111	Collector's Encyclopedia of **Weller Pottery**, Huxford	$29.95
3452	Coll. Guide to Country Stoneware & Pottery, Raycraft	$11.95
2077	Coll. Guide to **Country Stoneware & Pottery**, 2nd Series, Raycraft	$14.95
3433	Collector's Guide To **Harker Pottery** - U.S.A., Colbert	$17.95
3434	Coll. Guide to **Hull Pottery**, The Dinnerware Line, Gick-Burke	$16.95

3876	Collector's Guide to **Lu-Ray Pastels**, Meehan	$18.95
3814	Collector's Guide to **Made in Japan** Ceramics, White	$18.95
4565	Collector's Guide to **Rockingham**, The Enduring Ware, Brewer	$14.95
2339	Collector's Guide to **Shawnee Pottery**, Vanderbilt	$19.95
1425	**Cookie Jars**, Westfall	$9.95
3440	**Cookie Jars**, Book II, Westfall	$19.95
3435	Debolt's Dictionary of **American Pottery Marks**	$17.95
2379	Lehner's Ency. of **U.S. Marks** on Pottery, Porcelain & China	$24.95
3825	**Puritan Pottery**, Morris	$24.95
1670	**Red Wing Collectibles**, DePasquale	$9.95
1440	**Red Wing Stoneware**, DePasquale	$9.95
3738	**Shawnee Pottery**, Mangus	$24.95
3327	**Watt Pottery** – Identification & Value Guide, Morris	$19.95

OTHER COLLECTIBLES

2269	Antique **Brass & Copper** Collectibles, Gaston	$16.95
1880	Antique **Iron**, McNerney	$9.95
3872	Antique **Tins**, Dodge	$24.95
1714	**Black** Collectibles, Gibbs	$19.95
1128	**Bottle** Pricing Guide, 3rd Ed., Cleveland	$7.95
3959	**Cereal Box** Bonanza, The 1950's, Bruce	$19.95
3718	Collectible **Aluminum**, Grist	$16.95
3445	Collectible **Cats**, An Identification & Value Guide, Fyke	$18.95
4560	Collectible **Cats**, An Identification & Value Guide, Book II, Fyke	$19.95
4563	Collector's Encyclopedia of **Wall Pockets**, Newbound	$19.95
1634	Collector's Ency. of Figural & Novelty **Salt & Pepper Shakers**, Davern	$19.95
2020	Collector's Ency. of Figural & Novelty **Salt & Pepper Shakers**, Vol. II, Davern	$19.95
2018	Collector's Encyclopedia of **Granite Ware**, Greguire	$24.95
3430	Collector's Encyclopedia of **Granite Ware**, Book II, Greguire	$24.95
3879	Collector's Guide to **Antique Radios**, 3rd Ed., Bunis	$18.95
1916	Collector's Guide to **Art Deco**, Gaston	$14.95
3880	Collector's Guide to **Cigarette Lighters**, Flanagan	$17.95
1537	Collector's Guide to **Country Baskets**, Raycraft	$9.95
3966	Collector's Guide to **Inkwells**, Identification & Values, Badders	$18.95
3881	Collector's Guide to **Novelty Radios**, Bunis/Breed	$18.95
3729	Collector's Guide to **Snow Domes**, Guarnaccia	$18.95
3730	Collector's Guide to **Transistor Radios**, Bunis	$15.95
2276	**Decoys**, Kangas	$24.95
1629	**Doorstops**, Identification & Values, Bertoia	$9.95
4567	Figural **Napkin Rings**, Gottschalk & Whitson	$18.95
3968	**Fishing Lure** Collectibles, Murphy/Edmisten	$24.95
3817	**Flea Market Trader**, 10th Ed., Huxford	$12.95
3976	Foremost Guide to **Uncle Sam** Collectibles, Czulewicz	$24.95
3819	**General Store Collectibles**, Wilson	$24.95
2215	Goldstein's **Coca-Cola** Collectibles	$16.95
3884	Huxford's Collectible **Advertising**, 2nd Ed.	$24.95
2216	**Kitchen Antiques**, 1790–1940, McNerney	$14.95
3321	Ornamental & Figural **Nutcrackers**, Rittenhouse	$16.95
2026	**Railroad** Collectibles, 4th Ed., Baker	$14.95
1632	**Salt & Pepper Shakers**, Guarnaccia	$9.95
1888	**Salt & Pepper Shakers** II, Identification & Value Guide, Book II, Guarnaccia	$14.95
2220	**Salt & Pepper Shakers** III, Guarnaccia	$14.95
3443	**Salt & Pepper Shakers** IV, Guarnaccia	$18.95
4555	**Schroeder's Antiques Price Guide**, 14th Ed., Huxford	$14.95
2096	**Silverplated Flatware**, Revised 4th Edition, Hagan	$14.95
1922	Standard **Old Bottle** Price Guide, Sellari	$14.95
3892	**Toy & Miniature Sewing Machines**, Thomas	$18.95
3828	Value Guide to **Advertising Memorabilia**, Summers	$18.95
3977	Value Guide to **Gas Station** Memorabilia, Summers & Priddy	$24.95
4572	**Wall Pockets** of the Past, Perkins	$17.95
3444	**Wanted to Buy**, 5th Edition	$9.95

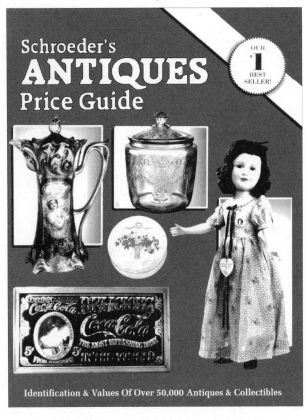